W0049958

# Focus on Computer Graphics

### Tutorials and Perspectives in Computer Graphics

Edited by W. T. Hewitt and W. Hansmann

Springer
*Berlin*
*Heidelberg*
*New York*
*Barcelona*
*Budapest*
*Hong Kong*
*London*
*Milan*
*Paris*
*Santa Clara*
*Singapore*
*Tokyo*

Peter Wisskirchen (Ed.)

# Object-Oriented and Mixed Programming Paradigms

## New Directions in Computer Graphics

With 68 Figures

Springer

*Focus on Computer Graphics*

Edited by W. T. Hewitt and W. Hansmann
for EUROGRAPHICS –
The European Association for Computer Graphics
P. O. Box 16, CH-1288 Aire-la-Ville, Switzerland

*Volume Editor*

Dr. Peter Wisskirchen
German National Research Center for Computer Science (GMD)
Schloss Birlinghoven, D-53757 Sankt Augustin, Germany

*Cover illustration by Ph. Slusallek, generated with an object-oriented renderer. From Computer Graphics Forum Vol. 14, No. 3 (1995), Conference issue Eurographics '95.*

CR Subject Classification (1991): I.3, D.1, D.3, J.6

*Library of Congress Cataloging-in-Publication Data applied for*

Die Deutsche Bibliothek - CIP-Einheitsaufnahme

**Object oriented and mixed programming paradigms** : new
directions in computer graphics / Peter Wisskirchen (ed.). –
Berlin ; Heidelberg ; New York ; Barcelona ; Budapest ; Hong
Kong ; London ; Milan ; Paris ; Santa Clara ; Singapore ;
Tokyo : Springer, 1996
  (Focus on computer graphics)
  ISBN 978-3-642-64676-8
NE: Wisskirchen, Peter [Hrsg.]

ISBN-13: 978-3-642-64676-8     e-ISBN-13:978-3-642-61062-2
DOI: 10.1007/978-3-642-61062-2

This work is subject to copyright. All rights are reserved, whether the whole or part of the material is concerned, specifically the rights of translation, reprinting, reuse of illustrations, recitation, broadcasting, reproduction on microfilm or in any other way, and storage in data banks. Duplication of this publication or parts thereof is permitted only under the provisions of the German Copyright Law of September 9, 1965, in its current version, and permission for use must always be obtained from Springer-Verlag. Violations are liable for prosecution under the German Copyright Law.

© 1996 EUROGRAPHICS The European Association for Computer Graphics

Softcover reprint of the hardcover 1st edition 1996

The use of general descriptive names, registered names, trademarks, etc. in this publication does not imply, even in the absence of a specific statement, that such names are exempt from the relevant protective laws and regulations and therefore free for general use.

Cover Design:Künkel + Lopka, Ilvesheim
Typesetting: Camera ready by authors
SPIN 10518851     45/3142 – 5 4 3 2 1 0 – Printed on acid-free paper

# Preface

The area of computer graphics is characterized by rapid evolution. New techniques in hardware and software developments, e.g., new rendering methods, have led to new applications and broader acceptance of graphics in fields such as scientific visualization, multi-media applications, computer aided design, and virtual reality systems.

The evolving functionality and the growing complexity of graphics algorithms and systems make it more difficult for the application programmer to take full advantage of these systems. Conventional programming methods are no longer suited to manage the increasing complexity, so new programming paradigms and system architectures are required. One important step in this direction is the introduction and use of object-oriented methods. Intuition tells us that visible graphical entities are objects, and experience has indeed shown that object-oriented software techniques are quite useful for graphics. The expressiveness of object-oriented languages compared to pure procedural languages gives the graphics application programmer much better support when transforming his mental intentions into computer code. Moreover, object-oriented software development is a well founded technology, allowing software to be built from reusable and extensible components.

This book contains selected, reviewed and thoroughly revised versions of papers submitted to and presented at the *Fourth Eurographics Workshops on Object-Oriented Graphics*, held on May 9-11, 1994 in Sintra, Portugal. In the year 1990, when Eurographics, the European Association for Computer Graphics, started a series of workshops on Object-Oriented Graphics, this topic was mainly used in the field of 2D graphics to build graphical user interfaces. In the meantime, elaborated object-oriented 3D-libraries and the first commercial products have appeared on the market.

The book contains two parts reflecting the current state of the art. Part 1, *Object-Oriented Design and Systems*, is about the design and implementation aspects of existing systems and prototypes. Experience shows that the use of object-oriented techniques in computer graphics is a widely acknowledged way of dealing with the complexities in graphics systems. Part 2, *Programming Paradigms for Graphics*, mainly reflects and analyzes problems when relying completely on pure object-orientation, and some papers propose mixed programming paradigms which may enrich the expressiveness of object-oriented languages.

The editor thanks all contributors for presentation and discussions, the members of the Programme Committee for careful evaluation, and Adelino da Silva for the local organization.

St. Augustin, May 1995                                                                  Peter Wisskirchen

# Contents

# Overview

Part 1, *Object-Oriented Design and Systems*, shows that the use of object-oriented techniques in computer graphics is a widely acknowledged way of dealing with the complexities in graphics systems. Part 2, *Programming Paradigms for Graphics*, mainly reflects and analyzes problems when relying completely on pure object-orientation.

## 1 Object-Oriented Design and Systems

In the last few years object-oriented graphics has outgrown its 2D orientation, and in the meantime complex algorithms and systems, such as elaborated renderers, as well as animation and multi-media systems, have been realized as object-oriented libraries.

In the first paper, *Fellner* presents a software architecture for a 3D rendering package which can operate in one of two modes: it either ray-traces a scene, creating photorealistic images, or it transforms the scene into a set of graphics primitives typically supported by a standard graphics package. The renderer is object-based rather than drawing-based and consists of an extensible set of objects that perform a variety of operations. The 3D objects as well as the imaging objects (such as Image, Screen, Light) are the building blocks that lend themselves to programmer customization through techniques such as subclassing. State-of-the-art functionality and advanced algorithms can be incorporated into this renderer with a minimum amount of programming, i.e., analysis/understanding of existing code and creation of new code. A thorough test of this approach has been carried out by using the renderer as the platform for teaching and for lab assignments in several undergraduate and graduate courses at two different universities. Experiences with this (inhomogeneous) user population prove that the system meets its design goal of being highly customizable and extensible.

The visualization system RayViS designed by *Groene* shows how that object-orientation is the key to design complex graphics systems exemplified here by the architecture of a highly elaborated ray tracer. The ray tracer is based on a well-defined overall protocol, extensible in various ways, and can easily be integrated in different application environments. RayViS is able to handle various primitive types combined in one scene. The illumination subsystem incorporates different shading methods, different light sources (point, linear, area, volume), and various ways to read in or build textures and let these vary geometric, material, and light source parameters. Besides this, several acceleration techniques are included to make the rendering process reasonably fast.

A top-down approach to the design of an object-oriented framework for curves and surfaces together with its C++ implementation is presented by *Slusallek, Klein, Kolb*, and *Greiner*. Object-oriented design offers the opportunity to use the inherent hierarchical structure of curves and surfaces to solve this problem. Starting from an abstract class of general differentiable curves and surfaces, this design is refined to various parametric representations of curves and surfaces. The resulting class hierarchy includes all of the standard curve and surface types and provides a powerful and uniform interface for applications. Examples from differential geometry, blending, and scattered data interpolation illustrate the approach.

Object-oriented design of graphical attributes is the core of *Beier's* paper. Beier describes an attribute concept that provides abstract, polymorphic, and rendering-independent attributes. This concept is implemented in his public domain 3D graphics system Yart. The article emphasizes the hierarchical modeling of primitives that may be expressed adequately by attributes and is based on the concepts of the traditional shading libraries such as GKS, PHIGS, and OpenGL. Requirements for an object-oriented modeling approach are formulated, drawbacks of current libraries are articulated, and innovative attribute concepts are introduced.

*Gemma* – the Graphical Environment for Multiple Users and Multiple Devices Architecture – is a design for a user interface architecture described by *Freeman* that allows users to bind together collections of devices for the task at hand, rather than being limited to virtual terminals. It provides mediated shared access to basic devices and higher-level virtual devices so that people can share computational facilities in the real world, rather than in a virtual world. Gemma uses object-oriented techniques to achieve the flexibility it requires, particularly inheritance and encapsulation, hiding distribution and allowing arbitrary devices to be connected together. Gemma was motivated by the observation that both computing systems and our understanding of human-computer interaction have changed since graphical interfaces were introduced, but that the layer which binds them together, the user interface system, has not changed as quickly.

*Palmer* and *Grimsdale* decribe the object-oriented animation system REALISM. It offers the user an environment whereby animation sequences may be developed using pre-defined libraries of objects and modifying their behavior to suit a particular task. It demonstrates the application of object-oriented techniques to computer animation. The classes in the system form a complex hierarchy, exploiting multiple inheritance and polymorphism to provide a rich expanse of capabilities. The two methods of influencing an object's behavior, through rules and constraints, offer dynamic methods of control whilst retaining the mechanism within the object's structure. The separate methods for geometry dependent and independent aspects lead to a more disciplined classification of an object's behavior. As a special problem, collision detection violating the encapsulation of the classes and creating heavy inter-object communications, has been solved by implementing a two-stage approach using a global table of bounding volumes as the first stage, and a direct peer-to-peer dialogue as the final stage.

*Dingeldein* describes in his paper an object-oriented approach to modeling multimedia. The model is independent of specific application domains, hardware and media types. It abstracts from the physical data sources and sinks. The model is implemented basically as a toolkit offering C++ classes to the programmer of multimedia applications and user interfaces. On top of this toolkit, some tools are realized to give non-programmers access to the features of the toolkit. There are media-dependent classes for modeling both media-data independent presentation (output) and interaction (input) aspects of multimedia objects. Furthermore, there are classes that define media data-independent relations and constraints between multimedia objects. Those relations can be spatial (layout definitions) and temporal (animation definitions). The media-independent classes use media-dependent classes (called Encodings) to access different data formats and connection classes to access media data storage. Using these classes, a multimedia application or user interface can easily be defined by connecting media objects and application objects.

## 2 Programming Paradigms for Graphics

The second part identifies research areas resulting from the field of computer graphics where object-oriented concepts must be enhanced, modified, or combined with other programming language concepts to meet the requirements articulated by different authors.

Due to the intrinsic object-based nature of computer graphics, the object-oriented paradigm seems to fit naturally as a tool for designing and using a graphics system. Although the object-oriented paradigm provides many highly desirable characteristics in computer graphics, there are other occasions where it is undesirable, if not impossible, to apply it effectively. The paper of *Egbert* and *Hilton* discusses the concept of object-orientation as it applies to computer graphics and identifies cases where a mixed programming paradigm approach to computer graphics may be more appropriate than a pure object-oriented model.

Recent developments in graphical user interface technology show an increase in complexity, with multiple input and output devices and a freedom for the end-user to be engaged in multiple dialogues simultaneously. Although existing models and programming languages come a long way, they lack the expressive power to describe such complex systems elegantly. With Talktalk, *Bouwman* and *de Bruin* present a Smalltalk extension with concurrency, interaction (access and output) protocols, as well as dialogues for easy specification of concurrent object-oriented (interactive) systems, supporting both delegation and inheritance. In Talktalk, objects are active, autonomous concurrent entities, which can communicate via synchronous as well as asynchronous message passing.

Although object-orientation is a suitable abstraction for computer graphics, significant problems exist in specifying relationships between objects, since relationships are not easily encapsulated within the objects concerned. Constraints, where the relationships between objects are maintained by the system, are an especially useful abstraction. Many existing constraint systems are forced to violate encapsulation and hence lose significant benefits of object orientation. This is because constraints are typically expressed by the programmer in terms of internal instance variables, which are then manipulated by the constraint solver to satisfy the constraints. *Hoole* and *Blake* present a solution which incorporates constraints while maintaining the benefits of object orientation. They present a solution which compromises encapsulation (this is unavoidable), but the violation is done in a controlled and localized manner. Solutions to the constraint set are arrived at by the constraint solver in consultation with constrained objects and are propagated back to objects strictly via their interfaces.

A different approach to integrate constraints into object-oriented systems is presented in the paper of *Veltkamp* and *Blake*. Here, the authors argue that a proper solution to the problem requires a radical separation of the constraint system and the normal object-oriented framework. They propose a way of dealing with these problems by means of two orthogonal communication strategies for objects: messages on the one hand, and events and data flow on the other hand. In this way, the process of constraint management does not interfere with the communication of the object-oriented world. Because of the global and compelling nature of constraints, this strict separation facilitates the design and debugging of constraints and the constraint system.

With TBAG, *Schechter, Elliott, Yeung*, and *Abi-Ezzi* propose a system architecture where the programmer is provided with one programming paradigm (namely, the functional paradigm) while the object-oriented paradigm is used for the implementation and extension. The programmer is presented with a simple, general interface that both is declarative and conforms to the functional programming paradigm. Pursuing a functional interface for developing interactive 3D applications is a novel concept that, in the author's experience, has been successful in providing a simple, powerful interface and a relatively straightforward implementation. The implementation of the system is highly object-oriented, relying heavily upon multiple dispatching. The system itself is extensible, and adding new geometric primitives and operations is straightforward.

# Part I

# Object-Oriented Design and Systems

# 1

# Extensible Image Synthesis

Dieter W. Fellner

Currently the two major obstacles for the limited growth of 3D application development to become a mainstream technology for everyday use are a) the computational and rendering requirements of 3D and b) the lack of a programming model that is appropriate for widespread use by developers who are not experts in the field of 3D graphics. But as the hardware gets faster, *software* will become *the* critical factor in the further growth of 3D application development.

In this paper we present a software architecture for a 3D rendering package which can operate in one of two modes: it either ray-traces the scene, creating photorealistic images, or it transforms the scene into a set of graphics primitives typically supported by a standard graphics package. The renderer is *object-based* rather than drawing based and consists of an extensible set of objects that perform a variety of operations. The 3D objects as well as the imaging objects (like Image, Screen, Light) are the building blocks that lend themselves to programmer customization through techniques such as subclassing. State-of-the-art functionality and advanced algorithms can be incorporated into this renderer with a minimum amount of programming (i.e. analysis/understanding of existing code and creation of new code).

A thorough test of this approach has been carried out by using the renderer as the platform for teaching and for lab assignments in several undergraduate and graduate courses at two different universities. Experiences with this (inhomogeneous) user population prove that the system meets its design goal of being highly customizable and extendable.

## 1 Introduction

3D graphics has not yet become a mainstream technology for everyday application and user interface development. One reason for this limited growth is that the computational and rendering requirements of 3D are beyond the performance capabilities of most machines. The other major reason for the slow proliferation of 3D is that software libraries available today do not provide a programming model that is appropriate for widespread use by developers not familiar with 3D graphics programming. The latest generation of RISC-based workstations and personal computers are quite capable of meeting the 3D performance challenge. As the hardware gets faster, software will become *the* critical factor in the further growth of 3D application development.

Currently available software libraries are of two types. *Hardware drawing libraries*, such as SGI's *GL*, HP's *Starbase*, and SUN's *XGL*, provide pixel and graphics primitive drawing commands as a software layer above hardware devices (typically a frame buffer). *Structured drawing libraries*, such as *GKS* [4], *PHIGS+* [5], HOOPS [13], and Doré [6] provide structured drawing commands that are abstracted from the low level hardware interface. All of these systems, however, are variants of display list technology. Designed to simplify the task of building applications using synthetic 3D graphics, these models imply that the same program organization and methods of user interaction are suitable for all graphics applications. While these techniques have served the graphics community well, they are being stretched by the size and complexity of today's applications. In addition, they appear to be inadequate for dealing with new issues such as multimedia, time-critical computing, and asynchronous user input.

The next generation of 3D software toolkits will be *object-based* rather than drawing based [14]. They will be composed of extensible sets of editable 3D objects that perform a variety of operations. Rendering will be one of the many operations that each object implements. The 3D objects will be building blocks that lend themselves to programmer customization through techniques such as subclassing.

This paper discusses a software architecture for a 3D rendering package independently developed to Inventor [11]. It can operate in one of two modes: it either creates photorealistic images by ray-tracing the scene, or it creates polygonal approximations of the scene and utilizes standard graphics packages like PHIGS+ or OpenGL [10] for the output to the display device.

The primary goal was the design of an *object-based* (in contrast to drawing-based) renderer consisting of a well structured and extensible set of objects that support all necessary operations to build a full-fledged rendering system for evaluation purposes during undergraduate and graduate teaching.

As the name *Minimal Ray Tracer* indicates, we tried to keep the renderer as minimal as possible. Nevertheless, experiences with the system prove that state-of-the-art functionality as well as advanced algorithms can be (and have been) incorporated into this renderer with a minimum amount of programming.

The last section gives a brief summary of our experiences with a quite inhomogeneous user population performing tasks which are typical for software engineers building, maintaining, or enhancing rendering or visualization packages.

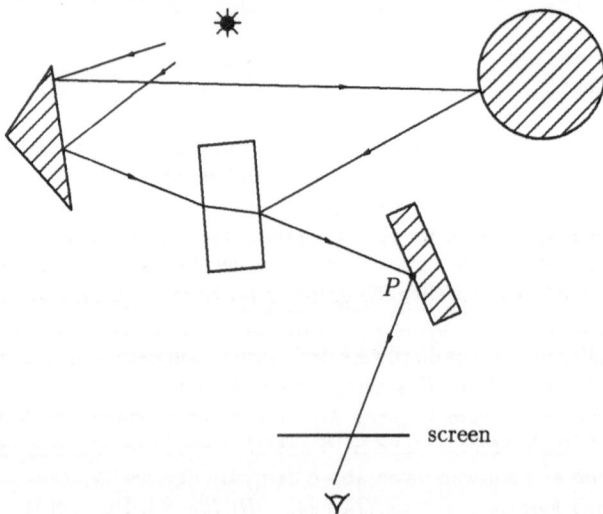

**Figure 1:** Ray-tracing: reflected rays and transmitted rays contribute to intensity at point $P$

## 2 Basic Concepts of Ray-Tracing

Since its development by Turner Whitted [12] *ray-tracing* has become a very popular technique to synthesize 'photorealistic' images [3]. The key concept is illustrated in Figure 1: Rays are cast from the observer through the center of each pixel onto the scene. If the ray doesn't hit any object, the pixel is colored with the scene's background color. Otherwise, the pixel color is evaluated from the color of the light emitted at the intersection point closest to the observer, say point $P$, in the direction of the ray.

To achieve a photorealistic impression the color at point $P$ has to be computed by evaluating the light coming from other objects or light sources and reflected or refracted by that object. This computation can be done by recursively tracing the reflected and transmitted rays. The resulting color of a point is the sum of the color computed locally and the colors contributed by the reflected and the transmitted ray. The equation reads:

$$I = I_L + c_{ref}I_R + c_{trans}I_T$$

with

| | | |
|---|---|---|
| $I_L$ | ... | intensity computed locally |
| $I_R$ | ... | intensity contributed by reflected ray |
| $I_T$ | ... | intensity contributed by transmitted ray |
| $c_{ref}$ | ... | constant to control reflection, $c_{ref} \in [0,1]$ |
| | | ($0$ = not reflecting, $1$ = perfect mirror) |
| $c_{trans}$ | ... | constant to control transmission, $c_{trans} \in [0,1]$ |
| | | ($0$ = opaque, $1$ = 100% transparent) |

To take care of shadows, so called illumination rays have to be sent from each intersection point to all light sources. If a light ray hits another object in the scene, the intersection point is in the object's shadow and thus cannot receive any light from that light source.

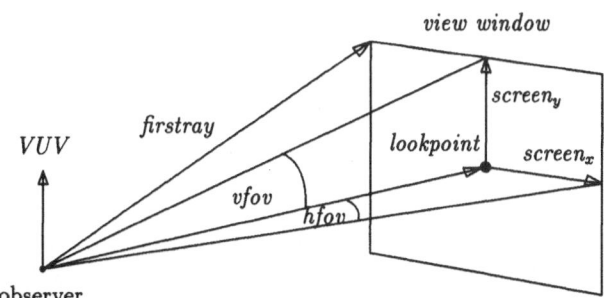

**Figure 2:** The modified pinhole camera model

Figure 2 illustrates the parameters used to define the modified pinhole camera model as commonly used in computer graphics with the parameters observer (*eyepoint*), *view up vector (VUV)*, *horizontal* and *vertical field of view (hfov, vfov)*, center of interest (*lookpoint*), and the screen dimensions *screen$_x$* and *screen$_y$*.

The world that finally appears on the screen lies within the infinite pyramid defined by the observer and the view window with the top cut off at the view window.

# 3  Architecture of MRT

The *Minimal Ray Tracer (MRT)* was not designed to compete with commercial rendering packages but to serve as a tool for teaching and as a testbed for the implementation of new algorithms (or, in case of student assignments, the implementation of existing ones) [2].

MRT currently operates in one of two modes: it either ray-traces the scene or it uses standard graphics packages like PHIGS or OpenGL for the display of an approximation to the scene. For the second mode the programmer does not need to worry about the functionality of or the interface to the underlying graphics packages (mapping of geometric objects to primitives supported, parameters of the camera model, definition of light sources, ...) – MRT can serve as an high-level object-oriented interface to these packages as well.

The programming language C++ [1] has been chosen due to its availability on almost all hardware and software platforms. Thus, a minimal familiarity with the language constructs of C will be assumed in the following.

For the discussion of the building blocks the various classes of the renderer are grouped according to their functionality.

## 3.1  Mathematical Elements

The basic data type representing all non-integral values is called t_Real.[1] It has been introduced to encapsulate machine specific details (e.g. machine accuracy for type double, handling of roundoff errors, ...) and to provide the flexibility to change the underlying representation of non-integral values in a convenient way. Introducing a new type of arithmetic (e.g. using rational numbers instead of floating-point arithmetic or using methods described in [9]) only requires the redefinition of this type together with the overloading of all standard mathematical operators and functions.

Class t_3DVector implements a 3D vector or 3D point and class t_4x4Matrix implements a $4 \times 4$ transformation matrix.

All classes, as well as the following ones, use the concept of operator overloading to enable the programmer to formulate the algorithms in a natural way. For example, $(P+Q)/2$ gives the point half way between P and Q and n = u*v assigns the vector normal to the plane defined by vectors u and v to vector n, such that u,v, and n form a right-handed system.

## 3.2  Color

Class t_Color implements the representation of a color together with a set of overloaded operators. This way rendering in more than three frequency intervals (by default red, green, and blue) or a different treatment of 'overexposed' pixels can be achieved by modifying this class only.

## 3.3  Geometric Objects

The base class of all geometric objects is class t_Object with the following virtual messages: t_BVol boundingVolume() returns the bounding volume (whose implementation is encapsulated in class t_BVol). t_Bool intersect() computes the intersection between the

---

[1]The prefix t_ has been introduced to avoid name conflicts with classes defined in other packages (e.g. class Color in InterViews).

object and a ray. It returns True iff an intersection can be found at a positive distance less than a given value (which stores the distance to the closest object found so far). t_Bool checkIntersect() just performs a Yes/No intersection test which is sufficient for the treatment of illumination rays and which, in most cases, can be done significantly faster than computing the intersection point. However, the default implementation is based on method intersect(). t_Bool checkBoxIntersect() is provided for the initialization of spatial data structures to accelerate the ray-object intersections. It determines if the object has a non-empty intersection with an axes-aligned box. The default implementation compares the box with the object's bounding volume. t_3DVector surfaceNormal() computes the normal to the surface at a given point (pointing outwards). triangulate() computes a triangular approximation of the object's boundary and stores it as a triangle strip list. This method is needed for visualizing the scene (and thus the object) using a standard rendering package like PHIGS or OpenGL. It returns True iff the triangulation changed from the last call (due to a different quality parameter). It will also return True if triangulate() has been called for the frist time. This enables the calling unit to determine if a refresh of the display has to take place.

It's worth mentioning that the whole scene as well as all sub-scenes are handled consistently as elementary geometric objects. I.e. class t_Scene is also derived from class t_Object and thus also provides the above messages. This illustrates the power of late binding and is an elegant way of handling arbitrary complex hierarchies of scenes: to compute the intersection of a ray and a particular scene the scene first tests for an intersection with its own bounding volume (computed after loading the scene description by message boundingVolume()) and then sends the message intersect() to all objects it contains which can either be elementary objects or scenes. The same mechanism applies to messages boundingVolume(), checkIntersect(), and triangulate().

## 3.4 Surface Properties

Class t_Surface is the base class for all illumination models and holds the surface parameters to implement the Phong illumination model. In addition to maintenance methods (to set and to read surface parameters) it provides the following virtual methods: diffuseCoefficient() returns the (local) diffuse reflection coefficient of that surface object at a given point. perturbNormal() provides a hook for derived classes to change the surface normal for a given point and object. shade() returns the color of the surface at a given point (computed globally) with the default implementation returning just the ambient light.

The ray tracer uses its own implementation of function shade() computing the Phong illumination model

$$
\begin{aligned}
I = \quad & k_a I_a & &\dots \text{ambient light} \\
+ \; & k_d \sum_{L_q} I_{L_q}(N \cdot L_{L_q}) & &\dots \text{diffuse reflection} \\
+ \; & k_s \left( I_s + \sum_{L_q} I_{L_q}(V \cdot R_{L_q})^c \right) & &\dots \text{specular reflection} \\
+ \; & k_t I_t & &\dots \text{transmitted light}
\end{aligned}
$$

with the local reflection vector $R$ and the local vector $V$ to the observer.

## 3.5 Light Sources

Class t_Light implements a positional light source and serves as the base class for all light sources. The key of defining new types of light sources like spot lights or directional light sources is the virtual function t_Bool lightEquPars(). Given an object, a point $P$ on its surface, and the level of recursion, it computes the vector $L$ to the light source, the distance to the light source, the scalar product of $L$ and the normal $N$ in $P$, and the brightness of the light source received at $P$. Message lightEquPars() returns False iff point $P$ is shadowed by any object in the scene.

## 3.6   Camera Model

Class t_Camera implements the modified pinhole camera model as shown in Figure 2. After being initialized with the viewing parameters message getRay() returns the initial ray from the observer through pixel $(x, y)$. Different camera models can be implemented by deriving new screen classes which redefine message getRay().

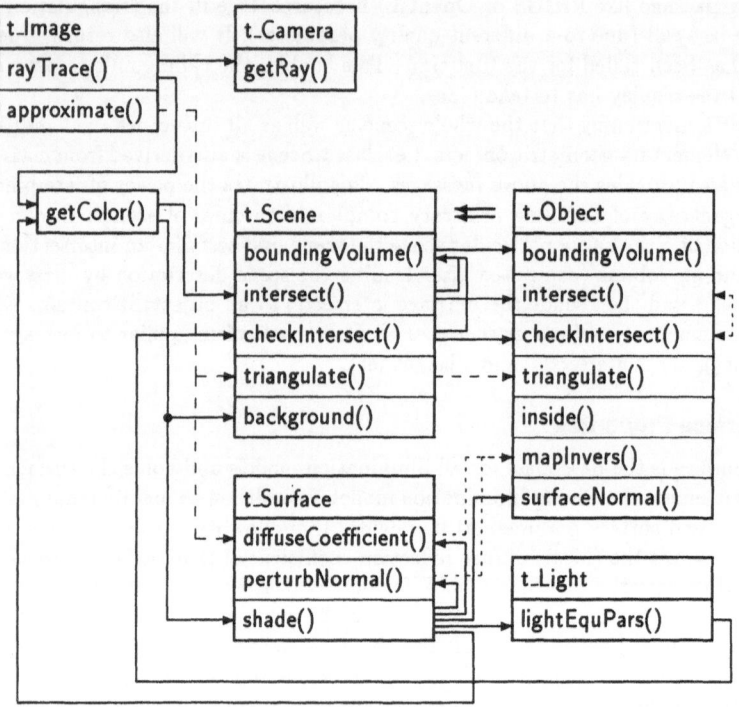

**Figure 3:** Building blocks of the Minimal Ray Tracer

## 3.7   Image Computation and Output

Class t_Image controls the main loop over all pixels to be computed. Protected messages gammaCorrect() and formatOutput() take care of gamma correction and formatting of output, respectively. Adaptive or stochastic anti-aliasing can be performed by derived classes (e.g. class t_AAAImage for Adaptive Anti-Aliasing) redefining virtual message rayTrace().

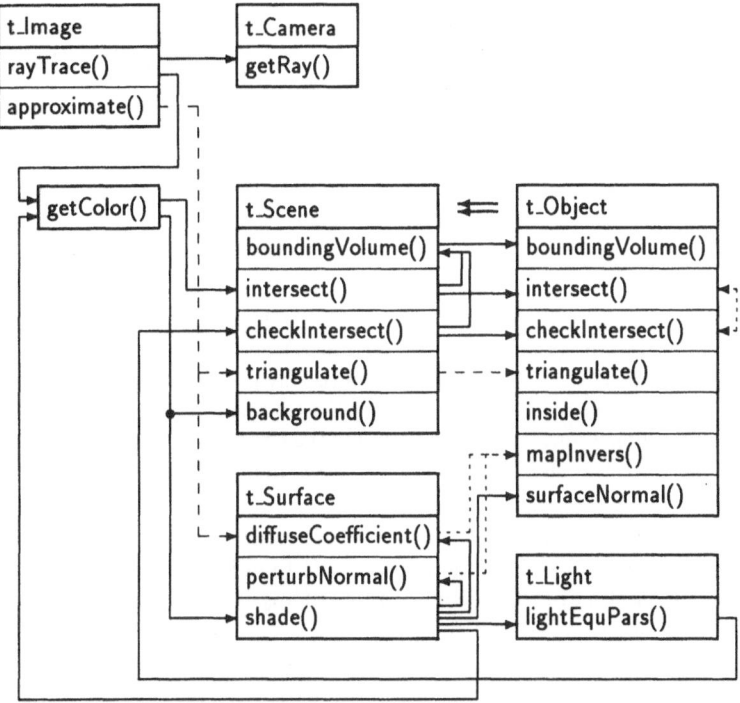

**Figure 4:** Building blocks of the Minimal Ray Tracer

## 3.8  Input

Extensibility for the input handling as well as support for different scene description formats is achieved by using compiler generation tools LEX and YACC for the parsing of the scene description files (which may be nested). Appendix A lists the syntax of the scene description grammar. For building the internal data structures and to implement the local scoping rules a set of classes is provided to stack surfaces, objects, groups of objects transformed by a transformation matrix, and include files.

Subscenes are automatically created whenever processing an included scene description and whenever a set of objects is embraced by a BEGIN ... END construct.

Bounding volumes of subscenes are computed automatically using the message unify() of class t_BVol which combines two bounding volumes into one.

## 3.9  Interface to Standard Graphics Packages

In viewing mode rendering is done by first extracting all parameters relevant to the underlying graphics package from the scene description (e.g. camera model, light sources, surface characteristics, ...). These parameters together with a list of triangle strips which have been created by message triangulate() sent to all objects are then passed to an object-oriented interface to the graphics package (e.g. PHIGS++) for the final rendering. In fact, message triangulate() is only sent to the object at the top of the hierarchy (see discussion of message intersect() in section 3.3).

## 4  MRT at Work

Without going into detail of the internals of the ray-tracing algorithm the main steps during the computation of an image are the following:

1. Processing of the scene description and construction (i.e. initialization) of all objects and associated data structures (e.g. hierarchy of bounding volumes).

2. Message rayTrace() of object image (an instance of class t_Image) loops over all pixels sending message getRay() to object screen to get an initial ray from the observer through the pixel.

   That ray is passed to function getColor() which computes the color of the scene seen along the direction of the ray. getColor() performs this computation by first computing the closest object intersecting the ray (i.e. sending message intersect() to object scene). For reasons of efficiency class t_Scene implements method intersect() by first sending message checkIntersect() to the bounding volume of the (sub)scene. If checkIntersect() doesn't report an intersection, message intersect() is not propagated further down the hierarchy.

   If the ray doesn't hit any object, getColor() returns the scene's background color (computed by sending message background() to object scene). Otherwise the color at the intersection point is computed by sending message shade() to the surface of that geometric object.

   shade() in turn evaluates the illumination equation for the ambient component and the diffuse and specular reflection component (by sending message surfaceNormal() to the geometric object and message lightEquPars() to all light sources). In case of a reflecting or transmitting surface, the colors along the reflected and transmitted ray are computed by a recursive call to getColor().

   In addition to method rayTrace() class t_Image provides methods for writing the computed picture to the output file. Method firstOutput() writes the header information and formatOutput() performs the gamma correction, if necessary, and writes the color information.

## 5  Introducing New Objects

In order to customize the renderer the application programmer only needs to know the basic functionality of a geometric object. In our case the following pure virtual methods of base class t_Object have to be provided for each new object:[2] boundingVolume() returns the bounding volume, intersect() computes the intersection between the object and a ray, surfaceNormal() computes the normal to the surface at a given point, triangulate() computes a triangular approximation of the object's boundary and stores it as a triangle strip list. It returns True if the triangulation changed from the last call (due to a different quality parameter) or if it has been called for the frist time.

Optionally, the following functions can be overloaded as well: checkIntersect() just performs an intersection test and has been introduced to speed up calculations of light rays as well as tests with bounding volumes. inside() returns the information if a given point is inside, on, or outside the object. The definition of this message is only necessary for objects

---

[2]We are employing the concept of *pure* functions to enforce the definition of these functions. Classes derived from t_Object which don't overload these functions remain abstract classes and thus cannot be instantiated.

allowed in CSG (constructive solid geometry) expressions. mapInvers() maps a point on the surface of that object onto a two-dimensional texture space defined over $[0, 1] \times [0, 1]$. By default, this message returns **False** indicating that 2D texture mapping is not supported for this specific object.

If a sphere was not already implemented, it could be introduced by the following definition of class t_Sphere:

```
class t_Sphere: public t_Object
{
  public:
    t_Sphere (const t_3DVector& center, t_Real radius, const t_Surface* surfId=NULL):
    virtual t_BVol boundingVolume () const;                      // return bounding volume
    virtual char* id () const;                                   // return Id 't_Sphere'
    virtual t_Bool intersect (const t_3DVector& point, const t_3DVector& dir,
                        const t_Object* from_obj, t_Real& dist,
                        t_Object*& to_obj);
    virtual t_3DVector surfaceNormal (const t_3DVector& point);
    virtual t_Bool triangulate (t_Real qualityControl = 0);
  private:
    t_3DVector centerpoint;                                      // object description
    t_Real rad;
};
```

Even though the above class definition is sufficient to introduce the object, we might want to add CSG functionality and 2D texture mapping with the two public functions

```
    ...
    virtual t_Real inside (const t_3DVector& point) const;           // return inside measure
    virtual t_Bool mapInvers (const t_3DVector& point_xyz, t_2DVector& point_uv) const;
    ...
};
```

The second and final step adds syntactic rules to the scene description grammar from which the parser of the scene description is generated:

```
object:                                      /* list of objects */
          CSG_UNION  surfnr csg_union         { ostack->push($2,$3); }
        | CSG_DIFF   surfnr csg_difference    { ostack->push($2,$3); }
        | CSG_INTER  surfnr csg_intersection  { ostack->push($2,$3); }
        | BEZIER     surfnr bezier            { ostack->push($2,$3); }
        | ...        ...
        | ...        ...         /* add sphere to list of objects */
        | SPHERE     surfnr sphere            { ostack->push($2,$3); }
        ;
sphere:   vector scalar /* center and radius */
                        { $$ = new t_Sphere(*$1,$2);
                          delete $1;
                        }
        | error         { yyerror("'SPHERE vector no' expected");
                          $$ = dummySphere();
                        }
        ;
```

These two steps are sufficient for any new object. No other parts of the ray tracer have to be studied or modified by the programmer.

Even though most users of a rendering system will only be confronted with the task of introducing new objects our renderer will also allow the introduction of new types of light sources or new types of 2D and 3D surface textures.

New types of light sources can be introduced by deriving a new class, say t_SpotLight, from base class t_Light and redefining the virtual function lightEquPars().

A new texture, for example, could be incorporated by deriving a new class from base class t_Surface overloading the definition of virtual method diffuseCoefficient(), which, by default, returns the diffuse reflection coefficient. For solid textures method diffuseCoefficient() will need a 3D point. For 2D textures the pointer to the object will be needed as well in order to perform the inverse mapping from 3D world coordinates into 2D texture space. Observe, that due to the concept of virtual functions there is no need to overload base class method shade().

Different techniques for ray accleration can be implemented by only providing new methods intersect() and checkIntersect() to class scene.

## 6  Experiences

This rendering package has been used as the platform for teaching and for lab assignments in several undergraduate and graduate courses at the Memorial University of Newfoundland, Canada, and the University of Bonn, Germany.

Besides the teaching of 3D image synthesis we used this package together with another Minimal Ray Tracer from [7] as well as RayShade to learn about the average time spent by a student on performing specific tasks like introducing a new object or implementing a new type of light source.

The ray tracer from [7] is written in C and provides less functionality compared to MRT with respect to scene structuring and input handling (compared to the original additional geometric objects have been introduced to make the two packages similar in functionality).

The results on the learning curve of the two minimal ray tracers over several courses were quite consistent and can be summarized by the relation $C : C++ \approx 3 : 1$ which means that, compared to the C++ version, it took our students approximately 3 times longer to perform their task in the C version. Even though the times converged with an increasing number of assignments, this is predominantly due to the relatively small size of these minimal ray tracers. I.e. students become more familiar with the whole package and the benefit of localized functionality characteristic for object-oriented design diminishes.

## 7  Conclusions

In this paper we presented an object-oriented software architecture for a 3D rendering package which significantly improves the readability of the underlying algorithms, drastically improves productivity, and, most importantly, consists of building blocks that lend themselves to programmer customization thus making 3D image synthesis more accessible.

Using the renderer as the platform for teaching and for lab assignments our experiences are consistent with [8] and they prove that the system meets its design goal of being highly customizable and extendable.

## Appendix A: Scene Description Grammar

The elements of the scene description file have to satisfy the following grammar. Reserved
keywords (terminal symbols) are written in upper-case (exception: INT, REAL, STRING,
and FILENAME stand for the according values), non terminal symbols are written in lower
case.

```
file:      param lights surf_obj_lst ENDFILE
           ;
param:     global screen
           ;
global:    /* nothing */
      | global OUTFILE    FILENAME /* default  "input-file".ppm */
      | global OUTFORMAT  INT      /* currently only 0 ( = ppm-format P6) */
      | global COLORRANGE number   /* R,G,B in [0,COLORRANGE] default 255 */
      | global MAXLEVEL   INT      /* maximum recursion level,  default 5 */
           ;
screen:    /* nothing */
      | screen  EYEP    vector                  /* default (100,100,-100) */
      | screen  LOOKP   vector                  /* default (0,0,0)   */
      | screen  UP      vector                  /* default (0,1,0)   */
      | screen  FOV     '<' number ',' number '>'   /* default <30,30>   */
      | screen  SCREEN  '<' INT ',' INT '>'         /* default <256,256> */
      | screen  GAMMA   '<' number ',' number ',' number '>'
                                                /* default <1,1,1>   */
      | screen  BACKGROUND  color               /* default (0,0,0)   */
           ;
/*================= lights */
lights:    /* nothing */
      | lights light
           ;
light: AMB_LIGHT  color            /* ambient light: color           */
      | POS_LIGHT  color vector     /* positional light: color, position */
      | SPOT_LIGHT color vector     /* spotlight: color, position     */
                  vector number     /*            direction, aperture */
           ;
/*================= surfaces + objects */
surf_obj_lst:              /* list of surfaces and transformed objects */
        surface
      | surf_obj_lst surface
      | transf_obj
      | surf_obj_lst transf_obj
           ;
/*================= surface */
surface:   SURFACE surfnr surftypes
           ;
surfnr:    INT   /* surfnr must be >=0 */
           ;
surftypes: /* nothing */ phong
      | PHONG         phong
      | STEXTURE      solid_texture
           ;
phong: number ';'     /* ambient coefficient - ka            [0,1] */
      color          /* diffuse surface color         [0,COLORRANGE] */
      number ';'     /* diffuse reflection coefficient - kd    [0,1] */
      color          /* specular surface color        [0,COLORRANGE] */
      number ','     /* specular reflection coefficient - ks   [0,1] */
      number ';'     /* specular exponent - c                  > 1 */
      coltyp         /* transmission coefficient - kt          [0,1] */
      number         /* index of refraction                    [0,3] */
           ;
```

```
solid_texture:                                    /* solid textures:    */
     ST_WOOD       st_wood                         /*    wood            */
     | ...         ...
     | ST_MARBLE   st_marble                       /*    marble          */
     ;
st_wood:
     number ';'           /* ambient coefficient - ka                   */
     vector               /* center of pattern                          */
     scalar ',' scalar    /* distance between and width of cylinders */
     color color ';'      /* light and dark color                       */
     color                /* specular surface color                     */
     number ','           /* specular reflection coefficient - ks       */
     number ';'           /* specular exponent - c                      */
     coltyp               /* transmission coefficient - kt              */
     number               /* index of refraction                        */
     ;
st_marble:
     number ';'           /* ambient coefficient - ka                   */
     scalar               /* texture scale factor                       */
     color color          /* marble colors 1 to 4                       */
     color color ';'
     color                /* specular surface color                     */
     number ','           /* specular reflection coefficient - ks       */
     number ';'           /* specular exponent - c                      */
     coltyp               /* transmission coefficient - kt              */
     number               /* index of refraction                        */
     ;
/*==================== object */
transf_obj:                        /* object transformed by optional matrix */
          opt_matrix object
          ;
object:
       INCLUDE FILENAME file               /* include file */
     | BEG surf_obj_1st END                /* BEGIN ... END block */
     | CSG_UNION     surfnr csg_union       /* CSG union */
     | CSG_DIFF      surfnr csg_difference  /* CSG difference */
     | CSG_INTER     surfnr csg_intersection /* CSG intersection */
     | BEZIER        surfnr bezier          /* cubic Bezier patch */
     | BOX           surfnr box             /* rectangular box */
     | CHAR_3D       surfnr char_3d         /* 3D character */
     | CONE          surfnr cone            /* circular cone */
     | ELLIPSOID     surfnr ellipsoid       /* ellipsoid */
     | GEN_CYLINDER  surfnr gen_cylinder    /* general cylinder */
     | PARALLEL      surfnr parallel        /* parallelogram */
     | QUADRANGLE    surfnr quadrangle      /* quadrangle */
     | SPHERE        surfnr sphere          /* sphere */
     | SR_ELLTORUS   surfnr sr_elltorus     /* elliptical hyper-torus */
     | STRING_3D     surfnr string_3d       /* 3D string */
     | SUPERQ        surfnr superq          /* general superquadric */
     | TRIANGLE      surfnr triangle        /* triangle */
     ;
csgobj: CSG_UNION      csg_union
     | CSG_DIFF        csg_difference
     | CSG_INTER       csg_intersection
     | BOX             box
     | CONE            cone
     | ELLIPSOID       ellipsoid
     | GEN_CYLINDER    gen_cylinder
     | SPHERE          sphere
     | SR_ELLTORUS     sr_elltorus
     | SUPERQ          superq
     ;
transf_csgobj:              /* CSG element: optional matrix, CSG object */
```

```
            opt_matrix csgobj
            ;
csg_union:  transf_csgobj transf_csgobj
            ;
csg_difference:
            transf_csgobj transf_csgobj
            ;
csg_intersection:
            transf_csgobj transf_csgobj
            ;
bezier: vector vector vector vector   /*  4x4 points:  00 01 02 03   */
        vector vector vector vector   /*               10 11 12 13   */
        vector vector vector vector   /*               20 21 22 23   */
        vector vector vector vector   /*               30 31 32 33   */
        /* normal vector in last subgrid defined by (v30-v00)x(v03-v00) */
        ;
box:    vector                        /* center                      */
        '<' number ',' number ',' number '>' /* 1/2 side length x, y, z */
        ;
char_3d: vector                       /* bottom left position        */
        number                        /* char height                 */
        '<' number ',' number '>'     /* stroke width, stroke depth   */
        STRING                        /* character                   */
        ;
cone:   vector vector number   /* center of basis, top, radius (>0 !!) */
        ;
ellipsoid: vector                       /* center                    */
        '<' number ',' number ',' number '>' /* main axes along x,y,z */
        ;
gen_cylinder:                   /* generalized cylinder              */
        vector vector           /*    center of bottom and top       */
        '<' number ','          /*    radius of bottom (>0 !!)        */
        number '>'              /*    radius of top (maybe <= 0)      */
        ;
parallel:   vector                  /* starting point               */
        vector vector               /* endpoints of spanning vectors, */
        ;                           /* vectors ordered counter-clockwise*/
quadrangle:
        vector vector vector vector /* corners ordered counter-clockwise*/
        ;
sphere:     vector scalar           /* radius and center             */
        ;
sr_elltorus:            /* Solid of Revolution:                      */
        vector          /*  center c                                 */
        '<' scalar ','  /*  ellipse parameters r0 (in direction o)   */
        scalar '>'      /*        and r1                             */
        scalar          /*  inner radius d (outer rad = d + 2*r1)    */
        vector          /*  orientation o (c and o define rotation axis*/
        ;               /*  with: r0, r1 > 0,  r1+d >= 0             */
string_3d: vector                      /* bottom left position       */
        number                         /* char height                */
        '<' number ',' number '>'      /* stroke width, stroke depth  */
        STRING                         /* character string            */
        ;
superq: vector                          /* center                    */
        '<' number ',' number ',' number '>' /* 1/2 side length x, y, z*/
        '<' number ',' number ',' number '>' /* exponent x, y, z       */
        ;
triangle:   vector vector vector   /* corners ordered counter-clockwise*/
        ;
/*==================== types*/
opt_matrix:                             /* optional transformation matrix*/
```

```
                    /* nothing */
                  | matrix
                  ;
matrix:                                           /* 4x4 transformation matrix*/
                  '(' number ',' number ',' number ',' number ','
                      number ',' number ',' number ',' number ','
                      number ',' number ',' number ',' number ','
                      number ',' number ',' number ',' number ')'
                  | TRANS '(' number ',' number ',' number ')'
                  | SCALE '(' number ',' number ',' number ')'
                  | ROT_X '(' number ')'
                  | ROT_Y '(' number ')'
                  | ROT_Z '(' number ')'
                  | matrix '*' matrix
                  | '(' matrix ')'
                  ;
/* all input of type vector is transformed by the accumulated
 * transformation matrix 'acc_tr_matrix', i.e.  v = v * acc_tr_matrix.
 * acc_tr_matrix is updated whenever parsing a sequence
 * "matrix BEGIN ... END", i.e.  acc_tr_matrix = matrix * acc_tr_matrix.
 * Thus a sequence of  "BEGIN m3 BEGIN m2 BEGIN m1 ... END END END"
 * is equivalent to    "BEGIN m1 * m2 * m3 ... END"
 * (mind reversed order of matrices)
 */
vector:    triple
           ;
coltyp:    triple                        /* red, green, blue in [0,1]      */
           ;
color:     triple                   /* red, green, blue in [0,COLORRANGE]*/
           ;
triple:    '(' number ',' number ',' number ')'
           ;
scalar:    number  /* scaled by an 'averaged' scale factor derived from */
           ;         /* the length of a unit-length vector transformed by */
                     /* the current transformation matrix                 */
number:       REAL
           |  INT
           |  '-' number                                   /* unary minus */
           |  '+' number                                   /* unary plus  */
           |  number '-' number
           |  number '+' number
           |  number '*' number
           |  number '/' number
           |  '(' number ')'
           |  SIN  '(' number ')'
           |  COS  '(' number ')'}
           |  TAN  '(' number ')'}
           |  SQR  '(' number ')'
           |  SQRT '(' number ')'
           |  EXP  '(' number ')'
           |  POW  '(' number ',' number ')'
           ;
```

Semantics:

- At least one light source and one surface have to be defined for a scene to be complete.

- Include-files follow the same structure, but the entries **param** and **lights** will be ignored.

- In case of multiple definitions only the last one is valid.

- The scope of a surface is the file it is defined in and all files it includes. Local surface definitions override all previous (global) definitions.

- An optional transformation matrix will be applied to all objects embraced between BEGIN and END. If the block contains more than one object, a subscene is created. This is an easy way of hierarchically structuring the scene.

Comments follow the C++ syntax and are either started by a double slash (//) extending to the end of the line or embraced by '/*' and '*/'. Nesting of multi-line comments (/*...*/) is not permitted.

## References

[1] Margaret A. Ellis and Bjarne Stroustrup. *The Annotated C++ Reference Manual.* Addison-Wesley, Reading, Mass., 1990.

[2] Dieter W. Fellner. *Computer Grafik*, volume 58 of *Computer Science Monograph.* B.I. Wissenschaftsverlag, Mannheim, 1988.

[3] Andrew S. Glassner, editor. *An Introduction to Ray Tracing.* Academic Press, London, 1989.

[4] ISO. *Information Processing Systems – Computer Graphics – Graphical Kernel System (GKS) – Functional Description, IS 7942*, 1985.

[5] ISO. *Information Processing Systems – Computer Graphics – Programmer's Hierarchical Interactive Graphics System (PHIGS), Amendment 1-3, IS 9592/Am. 1-3*, February 1992.

[6] Kubota Pacific Computer. *Doré Programmer's Guide*, 1991.

[7] R. Kuchkuda. An Introduction to Ray Tracing. In R. A. Earnshaw, editor, *Theoretical Foundations of Computer Graphics and CAD*, volume 40 of *NATO ASI Series F*, pages 1039–1060. Springer, Berlin, 1988.

[8] Lewis J. Pinson and Richard S. Wiener, editors. *Applications of Object-Oriented Programming.* Addison-Wesley, Reading, Mass., 1990.

[9] Arnold Schönhage, Andreas Grotefeld, and Ekkehart Vetter. *Fast Algorithms.* B.I. Wissenschaftsverlag, Mannheim, 1994.

[10] Silicon Graphics Inc. *The OpenGL Reference Manual – The Official Reference Document for OpenGL.* Addison-Wesley, Reading, Mass., 1st edition, 1993.

[11] Paul S. Strauss and Rikk Carey. An Object-Oriented 3D Graphics Toolkit. *Computer Graphics*, 26(2):341–349, July 1992.

[12] Turner Whitted. An Improved Illumination Model for Shaded Display. *Communications of the ACM*, 23(6):343–349, June 1980.

[13] Garry Wiegand and Bob Covey. *HOOPS Reference Manual.* Ithaca Software, 1991.

[14] Peter Wisskirchen. *Object-Oriented Graphics: From GKS and PHIGS to Object-Oriented Systems.* Springer, Berlin, 1990.

# 2

# RayViS – A Visualization System Based on Object-Orientation

Alwin Gröne

Object-orientation is the key to design complex graphics systems exemplified here by the architecture of the RayViS ray tracer. The ray tracer is based on a well-defined overall protocol, extensible in various ways, and can easily be integrated in different application environments. The flexible illumination subsystem allows a combination of many different shaders, textures, and light sources.

## 1 Introduction

The basic ray tracing idea is simple, well known [3, 4], and the achievable image quality is very attractive. Unfortunately, an implementation of this simple idea can become enormously complex. A ray tracer must be able to handle various primitive types combined in one scene. The illumination subsystem should incorporate different shading methods, different light sources (point, linear, area, volume), and various ways to read in or build textures and let these vary geometric, material, and light source parameters. Besides, several acceleration techniques have to be included to make the rendering process reasonably fast.

Many issues of complexity have been reasonably solved in our object-oriented design of a ray tracing based visualization system (RayViS). The majority of the paper will concentrate on architectural and protocol issues. Section 3 describes the main RayViS architecture as an interaction between abstract base classes. Section 4 answers the question, how to instantiate and use several ray tracers in one application. Relationships among RayViS objects are examined in Section 5, and Section 6 more closely examines the collaboration between shader and light source objects. Finally, conclusions are drawn in Section 7.

## 2 Previous Work

An abundance of literature is available on numerous algorithmic details of the ray tracing algorithm [4, 3, 11]. By far fewer publications can be found on how to incorporate all these algorithmic details in a single rendering system, especially not if done in an extensible, thoroughly object-oriented way. A few notable exceptions are mentioned in the following.

Both *rayshade* [8] and *pov-ray* [13] are popular public domain ray tracers. Even though they are implemented in traditional C, their design was partially influenced by object-oriented concepts. Both ray tracers are intended to be used as stand-alone programs that read a scene description file and output a pixel file. They can render various geometric

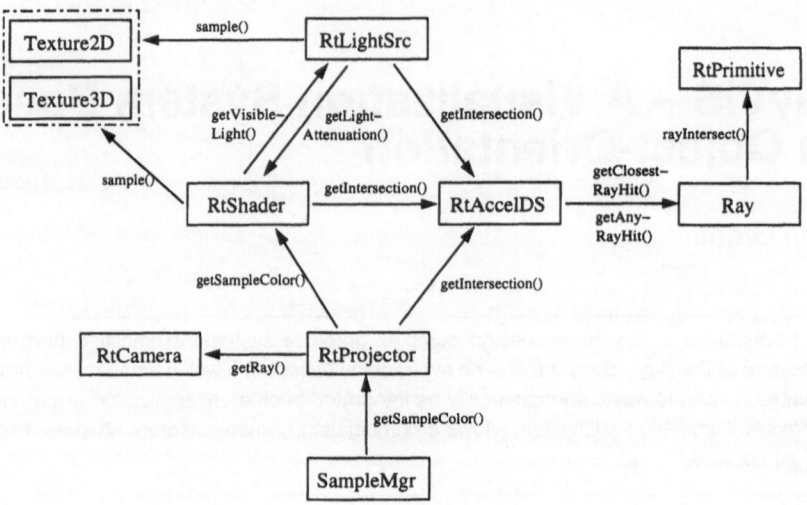

**Figure 1:** Main RayViS protocol

primitives and support different light sources and textures, but they restrict all shading calculations to a single Phong-like illumination formula.

The *radiance* system by Ward [12] is one of the most powerful ray tracers currently existing. *Radiance* is able to compute a physically correct lighting simulation und is especially useful for visualizing indoor scenes. Seen from a software architectural point of view, *radiance* is a collection of about eighty different programs, UNIX filters, and C-shell scripts.

Fellner [2] describes a small but extensible 3D rendering package that can operate in PHIGS as well as ray tracing mode. He emphasizes a clean object-oriented design of the renderer, which is used for teaching and lab assignments.

Other simple ray tracing architectures were outlined by Kirk and Arvo [7], Heckbert [6], and Leister et al. [9].

## 3  Main RayViS Protocol

Figure 1 shows the main ray tracing architecture as an interaction between abstract base classes as well as their most important methods. The sample manager (*SampleMgr*) is the uppermost control instance. He decides about order and method of pixel color computations. On request the projector (*RtProjector*) computes the RGB color of sample $(x, y)$. The corresponding ray (*Ray*) through $(x, y)$ is generated and initialized by the camera (*RtCamera*) and handed over to the acceleration data structure (*RtAccelDS*). Lets assume an octree (*OcTree*) was chosen. The octree computes the geometrically correct order of voxels traversed by the ray. All primitives (*RtPrimitive*) in a voxel perform an intersection test with this ray based on their private geometric representation. If an intersection point is found and is the closest one in the current voxel, traversing terminates and all intersection information (coordinates of intersection point, object normal, $(u, v)$-coordinates and pointer to shader) is stored in the ray object.

The ray is handed back to the projector, who then asks the shader (*RtShader*) of the intersected primitive to compute the RGB intensity in the intersection point. The shader is an 'intelligent' material and has access to the following parameters to perform the illumination calculations:

- the material constants are stored locally in the private shader data representation;

- the ray (member function parameter) has all geometrical intersection information;

- shaders for textured materials request the necessary texel information from the corresponding *Texture2D* and *Texture3D* objects;

- shaders for reflective and transparent materials generate secondary rays and emit them into the scene;

- each light source (*RtLightSrc*) is asked in turn to compute the light intensity arriving at the intersection point. The light sources do this by emitting one or more shadow rays.

If the ray is a primary ray, the intensity computed by the shader is given back via the projector to the sample manager.

## 4  Application Interface

For each ray tracer an application wants to use, an object of type

```
class RtDevice
{
  //...
  RtCamera      *camera;
  RtProjector   *projector;
  PrimitiveMgr  *primitiveMgr;
  ShaderMgr     *shaderMgr;
  LightSrcMgr   *lightSrcMgr;
  TextureMgr    *textureMgr;
  RtAccelDS     *accelerationDS;
};
```

has to be instantiated. The major purpose of this class is to act as a compound or wrapping device for the seven major data representation elements of each ray tracer.

The four manager classes are list classes. They are constructed as empty lists. The other three device element pointers point to their default objects:

```
accelerationDS = new OcTree;
projector      = new RtProjector;
camera         = new PinHoleCamera;
```

To render a scene, the internal data representation has to be set up properly first. The syntax to use is quite simple. The four manager classes allow an object to be added to their internal lists by using append-methods:

```
rtDev->primitiveMgr->append( new <DerivedRtPrimitive>(...) );
rtDev->shaderMgr->append( new <DerivedRtShader>(...) );
rtDev->lightSrcMgr->append( new <DerivedRtLightSrc>(...) );
rtDev->textureMgr->append( new <DerivedRtTexture>(...) );
```

The camera and projector parameters are set by

```
rtDev->camera->set<Param>(...);
rtDev->projector->set<Param>(...);
```

Two things remain to be done before rendering can start. Firstly, the acceleration data structure has to be build

```
rtDev->accelerationDS->build( rtDev->primitiveMgr );
```

and secondly, a sample manager has to be constructed

```
SampleMgr sampleMgr;
```

The sample manager is not part of the ray tracing device because this would restrict the usability of the ray tracer in certain application environments. If the sample manager is used, the simplest way to perform rendering is by using the methods

```
sampleMgr.putFirstPixelBlock( rtDev );
sampleMgr.putNextPixelBlock( rtDev );
```

## 5   Relationships Among Objects

An important question is: How do objects know of each other so that they are able to communicate and collaborate? The RayViS classes basically use three different solutions to answer this question.

One solution is to provide a reference to the RtDevice object as a member function parameter. This basically gives an object access to all seven device elements. In most cases access to only one or two device elements would be sufficient, but using always the same reference is more consistent and allows for changes of member function implementations without having to change member function interfaces. The device parameter solution is used, e.g., to give each shader access to the light source manager and thus to all light sources. It is also used to give the projector and all shaders and light sources a reference to the current acceleration data structure so that they are able to emit rays into the scene. If the user or application chooses a different RtAccelDS object, only the RtDevice object needs to be told explicitly.

A second solution to the communication problem stated above is to establish a parent/child or "is implemented in terms of" relationship, i.e., to make the child object a private data member of the parent object. This provides the parent object with an explicit access to the child object and is very useful for various geometric, illumination, and other parameters.

In some cases, however, the direct parent/child relationship is very inefficient in terms of storage. Three examples clarify the problem. Firstly, subdividing object space into disjunct subspaces causes fragmentation, i.e., many primitives will partially occupy more than one subspace. To store a primitive in each subspace is very inefficient concerning storage and ray traversal computations. Secondly, quite often different primitives have the same shader (material) parameters. For example, one thousand triangles shaping the famous Utah teapot may all be associated with a single teapot shader. To store the same shader one thousand times is not only very inefficient in terms of storage, but also difficult to handle if the teapot shader needs to be changed. Thirdly, a similar problem exists if several shaders refer to the same 2d texture, because textures often need several hundred KBytes of storage.

The RayViS solution is quite simple. Each (primitive, shader, light source, texture) object is stored exactly once by the corresponding manager (list) object. Relationships

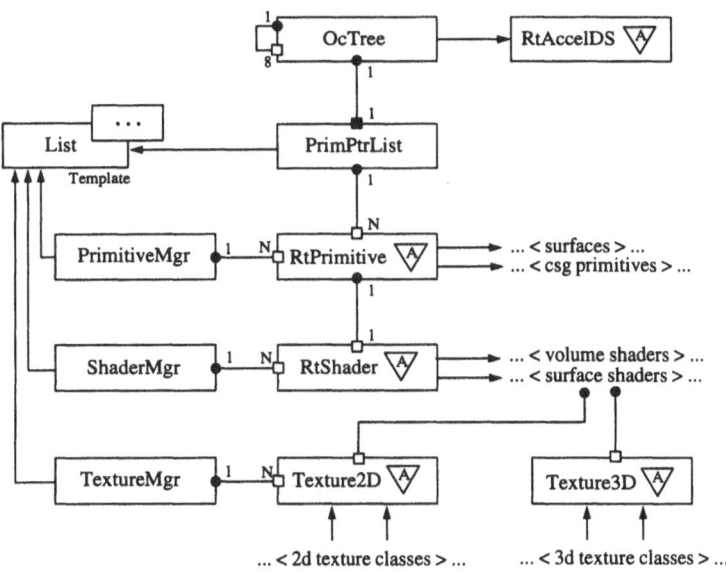

**Figure 2:** Part of the RayViS class diagram

are established indirectly via pointers, i.e., the acceleration data structure has pointers into the list of primitives, each primitive has a pointer into the list of shaders, and shaders for textured materials have a pointer into the list of textures (Fig. 2, notation similar to Booch [1]). Since this is a certain violation to the principle of data encapsulation, it is extremely important that the implementation assures a read only access via these parent/child pointers.

## 6    Illumination Calculations

An especially interesting part of the main RayViS protocol presented in Section 3 is the collaboration between shaders, light sources, and textures. The major aim of this section is to give more details on the uniform protocol for the communication between shaders and light sources.

### 6.1    Description of Illumination Problem

Most ray tracing literature states the illumination problem as a variation of the formula

$$\mathbf{I} = k_a \mathbf{I}_a + \sum_{i=0}^{n-1} f_{att,i} \left[ k_d (\mathbf{N} \cdot \mathbf{L}_i) + k_s (\mathbf{L}_i \cdot \mathbf{R})^m \right] \mathbf{I}_i + k_r \mathbf{I}_r + k_t \mathbf{I}_t \qquad (2.1)$$

but this formula needs a lot of additional explanation to demonstrate the whole complexity of the problem. Fig. 3 demonstrates the illumination problem graphically. Here, $\mathbf{P}$ is the point to be illuminated, $\mathbf{N}$ is the normal vector, $\mathbf{V}$ is the view direction, $\mathbf{R}$ is the reflected view direction, and $\mathbf{T}$ is the transmitted or refracted view direction. Three light sources are shown. One light source is entirely above the tangent plane, the second light source is partially above it, and the third one is entirely below the tangent plane. Each light

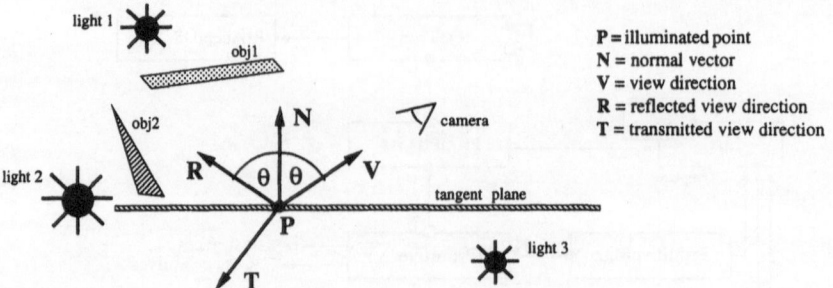

**Figure 3:** Illumination problem

source can be either zero-dimensional (point), one-dimensional (linear), two-dimensional (area), or three-dimensional (volume). Additionally, all light sources may have various light distribution parameters to influence the way they radiate light into the scene. The material in **P** may be either opaque or transparent. If it is opaque, light 2 contributes only partially and light 3 nothing to the intensity in **P**. If the material in **P** is transparent, the contributions of light 3 and of the lower part of light 2 have to be properly filtered.

Besides, other geometric objects in the scene may partially or entirely block the light from any light source. Again, the materials of these objects may be either opaque or transparent. The shaders of transparent objects must properly attenuate the intensity of shadow rays crossing them.

## 6.2  Assumptions and Concepts

Before presenting the RayViS solution to this problem, some principle assumptions and concepts should be mentioned:

1. There is no single best illumination formula that satisfies all needs and desires. It is the variety of different shaders, light sources, and textures that makes the ray tracing algorithm flexible and powerful.

2. All computations should be performed as locally as possible. The class to be chosen for any computation is the one with the most information available.

3. All shader classes are derived from a single abstract base class `RtShader`. The most important virtual method of this class is

   ```
   RgbColor getSampleColor( RtDevice& rtDev, const Ray& ray ) const;
   ```

4. All light source classes are derived from a single abstract base class `RtLightSrc`.

5. There is a uniform protocol by which any shader can request the intensity contribution from each light source, regardless of the geometric and light distribution parameters defining the light sources. This protocol is defined by the virtual `RtLightSrc` method `getVisibleLight`.

6. Any specific light source should make as few assumptions as possible about the nature of the shader requesting its intensity contribution.

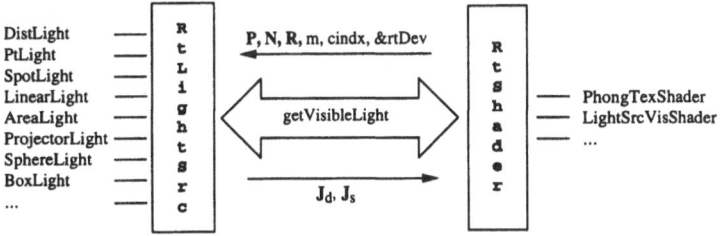

**Figure 4:** Illumination protocol

## 6.3 Illumination Protocol

The RayViS illumination protocol is outlined in Fig. 4. Each light source is given the following information:

**P** – The object space coordinates of the point to be illuminated.

**N** – The normal vector is needed to evaluate the dot product $\mathbf{N} \cdot \mathbf{L}$ (Lambert's law).

**R**,$m$ – The reflected view direction **R** and the specular power coefficient $m$ are used to evaluate the specular intensity contribution of the light source.

cindx – The shadow cache index will be explained below.

rtDev – A reference to the ray tracing device is necessary so that a light source has access to the current acceleration data structure and thus will be able to emit shadow rays.

Three values are returned by the light source. The first one is a boolean value informing the shader whether there is any contribution at all, i.e., whether the light source is at least partially above the tangent plane. The other two values are intensities:

$\mathbf{J}_d$ – This is a single RGB value determining the contribution of the light source to the diffusely reflected light in **P**. For a simple point light source this value will be

$$\mathbf{J}_d = f_{\text{att}}(\mathbf{N} \cdot \mathbf{L})\mathbf{I}_d \tag{2.2}$$

where $f_{\text{att}}$ is an attenuation factor, **L** is the light direction, and $\mathbf{I}_d$ is the emitted light source intensity possibly attenuated if the shadow ray crosses one or more scene primitives between the light source and **P**. For linear, area, and volume light sources $\mathbf{J}_d$ must be an approximation to the corresponding integral over all light directions **L** from **P** to the light source. It is a local decision of a light source whether this approximation is done by stochastic sampling, by evaluating a contour integral, or by any other approach.

$\mathbf{J}_s$ – This is the contribution of a light source to the specularly reflected light in **P**. For a point light source this value will be

$$\mathbf{J}_s = f_{\text{att}}(\mathbf{L} \cdot \mathbf{R})^m \mathbf{I}_s, \tag{2.3}$$

for extended light sources an approach similar to the diffuse case is taken. Thus, an extended Phong shader will not evaluate equation 2.1 but

$$\mathbf{I} = k_a \mathbf{I}_a + k_d \sum_{i=0}^{n-1} \mathbf{J}_{d,i} + k_s \sum_{i=0}^{n-1} \mathbf{J}_{s,i} + k_r \mathbf{I}_r + k_t \mathbf{I}_t. \tag{2.4}$$

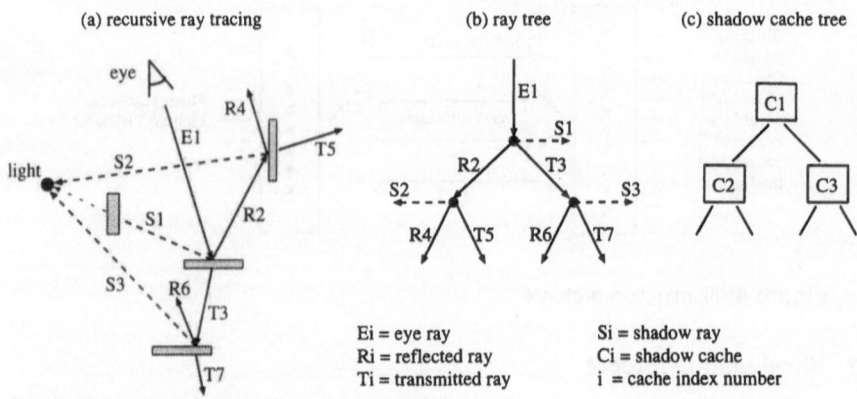

**Figure 5:** Binary tree of shadow caches

Each light source considers only that part of its light that is emitted above the tangent plane $(\mathbf{P},\mathbf{N})$. If the material in $\mathbf{P}$ is transparent, the shader asks each light source twice to compute its contribution: once for the positive half space $(\mathbf{P},\mathbf{N})$ and once for the negative half space $(\mathbf{P},-\mathbf{N})$. The second contribution is properly attenuated by the shader itself.

Two more very important details should be mentioned.

## 6.4  Shadow Rays

The RtDevice object contains the information whether shadows are switched on or off globally. If they are switched on each light source emits at least one shadow ray to sample the object space between $\mathbf{P}$ and the light source. Before doing so, though, the light source asks the shader manager whether there is at least one transparent primitive in the scene. If there is none, the light source asks the acceleration data structure to find any intersection of the shadow ray on its path to the surface point $\mathbf{P}$. If there is an intersection, the light along this shadow ray is totally attenuated.

If there are transparent primitives in the environment, computations are slightly more complex. In this case the light source asks the acceleration data structure to find the closest intersection of the shadow ray. If there is an intersection, the method `getLightAttenuation` of the corresponding shader does all further work. If the material is opaque, the shadow ray intensity is attenuated totally. Otherwise, it is the responsibility of this shader to emit a continued shadow ray and to compute a proper intensity attenuation. This is a good example for the general concept that computations should always be done where the most information is locally available.

## 6.5  Binary Tree of Shadow Caches

There is one protocol parameter whose importance has not been explained – the shadow cache index `cindx` (Fig. 4). Figure 5 outlines the general idea.

Each light source maintains a shadow cache [5] which stores the result of tracing the last shadow ray. If this shadow ray encountered a shadowing opaque object on its path from the intersection point to the light source, a pointer to this object is stored in the light cache. Otherwise, a null pointer is stored. Before the next shadow ray is traced, an intersection test is made between this ray and the object referenced by the shadow cache. The shadow ray is actually traced only if the test result is negative. The implicit assumption made above is that the environment primarily consists of diffuse objects so that successive shadow rays emanate from intersection points adjacent to previous intersection points.

The idea now is, only to use the shadow test results of the last shadow ray with the same position in the abstract ray tree [10]. The ray index representing this ray tree position is computed as follows:

$$
\begin{aligned}
\text{ray\_index( eye ray )} &= 1 \\
\text{ray\_index( reflected ray )} &= 2 * \text{ray\_index( parent ray )} \\
\text{ray\_index( transmitted ray )} &= 2 * \text{ray\_index( parent ray )} + 1 \\
\text{ray\_index( shadow ray )} &= \text{ray\_index( parent ray )}
\end{aligned}
$$

Instead of a single shadow cache, each light source maintains a binary tree of shadow caches, which usually is represented as a linear list and indexed by the above ray index. Notice that the shadow cache is not visible to the outside world, it is a pure internal implementation detail of a light source.

## 7  Conclusions and Future Work

The object-oriented way of thinking greatly helped to make the RayViS class system appear simple, even though it is not if we take a closer look at all the algorithmic details. C++ may not be a perfect language, but it doubtlessly is a great improvement over traditional C.

The work as presented in the previous sections is not the result of one clean design cycle, though. One major and several minor redesigns were necessary during the last two years. It seems to be nearly impossible to make a perfect object-oriented design if not all algorithmic details are known beforehand.

It is a well known fact that the extensibility of any class system has to be planned carefully from the very beginning. The extensibility of the RayViS visualization system is defined by the RayViS protocol in Fig. 1. It is possible to add new primitives (*RtPrimitive*), shaders (*RtShader*), light sources (*RtLightSrc*), 3D textures (*Texture3D*), acceleration data structures (*RtAccelDS*), and cameras (*RtCamera*) if the protocol defined by the corresponding base classes is kept.

Currently, we are working on the even more ambitious **DaViS** (Data Visualization System) project, of which RayViS will be one part. DaViS will solve many scientific visualization problems for physicists and mathematicians.

## Acknowledgements

Many thanks to Prof. W. Straßer for his long-term support of this research project. Special thanks to Armin Krauß and Gunnar Fratzke for implementing part of the acceleration data structures, the 3D textures, and the light sources.

## References

[1] Grady Booch. *Object-Oriented Analysis and Design.* Benjamin/Cummings Publishing Company, California, second edition, 1994.

[2] Dieter W. Fellner. Making 3D Graphics More Accessible. In J.G. Hosking, editor, *New Zealand Computer Science Conference '93*, pages 117–131, 1993.

[3] James D. Foley, Andries van Dam, Steven K. Feiner, and John F. Hughes. *Computer Graphics, Principles and Practice.* Addison-Wesley, second edition, 1990.

[4] Andrew S. Glassner. *An Introduction to Ray Tracing.* Academic Press, 1989.

[5] Eric A. Haines and Donald P. Greenberg. The Light Buffer: A Shadow-Testing Accelerator. *IEEE Computer Graphics & Applications*, pages 6–16, September 1986.

[6] Paul S. Heckbert. Writing a Ray Tracer. In Andrew S. Glassner, editor, *An Introduction to Ray Tracing*, chapter 7, pages 263–293. Academic Press, 1989.

[7] David Kirk and James Arvo. The Ray Tracing Kernel. *Proceedings of Ausgraph '88*, pages 75–82, 1988.

[8] Craig E. Kolb. Rayshade User's Guide and Reference Manual, Draft 0.4, January 1992.

[9] W. Leister, H. Müller, and A. Stößer. *Fotorealistische Computeranimation.* Springer-Verlag, 1991.

[10] Andrew Pearce and David Jevans. Exploiting Shadow Coherence in Ray Tracing. *Proceedings Graphics Interface '91*, pages 109–116, June 1991.

[11] L. Richard Speer. An Updated Cross-Indexed Guide to the Ray-tracing Literature. *Computer Graphics*, 26(1):41–72, January 1992.

[12] Gregory J. Ward. The Radiance Lighting Simulation System. Global Illumination, Siggraph '92 Course Notes, 1992.

[13] Drew Wells. Persistence of Vision Ray Tracer (POV-Ray), Version 1.0, Documentation, July 1992.

# 3

# An Object-Oriented Approach to Curves and Surfaces

Philipp Slusallek, Reinhard Klein, Andreas Kolb, Günther Greiner

Applications in computer graphics and geometric modeling generally require the integration of a variety of curve and surface types into a single system. Object-oriented design offers the opportunity to use the inherent hierarchical structure of curves and surfaces to solve this problem. This paper presents a top down approach to the design of an object-oriented framework for curves and surfaces together with its C++ implementation. We start from an abstract class of general differentiable curves and surfaces and in turn refine this design to various parametric representations of curves and surfaces. This design includes all of the standard curve and surface types and provides a powerful and uniform interface for applications. Examples from differential geometry, blending, and scattered data interpolation illustrate the approach.

## 1 Introduction

In this paper we present a top down approach to the design of an object-oriented framework for curves and surfaces together with its C++ implementation. We start from an abstract class of general differentiable curves and surfaces and in turn refine this design to various parametric representations of curves and surfaces [19, 25]. This design includes all of the standard curve and surface types, and provides a powerful and uniform interface for applications.

In Section 2 we present our approach to order the types of curves and surfaces into a hierarchical structure and review implementation features and selected curve and surface classes.

The main issue is to extract the operations that identify a certain class of curve and surface representations and set them apart from objects of other classes. This hierarchical structure serves as a reference for the derivation of a set of C++ classes implementing this hierarchy.

To an application programmer, this derived class hierarchy offers a unified view onto the various types of curves and surfaces representations. One only needs to know about the methods offered by the abstract classes and not about their internal implementation in derived classes.

Even more important in a research environment is our design decision to already supply most functionality at the abstract level by resorting to numerical techniques. As a result, a new curve or surface representation only requires to implement a method for point evaluation, and all other functionality is provided through numerical approximations in the abstract classes. Another benefit is the reuse of code in the class hierarchy, since similar functionality of certain curve and surface representations is already provided through common base classes (e.g. management of control points, operations on the parameter region, etc.).

The presented object-oriented framework is supposed to support a wide range of applications. Some examples are given in Section 3 which illustrate the power of this approach. These examples include visualization of differential geometry properties, the design of blending surfaces, and scattered data interpolation. In Section 4 the experience with this object-oriented approach is summarized and extensions and further research areas are discussed.

## 2  Design

We start with a general overview of curves and surfaces and explain how they can be grouped into a hierarchical scheme. We use this scheme as a guideline for the implementation of a set of abstract C++ classes. These abstract classes are used to derive the classes for concrete curve and surface types like a B-spline curve or a specific tensor-product patch.

### 2.1  Overview

An overview of our class hierarchy is shown in Figure 1. The important abstract classes together with some classes of special curve or surface types are given. Some less important classes have been removed from this figure to clarify the approach. Solid arrows mark derivations from super class to subclass. Dotted arrows mark classes that take a references to other classes, which either implement certain parts of this object (e.g. ParameterRegion for a surface) or which specify the class of objects that this class can operate on (e.g. CompositeCurve has ParamCurves as sub-curves).

The whole framework is implemented in C++ [5, 24], which enables an efficient and easy translation of our theoretical results to program code. At this point C++ is used almost exclusively for all projects within our group.

In the following subsections we present the more important classes of the hierarchical structure for curves and surfaces. For each class we describe the concepts implemented by this class and the set of methods providing this functionality.

Additionally, we identify those basic methods which must be implemented by all derived classes and those which may be implemented in the base class using the provided numerical methods.

### 2.2  Parameterized Curves

A parameterized curve $C$ is a mapping of an interval $I$ to $R^3$. This type of curve is so common in computer graphics that a class is certainly required. In our framework this class is called ParamCurve. The most fundamental methods for this type of curves are to obtain the parameter range $I$ and to evaluate the curve at a given parameter $t \in I$ to derive a point $C(t)$ on the curve.

Applications in Computer Aided Geometric Design (CAGD) and other areas often require methods to obtain the derivatives $C^r(t)$, curvature, torsion, arc length or the Frenét Frame at a given parameter value $t$. These methods can be implemented numerically, using only the point evaluation method of the curve.

To offer all this functionality for any curve that at least knows how to evaluate a point $C(t)$, we have chosen to implement this functionality in the abstract class ParamCurve.

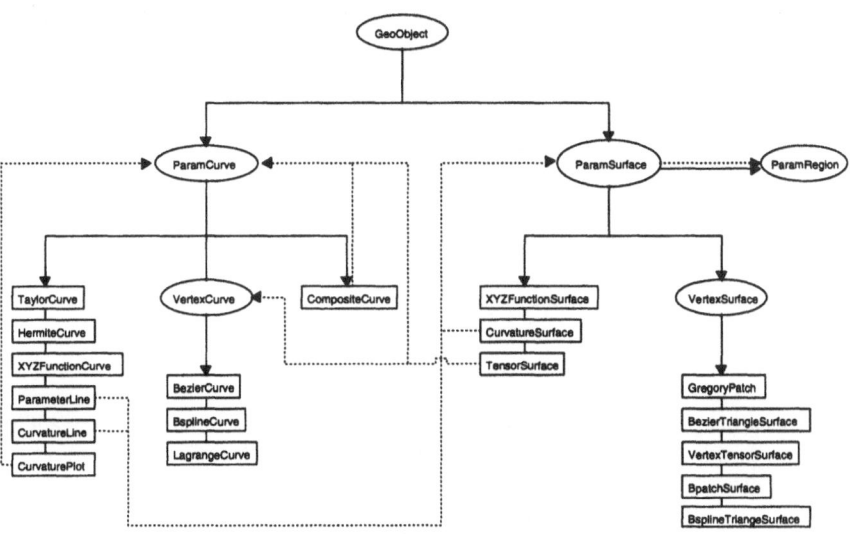

**Figure 1:** Schematic view of the class hierarchy. Ovals indicate abstract classes, rectangles actual implementations, solid arrows derivation in the class hierarchy, and dotted arrows references between related classes.

At this level the methods use numerical approximation techniques, to obtain results for a general differentiable curve. If a subclass of a curve provides more accurate or faster algorithms to obtain these results, then the methods can always be overridden.

This implementation on the abstract level frees the programmer of a new curve class from the burden to implement all these probably difficult algorithms and instead rely on numerical approximation. Other algorithms can then be substituted at a later stage of the design process.

Since we want to visualize the curve, we need a way to output the curve to a graphics display. We have therefore implemented a method to generate a piecewise linear approximation. The accuracy, that should be met by the approximation, is specified by the user or the application program. This accuracy description is a separate class, with methods to query for criteria like 'flatness', number of segments, etc., whichever is more appropriate for the given curve or surface type. Again a default implementation is provided by the ParamCurve class.

## 2.3  Vertex Curves

In CAGD many of the standard curve schemes are based on geometric control points. The shape of the curve is then derived from these control points by approximation or interpolation techniques. This common property of many curve types motivates another abstract class derived from **ParamCurve**, called **VertexCurve**.

This class handles methods like management and user interaction of the control points already on the abstract level. Thus instantiations like Bézier- or Lagrange curves do not need to handle those operations explicitly. Of course, if there are special needs which are not covered by the abstract methods, they can be met by overriding the appropriate methods. Only the specific algorithm to calculate a point on the curve using the control points needs to be implemented for these derived classes.

The set of control points is implemented as an object of a separate class, which is then referenced in the curve classes. Many curves also need a set of knot values (e.g. B-spline-, Lagrange curves), which is implemented in the same way. Because the class of control vertices or knot values is itself derived from `ParamCurve`, it shares all its functionality. This includes output, user interaction, and subdivision.

The method to obtain a linear approximation of a curve is overridden for many vertex curves. Instead of using the point evaluation method to obtain enough points on the curve for an approximation, we use the more efficient (recursive) subdivision schemes, which are available for many types of vertex curves.

## 2.4  Meta Objects

The application programmer who wants to use this framework often has many additional methods which he would like to implement for all surfaces. Changing the abstract classes in the framework might not be the best way to do this, due to a probable inflation of methods. Instead we have chosen to implement this functionality using classes of *meta object* (not to be confused with other definitions associated with the term "meta" in object-oriented languages). Instead of having their own representation of geometry, they derive their geometry from objects of other classes.

There is a large set of classes for meta objects, which reference other curves or surfaces and visualize their properties. For instance the class `CurvaturePlot` is a planar curve that plots the curvature of another curve over its arc length. Since `CurvaturePlot` is itself derived from `ParamCurve` any method of this class also works on it. Thus a `CurvaturePlot` applied to a `CurvaturePlot` is easy.

Another example for meta objects is the following: We could have implemented a method that returns the derivative of the curve $A$ over the whole parameter range as another curve object. Instead, we have used a meta object: A new meta object $B$ (of class `Hodograph` in this case) is instantiated with a reference to the curve $A$. Whenever a point of this curve $B$ is queried, it queries curve $A$ for the derivative and returns it. Thus hodographs [7, 10] are available for any curve type. Other functionality like offset curves are implemented using the same technique.

An alternative design to meta objects would have been the use of action tables [23]. This design allows a more general extension of arbitrary classes. Since this is not required in our case, we found that our concept of meta objects provides so much flexibility and functionality – while being simple and quick to implement – that we have used it throughout the framework.

## 2.5  Parameterized Surfaces

Parameterized surfaces are a bit more difficult and interesting. They are mappings from a subset $D \subset R^2$ to $R^3$. They are implemented in the class `ParamSurface`. All methods relying on evaluating the surface at a single point are nearly identical to the curve methods, except that we now have to calculate partial derivatives, etc.. Problems arise when a non-local method needs to be applied to a surface (e.g. triangulation), since the method needs knowledge about the whole parameter region over which the surface is defined. This is more difficult than in the one dimensional case.

Again the most fundamental method is to obtain a point on the surface corresponding to a parameter value $u \in D$. As in the curve class all the other local methods are implemented at the abstract level in the class hierarchy as numerical approximations using point evaluation. These methods include calculation of partial derivatives and cross derivatives, normal vectors, Gaussian-, minimal and maximal curvatures, and the Fundamental Forms [4, 8] of the surface. This functionality is offered for any derived class, but can again be overridden, if better algorithms are available for a specific type of surface.

## 2.6  Vertex Surface

Similar to curves, a large group of surface types use geometric control points to specify the geometry of a surface, which is adequately reflected as a separate abstract class called VertexSurface. But as for the parameter region, management of control points is more difficult for surfaces than for curves, due to the non-linear arrangement of the control vertices. Common arrangements form regular rectangular or triangular meshes, but arbitrary triangulations are also available.

Our implementation of this concept in an abstract class offers only linear access to the set of control vertices. This normally suffices to implement user interaction and other general operations, as we can access any set of control points regardless of their topology. The classes for the other topologies are derived from this class and offer different access methods and storage implementations to efficiently implement special arrangements.

Special instantiations of these surface types are tensor-product surfaces, triangular Bézier patches [6], and multivariate B-splines [9]. Again, we benefit from our hierarchical class structure, since for a new derived class only the point evaluation method must be implemented. All other functionality is already provided by the base classes.

## 2.7  Parameter Region

Non-local operations require knowledge about the domain of the surface. The problem is that the domain region is not a one-dimensional interval, but a region in two dimensions that could be non-connected and bounded by free-form curves. This is often the case for trimmed free-form surface.

In order to solve this problem, the concept of a parameter region is implemented in an abstract class ParamRegion. This class can be queried for such information as point in region, the border as a set of bounding curves, a 2D-bounding box, etc..

The region can also return a tessellation of itself. The tessellation can either be a simpler representation (bounded by piecewise linear curves) or a set of triangles. This offers support for many standard algorithms. Note, that this tessellation method does not know about the surface but only operates on the parameter region. Similar meshing methods are implemented for surfaces, which then have access to the surface properties to obtain an adaptive tessellation, e.g. based on the surface curvature.

In this section we have outlined our framework for curves and surfaces, its most important concepts, and their implementation as C++ classes. From these many other classes have been derived which either implement special curve and surface representations or which - as meta objects - operate on other geometric objects. Several advanced algorithms for tesselating parameter regions and surfaces have also been implemented.

## 3  Applications

In this section we illustrate the benefits of this object-oriented framework for three different applications:

For the visualization of concepts from differential geometry we have implemented several classes of meta objects. They allow the calculation of curvature and torsion for a curve as well as mean and Gaussian curvature for a surface. This enables the user to create curvature plots, lines of curvature, etc., thus supplying tools for quality control of curves and surfaces.

The second application is the construction of blend-surfaces through variational design. In this case we use the framework to obtain informations about the boundary conditions for a new blending surface. Given the position and cross derivatives at the boundary, we generate a smooth blending surface. The tools developed for the first application can be used for visualizing the smoothness of the resulting surface and thus determine its quality.

The last application illustrates how the framework can help designing new surface schemes for scattered data interpolation. The problem is to find a smooth surface interpolating a given set of unorganized points. Again, the visualization of the smoothness of the interpolating surface is vital for the development of good algorithms.

The hierarchical structure of curve and surface representations in our framework allows us to apply nearly all operations of these applications to any curve or surface. As a result implementing the applications was greatly simplified, because the algorithms need not deal with many special cases, as they were already handled in the specific methods of the framework (e.g. derivatives near the boundary of a surface).

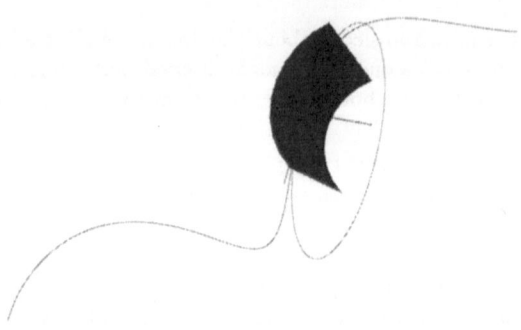

**Figure 2:** Visualizing differential geometry: A helix with a curvature circle, a Frenét frame, and a section of the torsion cylinder

### 3.1  Application 1: Visualizing Differential Geometry

Some properties of curves and surfaces can be visualized through appropriate geometric primitives. For instance, the curvature $\kappa$ of a curve at a given point can be visualized by displaying a curvature circle, also called the osculating circle. This circle lies in the osculating plane spanned by the tangent $t$ and the main normal $n$ and has the radius $\frac{1}{\kappa}$.

In an similar way we visualize the torsion $\tau$ of a curve by a cylinder through the point on the surface and with axis parallel to the binormal and having radius $\frac{1}{\tau}$ (Figure 2). Animating the curvature circle, the torsion cylinder, and the Frenét frame along the curve results in a method for displaying their variation.

A simple and convenient method for displaying the variation of the scalar curvature and torsion values is by means of a color-coded map. Another method for displaying the curvature is through curvature plots. The curvature plot is a two dimensional graph which plots the curvature as a function of the arc length of the curve. For surfaces, sectional curvature may again be visualized through curvature circles.

The variation of the scalar-valued Gaussian- and mean curvature, as well as minimal and maximal curvature over the surface can be visualized by means of a color-coded map (Figure 3). There are several other elaborated techniques which produce good results [2, 8].

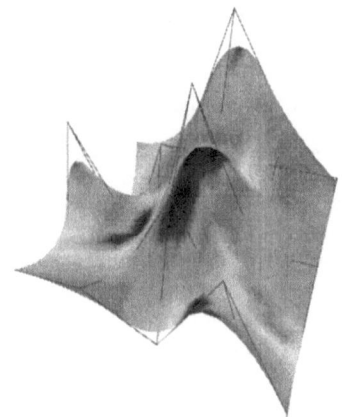

**Figure 3:** A B-spline surface with imposed color-coded Gauss-curvature

An informative method for analyzing the variation of the principal directions across the surface is to incorporate a family of lines of curvature [2] into the display. A line of curvature is a curve on the surface whose tangent direction at each point coincides with one of the principal directions (Figure 4).

The framework has proven to support this kind of application very well, because it is very simple to create various kinds of meta objects for visualizing different aspects of any of the supported surface representations.

## 3.2  Application 2: Constructing Blending Surfaces

Another application that uses this framework is the construction and visualization of blending surfaces. Given two *primary surfaces* the problem is to construct a smooth transitional surface. Such a surface is called a *blend surface*. Our method [14, 15, 16] is based on a variational principle or an optimization problem. These methods have become quite popular in recent years in different areas in computer graphics [21, 22, 26]. The main idea to construct the blend surface is as follows:

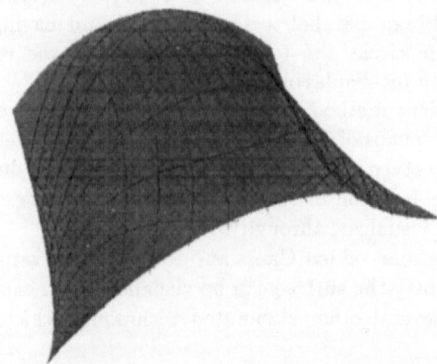

**Figure 4:** A Bézier surface with curvature lines visualizing the direction of minimum and maximum curvature at each point along the curve

- It gives a smooth transition to the primary surface at the boundaries, and

- a *fairing functional*, which somehow measures total mean curvature, is minimized.

The boundary curves and the derivatives along those curves are given by special curve objects, which live on each of the primary surfaces. They describe the geometry of the problem completely and together with the functional ensure a unique solution to the blending problem.

So far this method has been implemented for tensor product B–spline surfaces (TPS). For two primary TPS and specified boundaries (which are B-spline curves), a TPS is constructed such that it meets the primary surfaces at the boundaries. In addition, the cross-boundary derivatives of blend surface and a primary surface coincide at the boundary where they meet. The fairing functional $J$ which will be minimized is of the form [17]

$$J(F) = \int_\Omega \sum_{i\,\alpha\,\beta} w_{i\alpha\beta} \frac{\partial^\alpha S_i}{(\partial u)^\alpha} \frac{\partial^\beta S_i}{(\partial v)^\beta}$$

where $\alpha$ and $\beta$ are multi-indices of order $\leq 2$ , and $S_i$ ($i = 1, 2, 3$), denote $x$- $y$- and $z$ component of the surface $S$. The weight functions $w_{i\alpha\beta}$ depend on the geometry of the region to be blended and are chosen via a parameter transformation between the parameter space of the TPS (rectangle) and a more natural parameter space. This has the effect, that the fairing functional $J$ is a good approximation for the total mean curvature (in mean square sense). The details are given in [15].

The implementation of the blending operation relies on a set of classes that describe the boundary curves and the derivatives along those curves.

The boundary curves all lie on the blended surfaces. So they are implemented using curves that map a parameter interval to the two dimensional parameter region of the surface. This is the same technique which is used for trimming curves of parametric surfaces. This class `SurfaceCurve` for curves on surfaces offers additional methods to calculate derivatives of the surface along the curve. A `SurfaceCurve` object can be queried for a derivative and will return a new object of a class derived from `SurfaceCurve` called `SurfaceDeriv`. Evaluating a point on this curve results is the requested derivative.

Encapsulating the derivatives in another object allows us to trade accuracy for speed without changing any other algorithm in the framework: The class `SurfaceDeriv` can query the surface for derivatives at a few points and can then use interpolation to obtain intermediate results, which can result in large speedups. All this is invisible to the blending algorithm using this object.

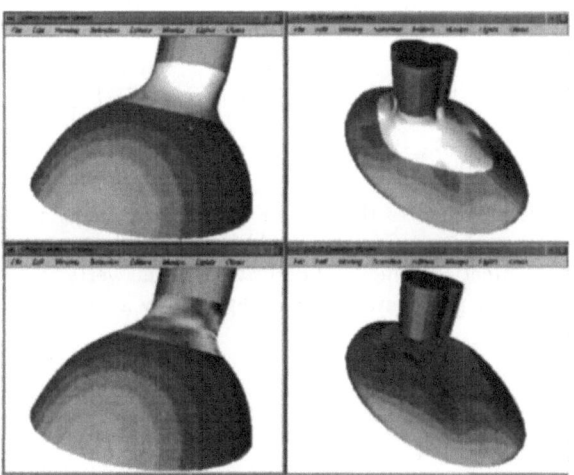

**Figure 5:** Two blend surfaces and their curvature plots

An example of a blending surface and its curvature distribution is given in (Figure 5). On the upper left side two primary surfaces (green) and the blend surface(red). On the upper right side the same setting with a curvature plot for Gaussian curvature for the blend surface. Below another setting of two primary and one blend surface. In this case the upper primary surface is an elliptical cylinder.

## 3.3  Application 3: Minimal Norm Network Interpolants

In various areas of research one is confronted with the problem of scattered data interpolation (to reconstruct a scalar valued function $F : \Omega \mapsto R$, $\Omega \subseteq R^2$, in two variables knowing its values only at a finite number of points $u_i \in \Omega$, where the points $u_i$ do not have any regular structure). It is generally difficult to ensure a priori that an interpolation scheme produces a surfaces with good overall shape. Therefore curvature plots are an indispensable tool for judging the overall quality of the resulting shape [18].

One approach to solve this problem is the so-called *Minimal Norm Network method* (MNN). This method has several advantages: it can be used on non-convex domains $\Omega$ and the shape of the interpolant can be controlled in a predictable manner.

The MNN method for constructing an interpolating function consists of three steps (for more details see [12, 20]):

1. The data points are used to construct a *triangulation* of the domain $\Omega$. Since thin triangles are not desired for numerical reasons, we usually take the well known *Delaunay* triangulation [11].

2. A *curve network* whose domain is the union of all edges of the triangulation is uniquely defined as follows: The single curves must meet with a certain degree of continuity. Furthermore, we choose among all these network functions those whose norm with respect to a given functional is minimal. The functionals are usually of the type:

$$\sigma(S) = \sum_{e \in T} \int_e \left\{ \left( \frac{\partial^2 F}{\partial e^2} \right)^2 + \alpha^2 \left( \frac{\partial F}{\partial e} \right)^2 \right\} de$$

or

$$\sigma(S) = \sum_{e \in T} \int_e \left\{ \left( \frac{\partial^3 F}{\partial e^3} \right)^2 + \gamma^2 \left( \frac{\partial^2 F}{\partial e^2} \right)^2 \right\} de,$$

where the triangulation $T$ is defined as a set of edges $\{e\}$.

3. The network is extended to the interior of each triangle by means of a *triangular interpolant*. For each vertex in the considered triangle, one patch is defined by interpolating the function values and derivatives in this vertex and along its opposite edge. The final triangular interpolant is obtained by a convex combination of these three patches.

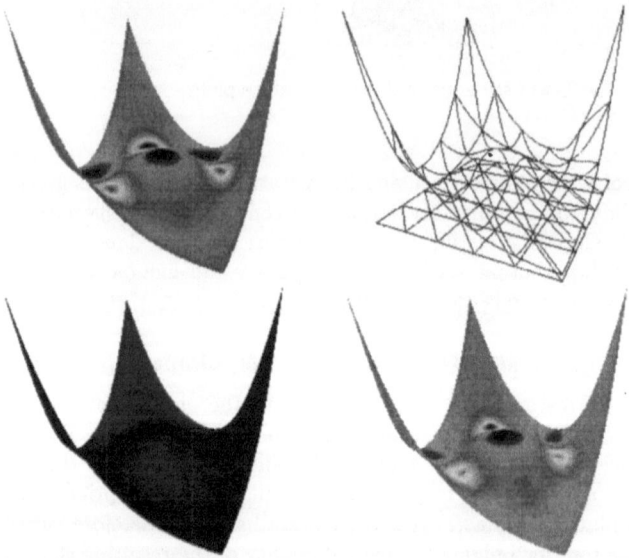

**Figure 6:** A curvature plot the original surface, the curve network, the MNN interpolant, and its curvature plot

A first preliminary implementation of this scheme showed quite good results as far as mean and maximum errors were concerned. However, after the scheme was introduced into this framework and analyzed using the tools for visualizing the curvature of the interpolating surfaces, the quality of curvature plots turned out to be quite poor. Thus, the visualization of curvature inspired us to do further investigation. This finally led to an improved MNN-interpolation scheme [20] with significantly better curvature distribution (Figure 6).

## 4  Conclusion and Further Work

We have presented a top-down approach to the design of an object-oriented framework for parametric curves and surfaces. Only the most fundamental method, point evaluation, must be supplied in order to integrate a new type of curve or surface into the scheme. All other methods are already implemented in abstract base classes. Thus the programmer is free to experiment without worrying about details such as implementing derivatives or similar operations, but still has the ability to use better methods as they become available.

A complete set of methods for curve and surface design and analysis with support for blending, scattered data interpolation, differential geometry, tessellation, and display is provided.

The support for surface manipulation based on differential geometry or other local operations which do not directly work on control vertices but on the surface itself, have not been studied [13]. This is certainly a very interesting research area, but it is yet unclear if and how these operators can be applied to arbitrary abstract surface classes.

## References

[1] R.H. Bartels, J.C. Beatty, and B.A. Barsky. *An Introduction to Splines for Use in Computer Graphics and Geometric Modelling.* Morgan Kaufman, 1987.

[2] J. Beck, R. Farouki, and J. Hinds. Surface Analysis Methods. *Computer Graphics & Applications*, 6(12):18–38, December 1986.

[3] J. Bloomenthal. Polygonization for implicit surfaces. *Computer Aided Geometric Design*, 5:341–355, 1988.

[4] M. P. do Carmo. *Differential Geometry of Curves and Surfaces.* Prentice Hall, Englewood Cliffs, N.J., 1976.

[5] Margaret A. Ellis and Bjarne Stroustrup. *The Annotated C++ Reference Manual.* Addison Wesley, 1991.

[6] Gerald E. Farin. Triangular Bernstein–Bézier patches. *Computer Aided Geometric Design*, 3:pp. 83–127, 1986.

[7] Gerald E. Farin. *Curves and Surfaces in Computer Aided Geometric Design.* Academic Press, 1988.

[8] R. T. Farouki. Graphical Methods for Surface Differential Geometry. In R. R. Martin, editor, *The Mathematics of Surfaces II*, pages 363–385. Oxford Science Publications, Oxford, 1987.

[9] Philip Fong and Hans-Peter Seidel. Control Points for Multivariate B-spline Surfaces over Arbitrary Triangulations. *Computer Graphics Forum*, 10:309–317, 1991.

[10] A. R. Forrest. Interactive Interpolation and Approximation by Bézier Polynomials. *The Computer Journal*, 15:pp. 71–79, 1972.

[11] S. Fortune. Voronoi Diagrams and Delaunay Triangulations. In D. Z. Du and F. Hwang, editors, *Computing in Euclidean Geometry*, pages 193–223. World Scientific Publ., 1992.

[12] R. Franke and G. Nielson. Scattered Data Interpolation: A Tutorial and Survey. In H. Hagen and D. Roller, editors, *Geometric Modelling: Methods and Applications*, pages 131–160, New York, 1991. Springer-Verlag.

[13] Priamos N. Georgiades and Donald P. Greenberg. Locally Manipulating the Geometry of Curved Surfaces. *IEEE Computer Graphics & Applications*, 12(1):54–64, January 1992.

[14] G. Greiner. Blending Techniques Based on Variational Principles. In J. Warren, editor, *Curves and Surfaces in Computer Vision and Graphics III*, Proc. SPIE 1830, pages 174–184. SPIE, 1992.

[15] G. Greiner. Surface Contructions Based on Variational Principles. In P.-J. Laurent, A. Le Méhauté, and L. L. Schumaker, editors, *Curves and Surfaces II*, Chamonix, 1993.

[16] G. Greiner and H.-P. Seidel. Curvature Continuous Blend Surfaces. In B. Falcidieno and T. L. Kunii, editors, *Modelling in Computer Graphics*, pages 309–317. Springer-Verlag, 1993.

[17] M. Kallay. Constrained optimization in surface design. In B. Falcidieno and T. L. Kunii, editors, *Modeling in Computer Graphics*, pages 85–94. Springer-Verlag, 1993.

[18] R. Klass. Correction of Local Surface Irregularities Using Reflection Lines. *Computer Aided Design*, 12(2):73–76, February 1980.

[19] R. Klein and Ph. Slusallek. An Object-Oriented Framework for Curves and Surfaces. In J. Warren, editor, *Curves and Surfaces in Computer Vision and Graphics III*, Proc. SPIE 1830, pages 284–295. SPIE, 1992.

[20] Andreas Kolb. Interpolating Scattered Data with $C^2$ surfaces. Technical report, Universität Erlangen, 1993.

[21] M. Lounsbery, S. Mann, and S. and T. deRose. Parametric Surface Interpolation. *Computer Graphics & Applications*, 9:97–115, 1992.

[22] H. P. Moreton and C. H. Séquin. Functional Optimization for Fair Surface Design. In E. E. Catmull, editor, *Computer Graphics*, pages 167–176. ACM Siggraph, ACM Press, 1992.

[23] Paul S. Strauss and Rikk Carey. An Object-Oriented 3D Graphics Toolkit. *Computer Graphics*, 26(1):341–352, July 1992.

[24] Bjarne Stroustrup. *The C++ Programming Language*. Addison Wesley, 2. edition, 1991.

[25] Allan H. Vermeulen and Richard H. Bartels. C++ Spline Classes for Prototyping. In *Curves and Surfaces in Computer Graphics II*, pages 121–131. SPIE, 1991.

[26] William Welch and Andrew Witkin. Variational Surface Modeling. In Edwin E Catmull, editor, *Computer Graphics*, pages 157–166. ACM Siggraph, ACM Press, 1992.

# 4

# Object-Oriented Modeling of Graphical Primitives

Ekkehard Beier

Object-orientation is a well-known paradigm to be applied in the field of computer graphics, e.g., to build class hierarchies of graphical primitives using inheritance. However, a clear framework for modeling primitives in an object-oriented manner is still unavailable. This article describes the functional requirements, the abstract realization, and a concrete implementation of a resulting object-oriented modeling paradigm that has its roots in display-list-based systems and takes advantage of multiple inheritance.

## 1 Introduction

The parameterization of graphical primitives can be accomplished in numerous ways, e.g., through the assignment of attributes like color, fillstyle or by spatial modeling operations like rotation or translation. Modeling will often be inherited inside hierarchies of primitives (hierarchical modeling). On the other hand, relations between arbitrary primitives can be maintained using (geometrical) constraints. Modeling may also contain temporal aspects. Sometimes, even global properties such as depth cues may be assigned to primitives.

This article will focus on the hierarchical modeling of primitives that may be expressed adequately by attributes and is based on the concepts of the traditional shading libraries such as GKS [13], PHIGS (PLUS) [14, 15], IRIS GL [9] and OpenGL [16]. Requirements for an object-oriented modeling approach will be formulated by analyzing the drawbacks of these libraries and by introducing innovative attribute concepts.

The realization and implementation of this approach will be explained. These concepts are integrated in the graphics kernel YART [2], which is available in the public domain. For more information have a look at *http://metallica.prakinf.tu-ilmenau.de/GOOD.html*.

## 2 Requirements for an Object-Oriented Modeling

### 2.1 Conformity with the Mental Model of Computer Graphics

The object-oriented paradigm defines *objects* as the integration of data and functionality. As shown in [18] these objects reliably match the mental model of the graphics programmer. This means:

- Graphical representations can be seen as entities or objects. They may be manipulated and attributed as wholes.

- They have their own attributes which influence the object and nothing else[1].

- Attributes may directly be assigned to or queried from the object itself (principle of locality). However that does not mean that objects cannot share physically existent attributes.

- Operations can be applied directly to the results of interactions (e.g., a pick operation). This is known as symmetry between input and output [18].

Conventional systems often violate the principles of locality and input-output symmetry. For instance, in PHIGS (PLUS) [14, 15] the attributes that are valid for a given structure cannot be queried because the temporary results of the traversing process cannot be accessed. The pick operation in PHIGS delivers a so-called pick path, from which the picked output object has to be extracted. Assinging an attribute to the picked object may cause fatal results in the central structure store because this structure could have been multiply referenced and an automatic individualization is not provided in PHIGS.

## 2.2  Part-Of Hierarchies

The modeling should support editable multi-level part-of hierarchies in an intuitive and object-oriented manner with inheritance of the modeling. This includes a uniform handling of elementary primitives and groups of primitives.

In contrast, traditional systems like GKS or PHIGS distinguish between both. For instance, in PHIGS some attributes may be assigned to groups (*structures*) only, while others are only applicable to primitives (*structure elements*).

## 2.3  Efficiency

Efficiency is also an important requirement, even in academic projects. The aim is to eliminate redundances. Assuming that modeling is only allowed via object *x29* (Fig. 1) and all internal polygons are defined in a common reference coordinates system, then it is efficient to reference attributes and modeling matrices of the father object instead of the instantiation of attributes for the part objects.

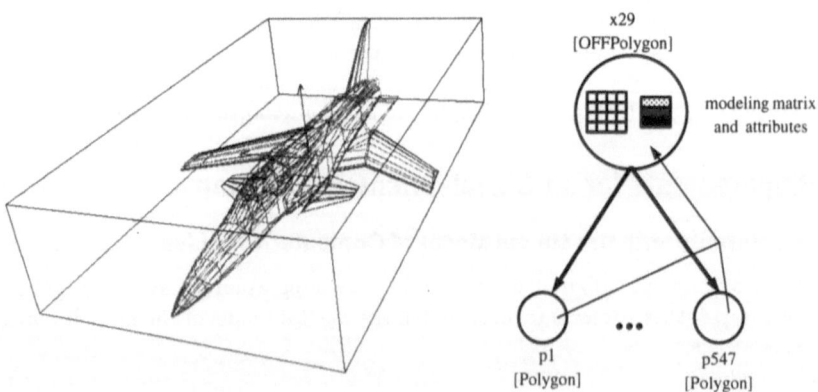

**Figure 1:** Sharing of modeling resources

---

[1]An exception is the inheritance of attributes inside a part-of hierarchy.

Classic display-list-based libraries make graphical scenes possible, which are very memory- (and run-time-) efficient, because they allow the creation of directed acyclic graphs of display lists. The price is the violation of the principle of locality as mentioned above and the loss of retraversing possibilities. Also, a time-consuming traversing process (attribute transfer, concatenation of modeling matrices) is necessary for the graphical output.

## 2.4  Naming Concepts

An object-oriented modeling approach should support some kind of a naming concept, allowing a flexible assignment of attributes. This includes the limitation of the scope of assignment of an attribute to a set of primitives, e.g., all primitives of a given type.

For this purpose PHIGS provides *name sets* consisting of inclusion and exclusion sets for some attribute types. However, in a complex multi-level graph history the filter concept of PHIGS is not powerful enough to specify that an attribute could be assigned to any predefined subset of the traversal list and not to the remainder of the list.

## 2.5  Abstract Modeling

In an extensible object-oriented graphics system a more abstract modeling mechanism is needed. This includes surface parameters which are more general and can be used for multiple kinds of rendering[2]. A modeling system that is not tailored to limited types of primitives reduces cognitive load and simplifies programming.

In contrast, PHIGS PLUS does not allow the definition of advanced surface parameters like transparency or refraction or even a surface mapping. Many of its attribute types are bound to one type of primitive.

# 3  Innovative Modeling Concepts

The following concepts gave useful inspirations for the modeling approach that will be introduced in Section 4.

## 3.1  C++ Encapsulation of PHIGS Attributes

The predecessor of YART was an object-oriented graphics system built around PHIGS PLUS. The C++ encapsulation of the PHIGS structures is depicted in figure 2. The structures were divided into four parts by using label elements. This division was useful for management jobs (destroying all children, clearing all geometry elements before recreation) and for implementing public and private attribute assignments. Some utility functions were defined for the convenient handling of the PHIGS attributes. For instance, when an attribute was assigned the *set()* function warranted that an attribute of the same type would be overwritten if there was already one. The universal attributes such as *Color* were put into the central structure store (CSS) using C++ polymorphic methods of the primitives. So, a color assignment to a *line* was realized by inserting a *pline_color* element into the CSS. A *pmarker_color* element was used in the *marker* class. The attribute value was retrieved by interrogating the CSS. Thus, many of the attributes of the C++ object could be placed directly into the CSS. The CSS may be implemented in hardware on high-end machines.

But the implementation of the attributes was dependent on the primitive type. Thus, a color assignment of a *line* object did not change the color of children with type *text*.

---

[2]However, the definition of such parameters is a difficult task considering the diversity of rendering approaches.

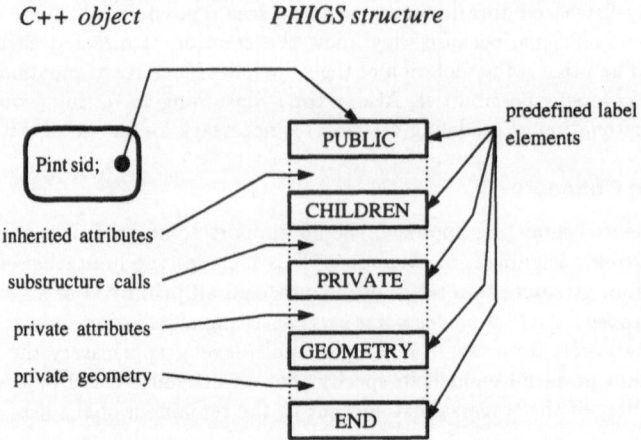

*C++ object*      *PHIGS structure*

**Figure 2:** Segmentation of a PHIGS structure in a C++ system

This was the result of the strong orientation toward PHIGS and the use of the CSS for attribute inheritance. Important abstract attributes such as *fillstyle* or *resolution* were not provided.

The PHIGS filters were represented by C++ pendants so that every filter attribute could be assigned separately to each object without knowledge of the other objects. The coupling with the PHIGS filters was realized thru the use of overloaded type cast operators.

## 3.2  Attributes in GEO++

GEO++ [18, 19] defines two kinds of graphical output elements: *parts* and *building patterns*. Building patterns consist of *groups* or *primitives* and may contain attributes. *Parts* are nodes of the object tree and may contain attributes as well. The building patterns represent ad-hoc quasi-classes that can be multiply referenced. The attributes of the groups will be used to address all objects of that group. A part object is unambiguous in the object hierarchy. Thus, attributes assigned to a part address exactly one object. GEO++ distinguishes between *default*, *group* and *part* attributes with the priorities:

$$p_{Part} > p_{Group} > p_{Default}$$

Thus, two hierarchy levels are provided regardless of the depth of the hierarchy. It would be more useful, to have as many attribute hierarchy levels as class hierarchy levels.

GEO++ also provides a type-orthogonal assignment of attributes.

## 3.3  Attribute Setting in X Toolkit

The X Toolkit [1] attributes (called *resources*) are used to manipulate widget[3] parameters such as fore-/background color, text font, and cursor. The attributes normally are inherited at widget creation time. Attributes can also be specified externally (resource file) in an object-oriented manner. As a precondition every widget has a name and a class. The widget is uniquely addressed by concatenating all parents of the widget tree.

Using an external resource description file attributes may be specified for

---

[3] A widget is a combination of a window and some semantics.

- single widgets

- all widgets of one class

- all widgets of one class in a subtree

- arbitrary groups of widgets

This is accomplished by using a canonical concatenation of widget classes and widget names. Two concatenation operators are provided, allowing the following examples:

- *background: red* – set backgrounds of all objects to red

- *XmForm\*background: blue* – set background of all objects in a widget tree which has an object of class *XmForm* as toplevel object (including the form widget itself)

- *form1\*XmLabel.background: yellow* – set the background of all objects of class *Xm-Label* in the subtree of widget *form1* to yellow

This approach has two essential advantages: every possible subset can be addressed[4] and the depth of addressing is equivalent to the class hierarchy and the object hierarchy. But the complete list of assignments has to be parsed to find the correct value for an object, since more than one specification may match a concrete widget. Thus, this mechanism is only useful to set the initial values of an object and not suitable for dynamic attribute manipulations. For that, all assignments have to be recorded and evaluated each time. But, as mentioned above, the correlation of attributes to certain classes is a useful way to set attributes in a complex hierarchy.

# 4  An Object-Oriented Modeling Approach

## 4.1  Separation of Geometry and Modeling

Our approach distinguishes between the *geometry* of a primitive and its *modeling*, the latter of these is organized by the assignment of *attributes* via specific *interfaces*[5]. A primitive owns one geometric representation that is the summary of the applied modeling. In result of the physical separation, both attributes and geometries may be multiple referenced. This separation corresponds to the traditional display list libraries. However, the following sub-sections will show the essential differences between the traditional concept and this new approach.

Multiple usage of modeling attributes guarantees memory (and run-time) efficiency and it is easy to maintain in object-oriented implementations (e.g., by usage of reference counters or with intelligent copy operators). If the attribute is stored inside the primitive an immediate attribute assignment is given. But, attributes also may be indirectly assigned to a primitive without being stored physically in it. For a given primitive in a hierarchy the value of a specific attribute type can be determined in the context of the primitive's ancestors and the priority rules of physically existent attributes.

---

[4]Note that the widget names can be chosen arbitrarily.

[5]An interface is the summary of methods which allow read and write accesses to an attribute as a whole or in part.

## 4.2  Abstract Attribute Types

The use of attribute types that are not related to a specific type of a primitive (*abstract* attributes) offers some advantages for the graphical programming:

- It simplifies the programming because the number of attribute types is much smaller than in PHIGS or HOOPS. This makes the creation of (WYSIWYG) user interfaces simpler and enables the development of generic user interfaces.

- For new primitive types that may be added to an extensible object-oriented graphics system there are predefined modeling alternatives that may be applied in a uniform manner. In contrast, PHIGS only provides recommendations about how to map specific attribute types (e.g., polyline color) to new non-portable primitives (GDP's) [12].

- The inheritance of abstract attributes inside hierarchies of primitives (*part-of hierarchies*) is quite natural and easy to realize. In opposite, in PHIGS a color attribute assigned to a text primitive (text color) will not affect children of type *marker*.

- The concrete implementation of composite primitives can be hidden. For instance, a class *Text3D* may be built from primitives of type *Polyline*, *Polygon* or *Spline* without affecting its external parameterizability.

Abstract attributes may be applied to the primitive's representation in a polymorphic manner. This is especially useful for composite primitives, providing a mechanism for an intelligent mapping of an assigned attribute to the parts of the primitive.

## 4.3  User-Defined Attribute Types

Application-specific modeling may be incorporated thru user-defined attribute types. This approach allows the definition of new attribute types in a portable manner and provides compatibility with the predefined attribute types. One class of potential candidates for new attribute types are physical properties.

## 4.4  Type-Orthogonal Assignment of Attributes

This approach allows the assignment of attribute types orthogonal to the primitive types. Assume a sphere is the top of a hierarchy containing text objects that are mapped around the sphere (Fig. 3). Then it is very efficient to assign the text attribute directly to the sphere and not to each of the text objects. Consequently, user-defined attributes may be assigned to predefined primitives.

Of course, the assignment of an attribute will not necessarily affect the geometry of the primitive. Thus, our sphere will not be changed by the assigned text attribute.

## 4.5  Multiple Inheritance

A given primitive type may inherit interfaces to different abstract modeling (and rendering[6]) types via multiple inheritance. Additionally, type-information that includes the supertypes, is provided. The type-information may be interrogated at run-time and can be used to implement a type-safe down cast in strongly-typed programming languages (e.g., C++ [7]).

---

[6]There is not necessarily a difference between modeling and rendering interfaces. The latter are used to display a representation of the primitive using a shading or ray-tracing algorithm, for instance.

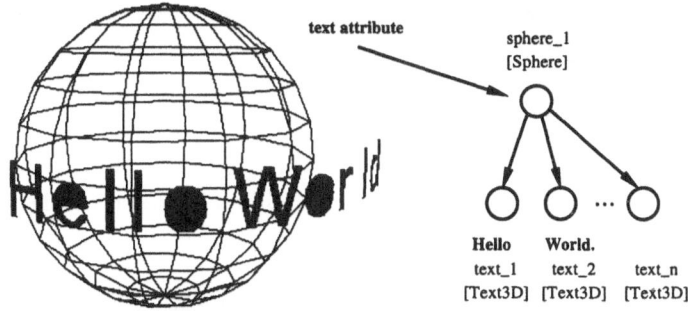

**Figure 3:** Type-orthogonal assignment of attributes

On the one hand, multiple inheritance offers a good mechanism integrating very different views of one thing. However, the inheritance solution lacks some flexibility because the inheritance relation is normally established at compilation time. On the other hand, the implementation of a particular modeling behavior for a given primitive type normally depends on both the abstract modeling type and the concrete primitive type (e.g., an analytically defined primitive). Therefore, it cannot be accomplished thru wrapper classes [8]. The same is true for the implementation of rendering protocols. Furthermore, the set of interfaces of primitives may be extended for subtypes. For instance, analytically defined primitives may additionally inherit modeling interfaces to control the tesselation into lower-level primitives. In contrast, multiple polymorphism approaches [6] do not provide a mechanism for the extension of very general method(s) defined for the base type(s) thus sacrificing extensibility.

In addition to the interfaces specific to the inherited modeling types every primitive offers a general attribute read and write method. These methods are essential for type-orthogonal assignment.

## 4.6   Trees Versus Direct Acyclic Graphs

In contrast to most display list libraries this approach allows only the creation of hierarchical trees of primitives. This is a limitation in comparison to the directed acyclic graph offered by the traditional libraries. However, hierarchical graphs are the key to maintaining the principle of locality, the type-orthogonal assignment and the extensibility of the set of attribute types. A given primitive may retraverse it's chain of ancestors to get information about the (logically) inherited modeling.

A physical hierarchical organization lacks memory and run time efficiency. However, this approach requests only logical trees. Multiple methods for increasing efficiency without loosing the advantages of the hierarchical primitives are available:

- Data which are not specific to a primitive (e.g., external data sets) may be shared between all primitives of this type.

- A geometric representation can be shared between various primitives if the modeling does not affect the representation directly. Also, a shared representation may be mapped to a temporary representation dependent on the modeling of a specific primitive. For instance, a display list can be called with different modeling matrices.

- A primitive may use a common representation as long as it does not change it. Otherwise, an individualization must be carried out to avoid side effects.

The logical hierarchical encapsulation of display lists with usage of multiple references and automatic individualization is described in [18].

# 5  Realization

This section describes the realization of the modeling approach without considering implementation details such as language binding, which will be contents of the next section.

## 5.1  Referencing of Attributes

As described above, a primitive may retraverse its hierarchy to inquire the value of a specific attribute. This solution is however not suitable for frequent inquiries. For instance, a ray-tracer may ask for surface parameters of a primitive and each pixel several times. Therefore, an attribute reference will be introduced here. Using a type-specific set of attribute references a primitive may bypass this retraversal for often needed attributes. Figure 4 shows an object scenario that illustrates the usage of the references.

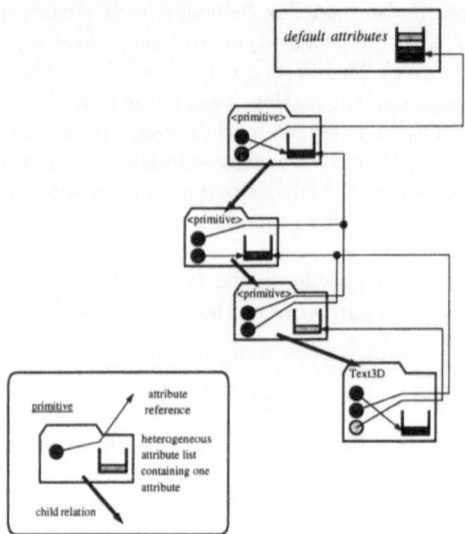

**Figure 4:** Usage of references to avoid retraversing the hierarchy

The semantics of attribute access is now as follows: A read access may invoke a retraversal if the desired attribute type is not referenced. Otherwise, the data will be read from the referenced attribute, which may be physically present in this primitive or not. A write access may directly modify the attribute if the primitive is its owner. Alternatively, an individualization could take place. An important goal is to implement this semantics below the API, i.e. invisible to the graphics programmer.

The update of the references is necessary if the hierarchy changes or new attributes were assigned to the primitive or its ancestors. This update process may be invoked immediately or globally before attribute inquires, e.g., when rendering. One option is to use a dynamically growing attribute context to transfer the attribute references down in the hierarchies. However, this mechanism and potential optimizations (e.g., attribute caches) are implementation details and may be realized in a number of forms.

It is important to mention, that the referencing is only necessary after changes and only partially. Otherwise, there is no traversing necessary. Virtually, all needed attributes are already bound to the primitives. This reduces the rendering efforts and improves the possibilities for multi-processing. In opposition, PHIGS and GL traverse the whole visible display list graph for each rendering process[7].

## 5.2  The Attribute Types

The super type of all attributes defines following common behavior:

- type information,

- a state flag and functions to set, reset and test the flag,

- a set-from-ASCII and a get-as-ASCII function[8],

- a method for persistent storing basing on the ASCII-get function,

- a list of types and names of primitives that the attribute is related to[9] and access functions,

- a copy and a compare operator,

- and access to a type-specific default attribute[10].

Subtypes define a concrete data value that will be stored in each attribute instance and therefore overload most of the above functions. Thereby, writing accesses to the data have to change the state flag.

## 5.3  The Attribute Interface Types

For each non-abstract attribute type there exists an abstract interface type that defines but does not implement the access functions specific to the attribute type. Both the attribute type and the types of primitives are derived from an interface type.

## 5.4  Predefined Attribute Types

In the above-mentioned graphics system, YART, there are four predefined attribute types. This was done to implement the basic YART primitives and to offer a means how to bootstrap higher-level primitives into the kernel. This also helps to maximize portability.

### The Surface Attribute

This attribute specifies the surface parameters relatively independent of a concrete shading model. It currently contains the Phong material coefficients [4], an emission color and a bidirectional reflectance density function (BRDF). The evaluation of these parameters

---

[7]At least they do so conceptually.

[8]This is useful for an interpretative language binding [3], for user-interface coupling and for metafile generation/evaluation.

[9]Initially, this list is empty meaning that the attribute is valid for all primitives. The scope of the attribute should include the primitive it was assigned to.

[10]There exists a global default attribute for each attribute type. The values of the default attributes may be set initially, e.g., via external setup. Using this, the graphics system may be easyly adapted to different platforms.

differs for the various kinds of rendering. Up to now, a Gouraud [11]/Phong shader, a ray-tracer [10] and a non-ideal diffuse radiosity [5] renderer have been implemented, which are working with this surface specification.

A surface attribute sets the global surface parameters for the primitive. These, however, may be overwritten in some cases by vertex-specific surface parameters.

### The Mapping Attribute

This attribute type can be used for the mapping of objects such as images or solid textures to the primitives. In this way, an extended description of surfaces can be obtained. The kind of mapping is implemented in the specific attribute type. A type $t_1$ may map the color values of a solid texture to the ambient and diffuse coefficients of a primitive dependent on the modeling coordinates of the primitive. Another type $t_2$ may map similar, but use the modeling coordinate system of the primitive's father. Using these, composite primitives can be built homogeneously from the same material. Finally, a type $t_3$ may use the world coordinates of the primitive. Thus, static primitives of the same type but at different places would generate a different solid texture.

Alternative mapping types are bump mappings, which manipulate the normal vectors of the primitives or image mappings. Rather than replace specific surface parameters of the primitives, extended mapping types may also manipulate it (e.g., addition, multiplication).

The evaluation of this attribute type by the renderer requires point-by-point inquiries of the surface parameters and callbacks into the modeling coordinates system of the primitive. Therefore, it is currently only supported by the ray-tracer in YART.

### The Resolution Attribute

The tesselation of high-level primitives such as analytically-defined ones, parametric curves and surfaces, into low-level primitives (triangle strip, polygon, quadmesh) can be controlled dynamically by using the resolution attribute. This discretization in the object space influences rendering time, memory need and rendering quality. A high resolution is useful for high-end images, because it leads to a good approximation of the mathematical shape. The visibility of spot lights and other non-linear phenomena can be improved. A low resolution has advantages for walk-thrus and other real-time applications, e.g. direct-manipulative interactions.

The resolution may also changed temporarily, for example where objects that are far away from the camera may get a very low resolution.

This attribute will not be considered by the ray-tracer for analytical primitives that overload the ray-tracing interface in order to use their analytical description directly.

The resolution can be specified in the range from 0.0 to 1.0. Currently, the extreme values 0.0 and 1.0 are undefined.

### The Fillstyle Attribute

The fillstyle attribute specifies two styles for area primitives: wireframe or solid representation. A wireframe display is useful for real-time requirements on low-end graphics workstations. Higher-level graphics platforms can display medium complexity scenes in solid mode even in real-time.

A future specification of this attribute type may include further styles like invisible or different bounding box modes. In the current YART implementation these are still realized as additional, non-inherited attributes of the primitives.

Figure 5 shows a scene with different values of attribute types *Fillstyle* and *Resolution*. The rendering was done on an entry-level SGI workstation (R3000 IRIS Indigo) using the

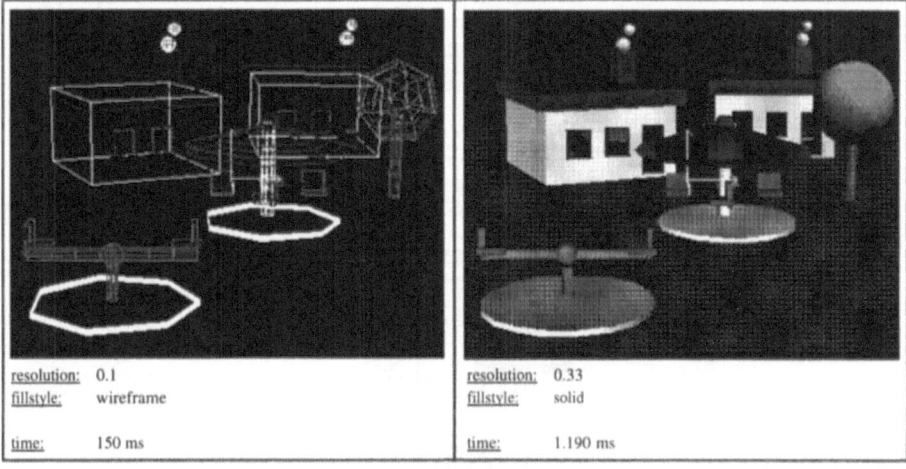

resolution:    0.1
fillstyle:     wireframe

time:          150 ms

resolution:    0.33
fillstyle:     solid

time:          1.190 ms

**Figure 5:** A scene rendered with different values for fillstyle and resolution

IRIS GL interface of YART. The time is the average of about 100 rendering processes. Each rendering process performs a complete update of attribute references and a propagation of attribute changes.

### 5.5   A Concrete Inheritance Graph

An inheritance graph for the current configuration of the YART graphics kernel is depicted in figure 6. The type *Primitive* is the supertype for all primitives and inherits the rendering interfaces as well as the modeling interfaces for the surface and the mapping modeling. The basic primitive types are derived from this class. The set of basic primitives encapsulate the rendering algorithm's and shading library's dependencies[11]. This is an important design feature allowing portability because of the independence of the most primitive types from concrete rendering aspects. The area primitives integrate the fillstyle modeling.

Application-specific primitives may be defined below the level of the basic primitives. These will be inherited from the basic primitive types or will use them in a part-of relation. In addition to the derivation from a more primitive type primitives may inherit additional modeling (or even rendering) interfaces. For example, the spline uses the resolution attribute to map itself into a (hidden) polyline that will represent the spline. Similarly, a sphere uses this attribute for its mapping into a quadmesh. Application-specific modeling aspects can be integrated in this manner.

## 6   Implementation

This section describes a C++ implementation of the concepts discussed earlier. The description will focus on the classes *Attribute*, *AttributeList* and *Primitive*. A sample implementation will conclude the section.

---

[11] However, higher-level primitives may reimplement the inherited implementation of a rendering interface. For instance, a sphere may implement the ray-tracing interface directly.

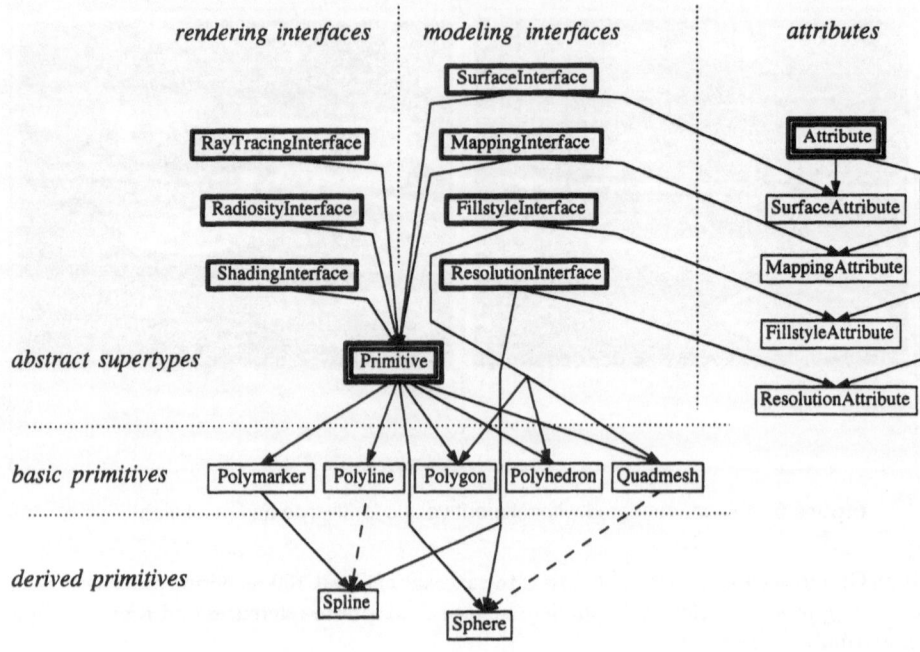

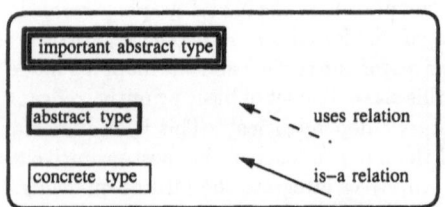

**Figure 6:** Integration of different modeling (and rendering) interfaces via multiple inheritance. The figure shows the current configuration of the YART graphics kernel.

## 6.1  The Class Attribute

The definition of the base class of the attributes conforms with the requirements outlined in Section 5.2 and is shown in Listing 1.

## 6.2  The Class AttributeList

Listing 2 shows the methods of the *AttributeList* class. An attribute list may be bound to a primitive. This allows retraversal during referencing. Additional methods realize a local attribute inquiry (*get()*) or an intelligent inquire, that looks in the current list or parent lists (*retraverse()*) for the specified attribute type relative to the primitive's type and name.

```
class RT_Attribute: public RT_GeneralListEntry {
    ... hidden members
  protected:
    RT_Attribute();
  public:
    virtual const char *getClass() const = 0;
    // the unique class name of the attribute

    virtual int isA(const char *) const;

    // modify/inquire change state:
    void changed();
    void reset();
    int isChanged() const;

    virtual int set(const char *) = 0;
    // set attribute value from a string representation
    // return 1 if successful set
    virtual const char *get() const = 0;
    // get attribute value as a string representation

    // store the attribute persistently:
    void print(FILE *) const;

    // set/get the names list:
    void setNamesList(const char *);
    const char *getNamesList() const;

    virtual void operator=(const RT_Attribute &) = 0;
    // copy one attribute into another
    // only attrs of the same type can be copied into another

    virtual int operator≠(const RT_Attribute &) const = 0;
    // test antivalency by value

    virtual const RT_Attribute *getDefault() = 0;
    // return the default attribute of the attribute class
};
```

**Listing 1:** Definition of the base class *Attribute*

The method *merge()* is useful for the implementation of a dynamically growing attribute context. Using this method a new attribute list will be copied into the context dependent on the name lists and a simple overwrite priority rule. The *print()* method is used to persistently store the attributes of a primitive.

Figure 7 illustrates the inheritance of an attribute context in order to bind the attribute references. It does not depict the management of the name lists and retraversing, the initial setup of the attribute context with the default attributes of the four predefined attribute types or other optimizations such as change flags or caches.

```
class RT_AttributeList: public RT_GeneralList {
  public:
    RT_AttributeList(RT_Primitive * = 0);

    void insert(const RT_Attribute *);
    // append it only if it not already exists
    // else modify the existing one

    RT_Attribute *get(const char *);
    // get the attribute with the specified attribute class
    // looking for it only in this list
    // returns attribute if successful - 0 else

    const RT_Attribute *retraverse(const char *, const RT_Primitive *) const;
    // get the attribute of the specified attribute
    // class that matches to the overgiven primitive
    // by retraversing
    // returns attribute if successful - 0 else

    void merge(const RT_AttributeList *);
    // merge an another list to this list
    // by usage of the "overwrite" priority rule

    void print(FILE *) const;
    // overload the standard list print
}
```

**Listing 2:** Definition of the heterogeneous attribute list class

As illustrated, children do not affect one another. As in PHIGS, the attribute context is duplicated for each child[12]. However, only the references are copied and not the entirety of existing attribute types.

## 6.3  The Class Primitive

In addition to modeling-specific methods, the base class of all primitives defines some virtual and non-virtual methods that allow extensible modeling. These will be described in the following sub-sections. Implementation-specific flags and methods that efficiently handle modeling and other resources (e.g. display lists), will not be mentioned.

### Creation of References

The overloadable method *createReferences()* may be used to create direct pointers to physically existing attributes. The method's argument is a constant reference to a temporaryly created attribute context. The corresponding method(s) of the super class(es) is/are called inside the method implementation. The method is called from the local or global update process.

### Checking of Attribute Values

As mentioned above, attributes may influence the appearance of the primitives. The virtual method *checkAttributes()* may be used to check certain attribute values and to

---

[12]Though, some PHIGS implementation optimize the duplication of the attribute context.

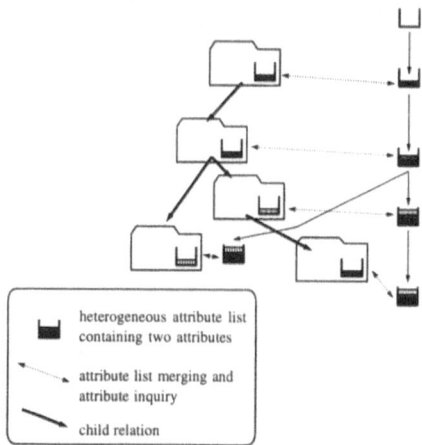

**Figure 7:** Attribute referencing using a dynamically growing attribute context

call semantics specific to the primitive. The change state of an attribute is recognizable thru the attribute's state flag, that is reset if the related primitives are updated. Inside the method implementation the corresponding method(s) of the super class(es) is/are called. The method is also called from the local or global update process.

**Updating a Primitive**

For efficiency, changes of attributes or in the hierarchies of primitives will not generate an immediate update of all joined primitives. For this purpose an *update()* method is provided that may be called for a primitive, e.g., before evaluating an attribute value. It may also be called globally; for instance via an iterator method for all primitives in the scene before rendering. Currently, this is done automatically in the rendering method of the camera objects. Since all manipulations via the direct-manipulative user interface cause an update, the primitives are always up to date. This is not a virtual method. However certain hooks to integrate specific semantics, e.g., the virtual method *create()* to create the geometrical representation are provided. The method automatically and recursively calls the update methods for the children.

**Generic Attribute Access**

The non-virtual methods *attribute()* and *get_attribute()* provide generic attribute access. The semantics of individualization and retraversing is hidden in the implementation of these methods.

## 6.4   A Sample Implementation of a Primitive

The definition of an analytical primitive *Cone* is depicted in Listing 3. The class is derived from the base class of the primitives and the class *ResolutionInterface*. In the private part of the class definition we find a *quadmesh* (used for the cone's mantle surface) and a *polygon* (used for the cover). Both are used as internal parts. An internal reference to a resolution attribute is also defined.

```
class RT_Cone: public RT_Primitive, public RT_ResolutionInterface {
    ...
    RT_Quadmesh *xmesh;
    RT_Polygon *xcover;
    RT_ResolutionAttribute *xresolution;

    void create();
public:
    RT_Cone(const char *, double RADIUS, double LENGTH);
    ...

    // specific methods:
    void radius(double);
    double get_radius() const;

    void length(double);
    double get_length() const;

    void open();
    void close();
    int get_open() const;

    // interface of Resolution:
    void resolution(double);
    double get_resolution() const;

    // overloaded generic attribute methods:
    void checkAttributes();
    void createReferences(const RT_AttributeList &);
};
```

**Listing 3:** Definition of an analytical primitive Cone

There are also cone specific methods (*radius()*, *get_radius()*, etc.). The interface to handle resolution modeling is implemented by overloading two methods inherited from *ResolutionInterface*. The methods *checkAttributes()* and *createReferences()* are reimplemented by the class.

Listing 4 shows example method implementations. Inside the *create()* method, the part objects are parametrized dependent on the resolution value. The method is invoked inside the update process if the non-virtual *geometryChanged()* method is called (e.g. in *checkAttributes()*). For that reason, changes to the resolution value invoke a call to *geometryChanged()*. Other attributes like *fillstyle* or *surface* influence the part objects directly and do not need to be maintained in the cone class. For resolution modeling the *set()* and *get()* methods do not manipulate the value directly. They operate on a referenced attribute as demonstrated in listing 4. The creation of an additional attribute reference besides the inherited attribute references is shown in the implementation of *createReferences()*.

```
RT_Cone::RT_Cone( char *_name, double _r, double _l ): RT_Primitive(_name) {
   ...
}

void RT_Cone::create() {
   // setup geometrical representation in dependence
   // of the resolution value:
   // max dim: 50, min dim: 4
   int dim =(int)( 46.0 * get_resolution() + 4);
   // parameterize quadmesh and cover,
   // compute normal vectors etc.
   ...
}

void RT_Cone::resolution(double s) {
   xresolution = (RT_ResolutionAttribute*)
      attributes→get( RTN_RESOLUTION_ATTRIBUTE );
   if (!xresolution) attributes→insert(
      xresolution = new RT_ResolutionAttribute);
   xresolution→resolution( s );
   geometryChanged();
}

double RT_Cone::get_resolution() const {
   return xresolution→get_resolution();
}

void RT_Cone::checkAttributes() {
   if (xresolution→isChanged()) geometryChanged();
}

void RT_Cone::createReferences(const RT_AttributeList &list) {
   RT_Primitive::createReferences( list );
   // create resolution reference:
   RT_ResolutionAttribute *tmp = xresolution;
   xresolution = (RT_ResolutionAttribute*)
      list.retraverse( RTN_RESOLUTION_ATTRIBUTE, this );
   if ( (tmp ≠ xresolution) || (*tmp ≠ *xresolution)) geometryChanged();
}
```

**Listing 4:** Implementation of some selected methods

# 7    Conclusion

The described modeling approach is implemented in the YART graphics kernel. Attribute handling is easier when using the Tk [17] based user interface for YART. Besides direct-manipulative interactions, this tool allows comfortable and intuitive attribute access via a tree widget. The widget supports additional maintenance functions such as displaying all physically instantiated attributes or the clearing of attributes. Figure 8 shows a screen dump of the various tools. In addition a shell tool is provided, allowing full access to the interpretative YART API including name lists, set operations, etc. This approach has been used for nearly a year and was found to be useful in several projects, even those with complex scenes, e.g., in a virtual reality tool. Nevertheless there is room for further optimization and conceptual improvement.

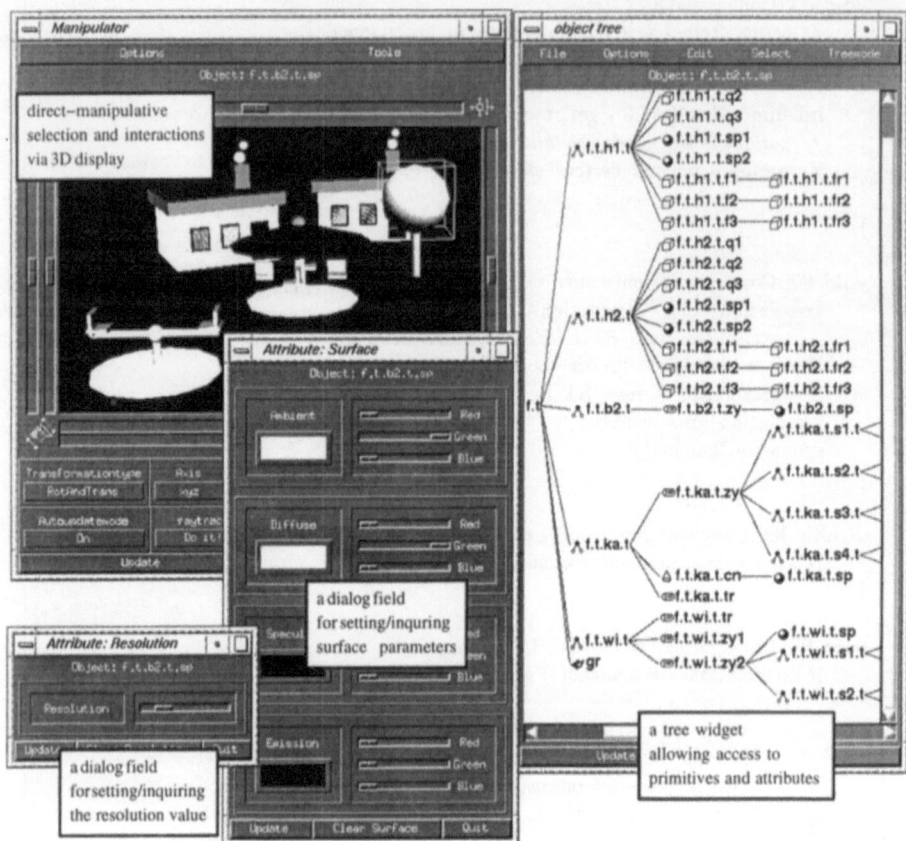

**Figure 8:** Attribute access via YART's user interface

# References

[1] P. J. Asente and R. R. Swick. *X Window System Toolkit*. Digital Press, 1990.

[2] E. Beier. *Objektorientierte 3D-Grafik*. Int'l Thomson Publishing, September 1994.

[3] E. Beier. Tcl meets 3D - Interpretative Access to Object-Oriented Graphics. In *2nd Tcl/Tk Workshop, New Orleans*, June 1994.

[4] P. Bui-Tuong. Illumination for computer generated images. *Communications of the ACM*, 18(6):311–317, 1975.

[5] M. F. Cohen, S. E. Chen, J. R. Wallace, and D. P. Greenberg. A Progressive Refinement Approach to Fast Radiosity Image Generation. In *SIGGRAPH'88*, pages 137–145. ACM SIGGRAPH, New York, 1988.

[6] C. Elliot, G. Schechter, R. Yeung, and S. Abi-Ezzi. TBAG: A High Level Framework for Interactive, Animated 3D Graphics Applications. In *SIGGRAPH'94*, 1994.

[7] M. A. Ellis and B. Stroustrup. *The Annotated C++ Reference Manual*. Addison Wesley, 1990.

[8] E. Gamma. *Objektorientierte Software-Entwicklung am Beispiel von ET++: Klassenbibliothek, Werkzeuge, Design*. PhD thesis, Universität Zuerich, 1991.

[9] Graphics Library Programming Guide. Technical Report 007-1210-040, Silicon Graphics Inc., 1991.

[10] A. S. Glassner, editor. *An Introduction To Ray Tracing*. Academic Press, 1990.

[11] H. Gouraud. Computer Display of Curved Surfaces. *IEEE Transactions on Computers*, 20(6):623–628, 1971.

[12] T. L. J. Howard, W. T. Hewitt, R. J. Hubbold, and K. M. Wyrwas. *A Practical Introduction to PHIGS and PHIGS PLUS*. Addison Wesley, 1991.

[13] ISO. Information Processing Systems – Computer Graphics – Graphical Kernel System (GKS). Technical Report ISO 7942:1985, International Organization of Standardization, 1985.

[14] ISO. Information Processing Systems – Computer Graphics – Programmer's Hierarchical Interactive Graphics System (PHIGS). Technical Report ISO/IEC 9592:1989, International Organization of Standardization, 1989. Parts 1 – 3.

[15] ISO. Information Processing Systems – Computer Graphics – Programmer's Hierarchical Interactive Graphics System (PHIGS), Plus Lumière Und Surfaces. Technical Report ISO/IEC 9592-4:1992, International Organization of Standardization, 1992. Part 4.

[16] J. Neider, T. Davis, and M. Woo. *OpenGL Programming Guide*. Addison Wesley, 1993.

[17] J. K. Ousterhout. *The Tcl/Tk Book*. Addison Wesley, 1993.

[18] P. Wisskirchen. *Object-Oriented Graphics - From GKS and PHIGS to Object-Oriented Systems*. Springer-Verlag, 1990.

[19] P. Wisskirchen. Objektorientierte Graphik. Handouts, April 1993.

# 5

# Gemma: An Open Architecture for Distributed User Interfaces

Steve Freeman

The *Graphical Environment for Multiple users and Multiple devices Architecture* (Gemma) is a design for a user interface architecture that allows users to bind together collections of devices for the task at hand, rather than being limited to virtual terminals. It provides mediated shared access to basic devices and higher-level virtual devices so that people can share computational facilities in the real world, rather than in a virtual world. Gemma uses object-oriented techniques to achieve the flexibilty it requires, particulary inheritance and encapsulation, hiding distribution and allowing arbitrary devices to be connected together. Gemma was motivated by the observation that both computing systems and our understanding of human-computer interaction have changed since graphical interfaces were introduced, but that the layer which binds them together, the user interface system, has not changed as quickly. An example window system, $SW$, and an example application show how Gemma's features may be exploited to provide a flexible, collaborative and mobile interactive environment.

## 1  Introduction

The general acceptance of graphical user interfaces has changed dramatically. Window systems, once considered exotic, are now a standard approach for interacting with a computer, but most architectures are built on ten-year old foundations and assumptions. On the one hand, application writers now have a more thorough and subtle understanding of how people work with computers in practice and are attempting to build more complex and flexible applications over existing window systems. On the other hand, computing infrastructures now include facilities such as high speed networks, flexible micro-kernel operating systems, and mobile computing. Thus, user interface requirements and computer systems have been changing faster than the layer which binds them together—the user interface system. It is both necessary and feasible to develop more open user interface architectures which support, for example, dynamic grouping together of interactive devices, dynamic association of users with device groups, devices shared between users, applications which can accept and distinguish between input from many sources, continuous media, and mobile devices.

This paper proposes the Graphical Environment for Multiple users and Multiple devices Architecture (Gemma), in which all the components of a user interface may be distributed; Gemma then provides mechanisms for collecting low-level devices into higher-level abstractions. An example window system, $SW$, shows how Gemma may be used to construct flexible, collaborative and mobile applications. After this introduction, I discuss some of the trends in user interface requirements and computing infrastructure which influenced the design of Gemma. The next sections describe Gemma itself and the *SW* window system. Then I discuss how Gemma can be used to assemble an application, how Gemma is related to other user interface systems, and the object-oriented techniques used in the design of Gemma. Finally, I draw some conclusions.

## 1.1   User Interface Requirements

Two decades of experience with user interfaces has improved our understanding of how people work with computers, particularly in groups. The assumption that applications and interfaces need only cater for a single user is now less tenable as the individual user sitting at a terminal driven by an individual machine (real or virtual) is proving to be only a special case of how people work. Grudin [20] notes that computers are not used in isolation but in an environment which includes a variety of sources of interaction, including books, telephones and other people; even explicitly single-user applications, such as the spreadsheet, turn out to be used by groups in practice [33].

One response has been the implementation of desktop conferencing systems ranging from window-sharing (such as ShX [3]), in which the output of a standard application is replicated to and the input multiplexed between several displays, to shared editors (such as Grove [11]), which allow users to share the *contents* of an application rather than its input and output streams. The single-user assumptions in current window systems, however, can hinder the development of multi-user systems. As Lauwers points out [25], the implementation of window sharing was more difficult with the monolithic X window system than with the *TheWA* window system in which input and output streams were managed by different processes. An alternative is to allow sharing *within* a user interface as in the Multi-device, Multi-user Multi-editor (MMM) [7], which provides a set of embedded editors shared on a single display with multiple input devices. It supports both multi-handed input and people sharing an output device—such as a wall-sized display; a user can dynamically take control of an input device so that it will take on his or her preferences and permissions, and actions driven by that device will be associated with that user. The study of the collaborative use of computers shows, firstly, that existing computers are either too desk-bound or too isolated for the way many people work in practice and, secondly, that once one has broken the assumption of the single-user terminal, almost any component of the user interface may be shareable.

Another trend is the integration of continuous media, such as video, into user interfaces particularly as digital implementations (such as [14]) become available; two interesting uses are to provide *media spaces* and to mix video and graphics. Media spaces (see [9] for a survey) use live audio and video to link people across a distance, supporting distributed groups by providing support for the informal interactions which help to bind co-present groups together. Each node (usually one per office) has a monitor and camera and a microphone and speaker which can be dynamically linked to the corresponding devices on other nodes; thus, two people can construct a "virtual office" by establishing a long-term video connection, or all the members of a group can watch the activity in some common area. Existing media spaces have been implemented by using computers to control analogue video, but digital video promises a more flexible medium, with lower costs for adding an individual to the space. Systems to mix graphics and video may provide digital annotation of real-world images, as in Ishii's *TeamWorkstation* [21], or video annotations of digital images [16]. In general, however, such systems use analogue hardware to mix the analogue and digital images, which makes the alignment and storage of the combined media difficult. The move towards digital audio and video reduces such problems but also increases the need for a user interface architecture which can integrate media with different characteristics.

Finally, human-computer interaction need not be limited to individual desktop displays. While virtual realities demonstrate increasingly complex modes of interaction with a computer, another approach is to distribute computing power around the users' environment. Instead of a single device onto which we overload all our computing activity, we may have many devices to support different activities; some devices are portable and all are linked by an ubiquitous communications system, hence Weiser's term *Ubiquitous Computing* [44]. Some devices may belong to a particular person and task whereas others, such as wall displays, are for public use but can be customised for those present at the time. Thus, people can work together by sharing in their physical world, passing hand-held devices to each other or writing together on a wall display, rather than in the computer's virtual world.

The implications for window-system design are that we can make fewer assumptions about how people interact with computers and that application writers need support for more flexible and complex applications with less predictable dialogues between person and machine. There are new media and interaction techniques which need to be integrated into user interface architectures, and people will need mechanisms to dynamically draw together collections of the myriad of available devices.

## 1.2  Computer System Trends

Computer systems, on the other hand, are becoming increasingly flexible. Gigabit per second networks are now available and Asynchronous Transfer Mode (ATM) protocols allow a single network to carry different types of traffic (described in [26]). Each client, when establishing a connection, negotiates with the network for the Quality of Service (QoS) it requires—defined in terms of, for example, bandwidth and maximum delay and jitter. Timeliness of delivery, for example, is more important than reliability for video data, whereas the opposite is true for text data. ATM networks provide application and system builders with a common infrastructure for multiple media so that different kinds of devices can be connected to, and communicate via, the same network.

As application demands become more complex it is decreasingly likely that they can be satisfied by a general purpose, monolithic operating system. The current solution is to use an efficient micro-kernel (kernel) operating system which provides processor scheduling, core memory management, and inter-process communication. Services, such as file systems and high-level communications, run as user-level processes rather than in the kernel, which improves modularity and allows flexibility and specialisation when configuring a machine. As shown in [6] and [27], even device drivers may be run at the user level. Thus, modern operating systems provide a platform for tying multiple hosts and devices together, rather than managing a single machine. This degree of partitioning, however, has not always been extended to higher level software. Most current user interface systems are monolithic, assuming a static collection of devices bound into a desktop terminal, but modern operating systems show that very little functionality *must* be embedded in the kernel.

Finally, the development of mobile computing shows that we cannot even rely on machines to stay in the same place. Xerox PARC, for example, has developed hand- and notebook-sized portables which communicate via infra-red and radio respectively [44], and the Active Badge [43] is a wearable input device which can be used to trace the wearer's location. The PenPoint notepad operating system [10], on the other hand, can handle arbitrary disconnection from a network file system by storing changes locally and resolving the differences when the notepad is reconnected. The rise in mobile computing signifies another potential direction away from current desktop-bound computing.

## 2    Introduction to Gemma

Gemma is a user interface architecture intended to provide better support for the user requirement issues and take advantage of the computer system advances described above. It is based on networked devices which provide input and output services to clients. These clients can then assemble low-level devices to provide higher-level services, such as windows, to application clients. Gemma is intended to support interactive systems which are not confined to virtual terminals, but use collections of independent devices which may be bound together for the task at hand.

### 2.1    User Requirements

A first step towards a design is to clarify the activities to be supported. Consider a group of people in a room, working on related tasks, who occasionally want to share devices and applications, without performing complex dialogues to establish a connection, and who want to be able to identify who performed each action; they also want to use multiple devices for simultaneous multi-modal input. The following scenarios provide several interesting user-level requirements:

1. The group holds a design meeting around the wall display. Users write and draw on the display with their pens and the meeting software keeps track of each person's contribution. One person has forgotten his pen and must share his neighbour's, so there must be easy mechanisms for changing the association between person and device. In addition, some people have their own notepads on which they make notes that they sometimes transfer to the display.

2. A user has a problem, so he asks a colleague for help. She comes to his desk and they discuss the problem, both making annotations on his desktop display. As they need to look at more information, she brings over a couple of notebook displays which they add to his desktop, but there is still not enough space so they transfer his desktop image to the wall display.

3. In a design class, each student has his or her own drafting display. The teacher wanders around the room correcting and annotating the students' designs with his own pen. His marks are distinguishable from the students' and can be shown or hidden independently. Sometimes he refers to a document in his own persistent storage; the system can pop it up by identifying him as the origin of the input gesture.

These scenarios assume a hardware environment of a room full of output devices: a wall-mounted display, desktop displays, many portable displays ranging in size from a notebook to a badge, and several loudspeakers; there is also a range of input devices: keyboards, pens, mice, position sensors and so on. Many of these devices are mobile.

The user-level requirements can be reduced to the following (the numbers in parentheses refer to the relevant scenarios): mobile input devices, ownership of input devices, and shared displays and applications (1, 2, 3); dynamic grouping of displays (1); and mobile displays (1, 2).

## 2.2  System Requirements

The user requirements place several demands on the user interface architecture of which the first is to allow dynamic association of input and output devices. Current user interface architectures view the set of user interface devices as static, but this is too limited as devices become mobile and *group interfaces* become more common. Users could, instead, define relations between sets of devices to combine them together. For example, two people editing together may each define a compound device consisting of their own input devices and the shared screen; the input focus for the keyboard of each compound device is determined by its related mouse. This approach also requires that the user interface software be able to make connections to new devices and handle the loss of existing connections.

Some devices may be shared between users, such as wall-sized displays or touch screens divided into virtual windows [10], or shared between applications—for example, a mouse driving telepointers on several displays or two window systems sharing a screen. Thus, devices must be able to support multiple clients and provide access to special attributes, such as portability or the display of video, without subverting the architecture. Similarly, the user interface software must be able to manage input from multiple sources, providing built-in support for the association of devices with roles—for either different users or different functions.

Users must be able to dynamically associate themselves with compound devices. At its simplest, this is equivalent to current login procedures where a user acquires control over a fixed combination of devices (a terminal or workstation) by typing an identifier and password. A more general approach, however, allows users to establish a connection to a group of devices, such as all those within a given room, where the group may change during the connection period. Flexible grouping of devices allows, for example, a user to move between displays while keeping the same set of input devices; this at least would help those with several machines on a desk who have nowhere to put all the keyboards. It also makes easier the impromptu lightweight collaborations which studies such as [38] show to be a feature of teamwork. Thirdly, it allows users to join in each other's interactions without interrupting a session, and facilitates transitions between modes of input—such as from one-handed to two-handed. Finally, it must be possible to locate and connect to all these disparate components.

The architectural requirements can be reduced to: a general mechanism for grouping input and output devices into compound devices; provision for sharing compound and basic devices and for controlling access to particular attributes of a device; and, the ability to identify devices and the sources of events.

## 2.3  Distributed User Interfaces

This paper claims that Gemma supports *distributed user interfaces*, but this term can be understood in three ways—with different implications for the software architecture to support it:

- *distributed* user interface: this is the conventional meaning in which the user interface for a single display is implemented across several machines, examples include the X Window System and NeWS.

- *distributed user* interface: groupware applications and architectures tie together multiple users who may be physically separated. Each person, however, is the sole user of a particular display, and users must communicate with each other *via* the computer system.

- *distributed user interface*: this is a more radical sense in which the user interface is not limited to a particular machine on a single desk but is made up of many communicating devices scattered around the users' environment. Users can bind together the input and output devices they need for the task in hand as the need arises.

It is this last sense which Gemma is particularly designed to support; the other two are special cases of this wider approach.

## 3   Low-level Services

Gemma needs a practical means for representing physical input and output devices, which may be shared or mobile, to programmers, so we use proxy objects, such as Birrel et al.'s network objects [8]. A proxy object contains no state but provides an interface to the *real* object which may be in another address space; different proxies may represent different aspects of a common object. Proxy objects provide a mechanism for distributing data and events across address spaces within the discipline of a type system. The motivation for an object-oriented approach are discussed further in Section 5.3.

Lantz [24] points to the advantages of using separate processes to manage the input devices and display, so low-level Gemma devices are categorised as input or output with as few assumptions as possible made about the user-level interactions they are to support. These device objects may be gathered together by higher-level objects to provide more complex devices, such as a conventional window server or a virtual terminal, for other clients.

### 3.1   Devices

The core Device[1] type is concerned with locating a device service and establishing a connection to it. The init method (similar to a C++ constructor) establishes the name of the device to connect to and the identity of the client; the connection can then be controlled with the open and close methods.

```
Device =
  init(deviceId, clientName)
  open()
  close()
  callbacks{description}
```

The device identifier is an arbitrary value which may be looked up by sending a description to a name service, or trader in ANSA [4] terminology; a description, briefly, consists of a type name, a name space in which to look and optional properties to further constrain the search. This implies that the description of a device is independent of its identifier, so the client can define callbacks to be notified should the description change. For example, if a device's location forms part of its description, the client could be notified when the device is moved. Devices, once defined, may also be exported to a trader to make them accessible to other clients.

---

[1]The object notation used is indicative only and the conventions should be obvious; it assumes single inheritance. A type is defined as:
```
type = [supertype] [data fields] [methods] [callbacks]
```
Methods have the form: [*result* |-] method_name ([*parameters*]), and callbacks are: callbacks {[*parameters which may change*]}.

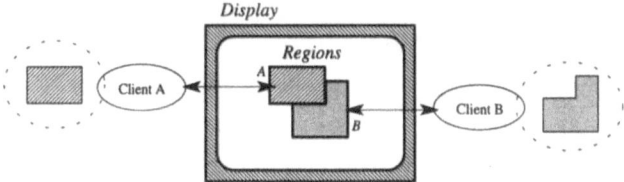

**Figure 1:** Arbitrary regions give the illusion of overlapping windows The basic Display object allows clients to request a region with a given area. When creating a region, the client may give it a name, in which case other clients of the display may share it by using the name to request access.

## 3.2  Display Servers

A display server provides controlled access to arbitrary regions of its screen without imposing a model of a window structure—as Took shows [41], not every user interface system need have overlapping windows. A window server can then establish itself as a client of a display server, requesting regions of the framebuffer which represent parts of overlapping windows, as in Fig. 1. Another window server may also be a client of the same display, making its own requests for space, so the server must arbitrate between conflicting requests and notify other clients when they lose part of their allocation. So, individual window servers must now be prepared to handle messages which change its output region, but a display can support arbitrary multiple window systems simultaneously.

```
Display = Device
  region <- requestRegion(area, name)
  region <- shareRegion(name)
```

A Display.Region, then, gives the client rights over an arbitrarily-shaped area of the display, such as the ability to change its shape, and allows the client to be notified of changes to the region's state.

```
Display.Region =
  requestArea(area)
  callbacks{regionChanged, disconnected}
```

Clearly, an interface which provides only the allocation and deallocation of areas of a display is of limited use. Clients must be able to write to the display so a Sun Pixrect subtype, for example, could be implemented to provide basic drawing operations for the client:

```
PixrectDisplay.Region = Display.Region
  rop()  -- raster operations
  polypoint()  -- draw a set of lines
  setcolourmap()  -- set colourmap
  etc...
```

A client may hold more than one connection to a display server at once, so a client can open multiple connections to represent multiple characteristics. This avoids the need for multiple inheritance when a virtual device with several characteristics is needed, as a client can open several connections to the same named region from multiple interfaces. Multiple interfaces also allow access to individual facilities in the server to be controlled for each client. For example, in Fig. 2, a server supports the Display and PixrectDisplay types and

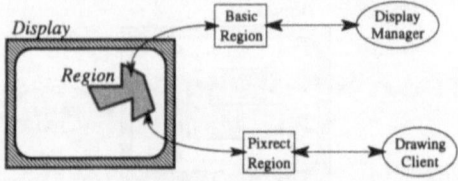

**Figure 2:** Multiple interfaces to a Region

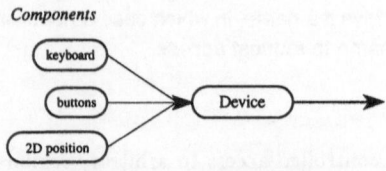

**Figure 3:** Assembling an input device from components

a client requests a named Display.Region which it can manipulate. Another client asks to share the region using the PixrectDisplay interface and receives a connection which is a PixrectDisplay.Region. Both regions (the Display and the PixrectDisplay) refer to a common structure in the server, but have access to different aspects of it. This differs from X, for example, where a client, once connected to the server, has access to all its facilities.

Another example is an Overlay interface which would allow one client to make annotations over another client's window without altering the underlying image.

## 3.3 Input Servers

As with display servers, input servers provide controlled access to devices which may be shared between clients. Although there are fewer cases for input than for output where an input device needs to be shared, examples include the abstraction of multiple pens on a Liveboard from common input sensors and Mermaid [34] implements a multi-user application by distributing low-level input events. Unlike displays and regions, there are difficulties in using multiple objects to represent aspects of a single input device as every client of the device must receive the component events in the same order. The solution is to allow users to add components to a virtual device, rather than abstract them from it. Fig. 3, for example, shows a conventional input device assembled from keyboard, buttons and 2D position components. A virtual input device provides a synchronisation point for the component devices it manages and timestamps events as they pass through it. A virtual input device may, of course, be exported to form a component of a higher-level compound device.

A basic InputDevice.Event is defined as consisting of a timestamp, the identity of the virtual device, the identity of the source component, and the event data itself. A Component is then defined as a type of Device:

```
InputComponent = Device
  enable()              -- turns the input stream on or off
  event <- getState()  -- immediately returns the most recent event
```

The InputDevice type itself is similar, with methods to add and remove components, except that the getState and nextEvent methods return a compound event which includes the current state of all the components. This simplifies co-ordination between input sources in multi-device interfaces, such as MMM, and also allows the compound input stream to be distributed or shared.

```
InputDevice = Device
  event <- getState()
  event <- nextEvent()
    -- blocks the client thread until a new event arrives
  addComponent()
  removeComponent()
```

A simple example of the use of some of these features is the definition of a device which gives absolute 2D co-ordinates. An absolute device may need calibration, so we allow a client to define a mapping from 2D space to another:

```
Absolute2D = InputComponent
  setCalibration(mapping)
  callbacks{mappingChanged}
```

The input stream from the mapped device may now be shared or distributed without writing application-specific code; note that this definition includes a callback to notify clients when the mapping has changed.

### 3.4  Continuous Media

Gemma also provides a structure for handling continuous media, such as video, which must distinguish between in-band data (the video frames themselves) and out-of-band data (control of the stream). In common with other continuous media architectures, such as the Touring Machine [23], Gemma provides an object to handle application-level data, such as the frame count, and to control a Video.Sink object; the Video.Sink, in turn, manages communications-level activity, such as jitter control. Thus, a video region establishes a link between a video sink and a display and provides access to application-level out-of-band data:

```
VideoDisplay.Region = Display.Region
  setSink()        -- attaches media object to region
  callbacks{frame} -- notifies client of frame count
```

For example, in Fig. 4, the display manager controls the shape of the region, an overlay region allows a pointer device to drive a cursor, and the video region tells the video sink to which parts of the screen to send images; this provides the user with a pointer-driven cursor over a moving video image.

### 3.5  Summary

Low-level Gemma, then, provides an infrastructure for managing distributed input and output devices. Output devices may support multiple virtual devices, and different virtual devices may export different aspects of a base device. Virtual input devices, on the other hand, may be assembled from more basic components and provide a synchronisation point for input from those components. Finally, continuous media are controlled by virtual devices which provide a handle for control of the medium—the data themselves are managed by communications objects.

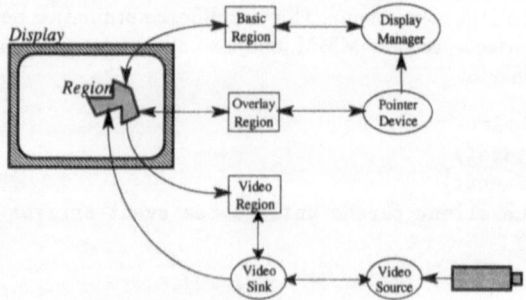

**Figure 4:** A Region with a video interface

Gemma supports some of the architectural requirements described in Section 2.1: the basic device type makes devices accessible to arbitrary clients and notifies those clients when the status of a device, such as its location, changes; clients may share a device by importing the same device object; the output model provides controlled access to facets of a display device; the input model allows input devices to be assembled into compound devices; and, the model supports continuous media. Other requirements, such as the association of input and output devices and compound output devices, are supported in the window system described below.

## 4    A Simplistic Window System

Low-level devices are too primitive for building all but the simplest applications, so we need a level which will bind them into more complex services. In particular, logical devices at this level provide a synchronisation point for their components: in space, by defining a mapping between input and output device co-ordinates, and in time, by timestamping events. These are the objects usually described as servers in window systems; they provide higher-level services from the low-level devices they import. This level defines how the input and output devices are to be combined, and presents a logical set of devices to the application level above it.

The simplistic window system, $SW$, described here is intended to demonstrate how a window service might be constructed using Gemma. It is to support an environment in which there are many input and output devices scattered around a room which may be combined arbitrarily. For example, the first time a person uses an identifiable pen on a display, the application should be able to identify and validate this new source of input. Similarly, $SW$ should support a user adding a portable screen to an existing set of screens, so that the logical display can be dynamically enlarged.

$SW$ uses two techniques to support these requirements: a common window abstraction at all levels of the hierarchy which can also bind physical displays together, and the ability to group input devices and attach them to a window at any level of the hierarchy. $SW$ provides a model within which multiple distributed devices can be combined into a higher-level user interface, using the window as a co-ordination point to provide timestamping and alignment between devices.

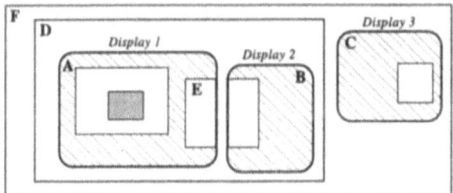

**Figure 5:** A logical hierarchy of windows. Windows A, B and C represent the top level of displays 1,2, and 3 respectively. A and B are children of a logical window D which is used to bind displays 1 and 2 together, so that window E can cross between them. C and D are children of a logical window F which represents a common domain for access control and handling unexpected events.

## 4.1  Windows

The basic component in $SW$ is the **window**—an arbitrary area of 2D space that may contain child windows. This general definition does not require a top-level window to be associated with a physical display—it is not always the case that the top-level window is the "closest" to the output device. A top-level logical window may handle drawing requests by either refusing to accept the request and raising an exception or by passing it down to the relevant child. For example, a logical window may contain a set of displays around a room with an arbitrary policy for defining the spatial relationships between the children (Fig. 5). A logical window may allow paint operations to span two children, so two physical displays could be tiled together to make a larger virtual display; the parent forwards its paint requests to the children who overlap the image being drawn.

The use of a single abstraction means that applications need only be concerned with manipulating a single top-level window. An application may be moved between displays by reparenting its top-level window, and the role that a display plays with respect to neighbouring devices may also be changed by reparenting the window associated with that display.

### Distribution

Windows can be distributed by inserting a network window between parent and child that relays events and requests between the two; import/export facilities are provided by subclassing the basic window type from a Gemma Device.T. This is similar to Trestle's cross-address-space filter [29], except that the child window does not have to be attached to a parent window—if exported, it can maintain its existing state and be attached to another parent, local or remote. This allows a process to export its significant windows, such as the bottom-level window of a display or the top-level window of an application, which other applications may then import and use as an interaction device. In addition, a window subclass, such as one which manages the layout of its children, may encapsulate its specialised behaviour in an object like a Silica contract [36]; a network version of this object may then be driven from another process (Fig. 6). This is similar to the X window manager where some of the functionality of the window system is implemented by a remote process using a specialised protocol.

### Input Handling

Conventional window systems attach their input devices to their top-level window, but this is less meaningful in $SW$ where the top-level window may change. The solution is to allow clients to attach input an input device to arbitrary windows in the tree. The device

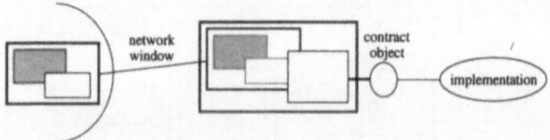

**Figure 6:** Two mechanisms for application distribution. Network windows to connect parent and child in different address spaces and a contract object to encapsulate, and distribute, the behaviour of the contents of a window.

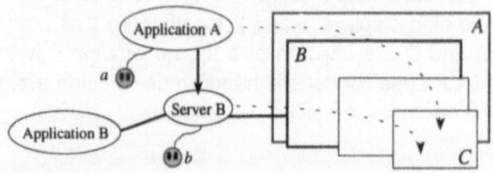

**Figure 7:** Event dispatching in different window levels. Server B uses mouse b and window B, which is the top-level window of a display device, and provides a window service to application B. Application A creates a virtual window A, which includes window B, and accepts input from mouse a; input events and output requests which fall into the domain of window B are passed on to server B.

then uses the window to which it is attached as the root of its window tree; the window determines the device's scope. For example, selections made with a device are retained at the level of the window to which the device is attached.

In Fig. 7, for example, application B sees a window service which includes window B and mouse b, application A creates an internal window hierarchy of which window B is a member; server A sees only events from mouse a, while server B sees events from both mice. The approach allows input to be managed at multiple levels in a window hierarchy; in Fig. 8 (c), mouse b may only move within window B, whereas mouse a can cover both windows. In the example of the drafting class, all the drafting boards are children of a common logical window; input from the students' pens is handled at the level of the individual board, whereas the teacher's pen is registered with the top-level window so she does not have to establish a separate connection with each board.

This approach also allows clients to determine whether event handling for two neighbouring displays should be kept separate or combined in a larger virtual display (Fig. 8, (a) and (b)). In the latter case, a client can make both displays descendants of the same logical window and associate the input devices with that ancestor.

## 4.2  Input Devices

Users need a mechanism for grouping arbitrary sets of devices to provide an event order across the devices and an input focus for non-positional events such as key presses. In addition, other clients may wish to receive a copy of the event stream from an input device once it has been calibrated with a display, so $SW$ defines a further virtual device which, of course, may be exported for other clients. When attached to a window, events from the component devices are distributed through the window hierarchy as if from a single device—although a client can unpack the original source of the event. An $SW$ input device may include an arbitrary number of pointing components, of which one may be nominated as the focus pointer which is then used set the input focus window; the default input focus

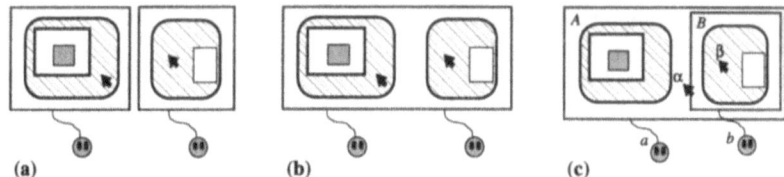

**Figure 8:** Cursors and windows. In (a) the pointers are restricted to their respective displays; (b) the displays are part of the same logical window and the pointers have access to both. In (c) mouse a is attached to window A and drives cursor , mouse b is attached to window B and drives cursor ; cursor is restricted to window B, but may enter window A or B.

window is the one to which the device is attached. This arbitrary combination of input sources allows, for example, a person at a digital drafting board to *SW*itch between two or three different pens with one hand to represent different drawing functions, with a button device in the other hand to provide modifier keys common across all the pens. Each pen can be represented by a different *SW* input device, all of which include a copy of the button device.

MMM shows that multi-user and multi-device interfaces need to be able to make associations between devices and users and roles. MMM runs within a single address space and so can maintain internal device and user tables, but *SW* needs to maintain device associations between displays. This assumes that some input devices have an identity which they carry with them, like an IP address, which is a property of the physical device rather than the virtual devices implemented over it. To make these associations available across hosts, *SW* holds them in a device registry which is accessible over the network; the need for rapid response may mean that device registry data needs to be cached locally, but this matches the intended use. Clearly, at most one user can own an identifiable device, although there may be multiple clients receiving events from it. *SW* also includes a user registry which holds details about users, including their application preferences.

The device registry is also used to control user access in a shared interface. The event mechanism attempts to dispatch positional events from leaf to root (unless the device has been grabbed). Each window has an acceptOrRejectEvent method which either accepts the event and returns TRUE or returns FALSE; where a window contains children, acceptOrRejectEvent should first try to pass the event to any child which is appropriate before considering it for its own window. Thus, the interpretation of an event and access control is localised to the application in charge of each window. Client applications can retain an access list of users who may make changes to an application's appearance or its data and check the owner of the source device with the list before accepting an event. A possible implementation of acceptOrRejectEvent for a leaf application checks whether the owner of the input device has write permission in the window before allowing him or her to change the input focus to the window:

```
PROC AcceptOrRejectEvent(event: Event): BOOLEAN =
    -- get the device from the event
    device <- event.device()
    -- try to find owner of device
    owner <- LookupOwner(device)
    IF NO owner THEN RETURN FALSE FI
    deviceRec  LookupLocalDeviceRec(device)
```

```
-- get data about this device from the local cache
   or create a new record
IF event = Event.AcquireFocus THEN
   -- only set input focus to window if device owner may write in it
   IF owner.writePermission() THEN
     AcquireInputFocus(device, event)
     RETURN TRUE
   ELSE
     RETURN FALSE FI FI
-- events are put onto window's input queue to be
   processed by window's event thread
AddEventToInputQueue(event, deviceRec, owner)
RETURN TRUE
END
```

### 4.3  Summary

*SW* provides a mechanism for grouping sets of input and output devices. Clients of low-level Gemma can dynamically assemble compound devices from more basic devices and make them available to other clients in turn. *SW* windows provide a common abstraction for determining interaction scope; they can be extended above the hardware to create logical combinations of displays and define co-ordination points between input and output devices. *SW* input devices gather component devices together to provide an order on events from those components and route non-positional events. Finally, the input mechanism provides for default handling of unfamiliar devices and uses networked device and user registries to store user state and preferences.

## 5  Discussion

### 5.1  Applying Gemma and *SW*

How, then, might Gemma be used to actually build an application? This section describes how the design meeting example from Section 2.1 may be implemented, showing that a Gemma application can be written independently of a particular combination of hardware and that its behaviour can be changed to match external circumstances by connecting to a different set of virtual devices.

The implementation breaks down into two parts: the use of the shared wall display and the communication with the notepad displays. For the first part a local *SW* server implements a top-level window that it attaches to the display; one of its sub-windows is driven by the application. There is also a Device Watcher which manages the pen sensor and implements virtual devices for the physical devices it detects (Fig. 9).

As a user moves a pen into the range of the sensor, its presence is noted by the Device Watcher which then contacts the Device Registry to get its details and claim ownership; if the device is registered at another site, that Device Watcher can be notified to allow it to clean up its data. The Device Registry also records whether a device currently is owned by anyone; if not the device may simply be presented on the display to be used anonymously until someone acquires it. Otherwise, the use of the pen may, for example, be treated as a form of login and the user asked for further validation, or the pen may be added to the user's state in an existing session. The Device Watcher then feeds events from its devices to the *SW* server which places them on its input queue for dispatching

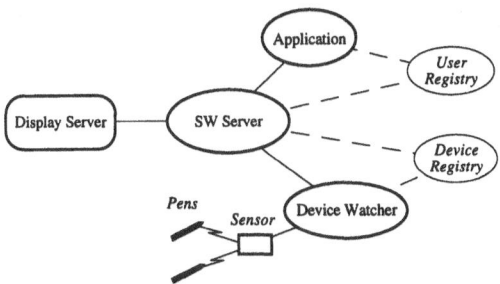

**Figure 9:** Using $SW$ and Gemma to manage a shared wall display. Remote connections are shown by a dotted line and wireless connections by a zig-zag.

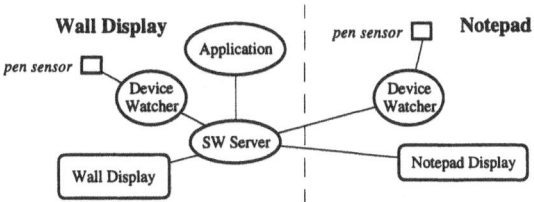

**Figure 10:** The connections for combining a wall display and a notepad into an $SW$ window. Notepad input events are forwarded to the $SW$ server which, in turn, dispatches output requests to the two displays.

to its applications.

The second part implements the communication with the notepad displays. Much of the time, notepad owners will be working independently of the main display, but occasionally they will want to transfer work between the notepad and the display and to use the notepad as an input device for the wall display. One approach is to include both the wall display and the notepad in a common $SW$ window—the notepad area is treated as if attached to an edge of the wall display area. Graphical objects may then be dragged from one display to the other, even though the two displays are physically separate; once an object has been moved to the main display it can then be picked up with another device. Fig. 10 shows how input events from the notepad may be diverted to the common $SW$ Server process which, in turn, drives the notepad display. All the pens are absolute pointing devices, so their input events can be mapped so that their range is limited to the area of the display with which they are associated. The application is removed from the details of the hardware and sees only an oddly-shaped top-level window with input coming from multiple users.

Another approach is to use simple cut and paste by associating the selection with the user, rather than the window server, and storing it with the User Registry; the selection may then be retrieved from the User Registry if the user pastes to another display. Thus, a user can make a selection on his or her notepad and paste to the wall display with any pen with which he or she is associated. This is similar to a technique used in some meeting room systems, such as the Capture Lab [30], which allow users to maintain their copy buffer when switching between control of their personal machine and of a common display. A further step is to allow the owner of a notepad to switch between using it as a local device and as a pointer for the wall display. When used as a pointer, the notepad display replicates a part of the main display which can be panned around using a local

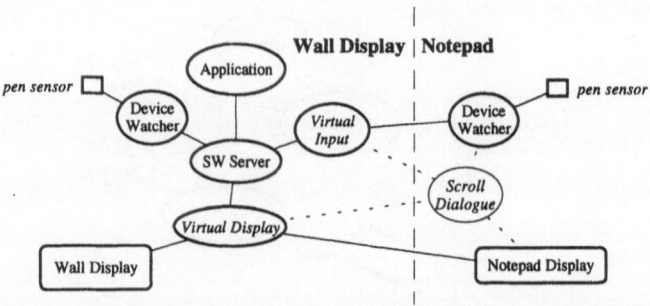

**Figure 11:** The connections for using a notepad as a pointer on a wall display. The Scroll Dialogue process allows the user to control which part of the wall display the notebook replicates.

dialogue area; the notepad owner can interact with the replicated area as if drawing on the wall display.

Figure 11 shows how this may be achieved. The *SW* Server draws to a Virtual Display device which replicates parts of the display image to its connected displays. The input from the notepad pen is sent to a Virtual Input process which maps its co-ordinates to that part of the virtual display which is visible on the notepad. The Scroll Dialogue process manages a dialogue box on the notepad which provides an interface to allow the user to move around the virtual display; as the user scrolls, the scroll dialogue notifies the virtual input and output devices of the change of view. If the user switches to a local application, the Scroll Dialogue notifies the virtual devices to suspend their connections with the notepad. Once again, the application sees only a display with input coming from a variety of sources.

## 5.2  Related Work

With the spectacular exception of NLS/Augment [12], which included shared hypertext and computer support for meetings, most graphical user interface systems have been motivated by the notion of the personal computer; Kay's influential Dynabook [22] was to be dedicated to the person carrying it. As a result, these systems have embedded assumptions about the style of user interaction they are to support, typically combining the standard mouse, keyboard and display.

Some early window systems were actually more flexible than their successors. The Adagio workstation [40], for example, used multitasking and message passing to support a graphical environment. There were device tasks which controlled access to a particular device, application tasks which implemented programs,and a central switchboard task which routed messages between the other tasks. Adagio provided several features also present in Gemma, such as: the ability dynamically to connect input devices to an application, sharing devices between clients, and virtual devices. It was, however, designed to support only a particular application, robotics, and was not distributed. Lantz et al.'s TheWA [24] also used multitasking and message passing, on the V operating system, to implement a user interface system. An Input Server process imposed a sequence on events from its input devices, each managed by a separate thread, and there was an Output Server process for each output medium, such as graphics or audio; input and output were kept separate except to provide input device feedback. Both TheWA and Adagio, however, were designed for a single user at a desk-based workstation, and only TheWA had even limited support for making interactive components available to other workstations.

More recently, X's hegemony has brought the benefits of a standard environment and a large user community, but its limitations have inhibited some developments. X, for example, does not allow a client to retrieve all of the state of a window, as there is only supposed to be one client of a given window, which makes window sharing particularly difficult [15]. Some researchers have had to add levels of indirection: implementing pseudo-servers on top of X [32, 39], a virtual window system below X [35], or something of both [13]. Similarly, those wishing to make X useful to people with disabilities have needed better access to input and output devices [42]. For many applications X is too monolithic, trading flexibility for convenience, as is NeWS [18], and neither provides facilities for sharing within an interface. A Gemma environment, on the other hand, may make any of its components, physical or virtual, available to multiple clients while still providing window system features.

Many virtual reality systems, however, do not have the same pragmatic restrictions and two in particular, VUE [5] and MR [37], are based on a set of communicating processes. Devices are managed by servers, possibly on separate hosts, that interpret between the specific device and the internal system protocols and may provide facilities such as smoothing; both teams found that the use of networked devices helped to structure the system and provide flexibility with little performance cost. Other servers perform functions such as maintaining the state of the virtual world, interpreting input events, and rendering images. Both systems, however, are designed to support a particular approach to user interaction, in which the user is immersed in the computer's world, unlike Gemma, in which computing devices are immersed in the user's world. For example, MR uses shared files to describe system-wide dependancies, such as available servers, assuming that a the components of a session will be static during its lifetime, whereas Gemma uses a name service.

Finally, the Fresco protocol [28] is concerned with the fine-grained, transparent distribution of graphical applications in which the components of an application's user interface, such as spreadsheet cells or a generated image, may be managed by processes on different hosts. Like Gemma, Fresco defines an environment in which the components are defined as pure virtual classes that may then be instanciated as either local objects or proxies for remote objects. Fresco, however, is largely concerned with distributing parts of an application that is manipulated through a conventional workstation, whereas Gemma is concerned with distributing the components of the workstation itself.

## 5.3  Object-Oriented Issues

Gemma manages a set of discrete components, both physical and virtual, which maintain internal state and communicate with each other. A component may run its own thread and may be one of several components which share a common resource. Furthermore, some components are available to clients in other address spaces and so must be named to be accessible, and some components may be persistent between instances of the service. These requirements suggest that an object-oriented approach, in which Gemma components are managed by software objects, maps well onto the basic problem. Gemma exploits two object-oriented techniques in paticular: inheritance and encapsulation.

Gemma's flexibility depends on applications being able to connect to arbitrary devices as the need arises, so applications should have a few dependencies as possible on the details of their devices. Two techniques help to achieve this: polymorphism, in this case based on inheritance, and encapsulation. Gemma objects are defined as pure abstract types (their internal structure is not directly accessible from the application), that are then subclassed to provide particular implementations. Applications are written in terms of the common supertypes and so look the same to the caller whether an object is local or is a proxy for a remote object. Thus, the distribution of any particular object is managed transparently to the application, while applications will, by default, be capable of handling remote devices. This approach is used in distributed object systems, such as Network Objects [8] and CORBA [19], and has an incidental advantage that the local implementation can be used as a foundation for the server implementation.

Gemma's component types are defined in an inheritance tree, which has several advantages. Firstly, it expresses relationships between component types, some of which are specialisations of each other—an Absolute2D component is a type of 2D component which is a type of InputComponent. This encourages code reuse both in the definition of component behaviour and, with inheritance polymorphism, in the applications that use the components. Clients of components can be written in terms of the most general supertypes they are prepared to accept, only unpacking further type information as the need arises. Secondly, an inheritance-based classification of component types helps to provide the basis of a common infrastructure by moving shared features into the supertypes. Again, this improves flexibility as an application may operate on any component type which matches its requirements. Thirdly, abstracting out aspects of a component's functionality, such as the media objects in Section 3.1 or contract objects in Section 4.1, provides a clean separation between a component's features. Again, these objects are defined as abstract supertypes which are made concrete in the leaf types and so the implementations can easilsy be substituted.

Finally, there are three main ways in which Gemma gains from the use of encapsulation. Firstly, as a basic software engineering approach it reduces dependancies between program components. Secondly, encapsulation makes easier the handling of special cases; for example, the client and server ends of a distributed object can establish a separate communication path without affecting any other components. Thirdly, it supports the association of state with components, rather than storing state globally. This makes distribution easier and provides a better match to the environment, in that there may be no single authority (such as a workstation) for the state of an interaction in a Gemma system.

## 5.4  Conclusions

Gemma is design for an architecture which provides a highly flexible user interface environment, in which users can combine input and output devices as the need arises in their own world, rather than in the computer's. To achieve this flexibility, Gemma relies on object-oriented techniques. In particular, it uses encapsulation to hide implementation details, particularly distribution, and to avoid global state. Gemma also uses inheritance to express the relations between device types, to support reuse and incremental change, and to provide polymorphism. Object-orientation is a natural model for a system built up from many communicating discrete components, many of which share common features. Devices are represented by objects that publish the interfaces, possibly more than one, they will support. These interfaces are imported by clients either to implement a virtual device, which is then published in turn, or to assemble a user environment. Applying this approach throughout a user interface architecture provides a flexible architecture in which, for example, the way users interact with an application object may be changed by attaching it to different virtual devices.

The greatest benefits of the Gemma approach, however, will accrue when a significant proportion of the people in an organisation can operate within it, sharing devices and applications—the critical mass issue is similar to that for CSCW applications [31]. Thus, it may be some time before Gemma can fully be validated.

## References

[1] ACM. *Conference on Computer Supported Cooperative Work, Los Angeles, CA*, September 1990.

[2] ACM. *ACM Symposium on User Interface Software and Technology, Altanta, GA*, 1993.

[3] M. Altenhofen, B. Neidecker-Lutz, and P. P. Tallet. Upgrading a window system for tutoring functions. In *ARGOSI Workshop on Distributed Window Systems*. EuroGraphics, EuroGraphics, December 1991.

[4] ANSA. *ANSA Reference Manual*. APM Ltd., Cambridge, UK, 1989.

[5] P.A. Appino, J.B. Lewis, L. Koved, D.T. Ling, D.A. Rabenhorst, and C.F. Codella. An architecture for virtual worlds. *Presence*, 1(1):1–17, Winter 1992.

[6] François Armand. Give a Process To Your Drivers. Technical Report CS/TR-91-97, Chorus Systèmes, 1991.

[7] Eric A. Bier and Steve Freeman. MMM: A User Interface Architecture for Shared Editors on a Single Screen. In *ACM Symposium on User Interface Software and Technology, Hilton Head, NC*, pages 79–86. ACM, 1991.

[8] A. Birell, G. Nelson, S. Owicki, and T. Wobber. Network objects. In *Symposium on Operating System Principles*, NY, 1993. ACM.

[9] S.A. Bly, S.R. Harrison, and S. Irwin. Media Spaces: bringing people together in a video, audio and computing environment. *Communications of the ACM*, 36(1):28–45, January 1993.

[10] Ed Brown, W.A.S. Buxton, and K. Murtagh. *Windows on Tablets as a Means of Achieving Virtual Input Devices*, pages 675–681. Elsevier, Amsterdam, 1990.

[11] C.A. Ellis, S.J. Gibbs, and G.L. Rein. Groupware: some issues and experiences. *Communications of the ACM*, 34(1):38–58, January 1991.

[12] D. Engelbart. *The Augmented Knowledge Workshop*, pages 187–232. In [17], 1988.

[13] S. Feiner, B. MacIntyre, M. Haupt, and E. Solomon. Windows on the World: 2D windows for 3D augmented reality. In [2], pages 145–156.

[14] S.M.G. Freeman and M.S. Manasse. Adding digital video to and object-oriented user interface toolkit. In Mario Tokoro and Remo Pareschi, editors, *Object-Oriented Programming (ECOOP)*, volume 821 of *Lecture Notes in Computer Science*, pages 493–512, New York, 1994. Springer-Verlag.

[15] James Gettys, Philip L. Karlton, and Scott McGregor. The X Window System, Version 11. *Software—Practice and Experience*, 20(S2):S2/35–S2/67, October 1990.

[16] S. Gibbs, C. Breiteneder, V. de Mey, and M. Papathomas. Video Widgets and Video Actors. In [2], pages 179–186.

[17] Adele Goldberg, editor. *A History of Personal Workstations*. ACM, New York, 1988.

[18] James Gosling, David S. H. Rosenthal, and Michelle J. Arden. *The NeWS Book: an introduction to the Network Extensible Window System*. Springer-Verlag, New York, 1989.

[19] Object Management Group. Common Object Request Broker Architecture and Specification. Technical Report 91.12.1, OMG, 1991.

[20] J. Grudin. Interface. In [1].

[21] H. Ishii. TeamWorkStation: Towards a Seamless Shared Workspace. In [1], pages 13–26.

[22] A. Kay. *Personal Dynamic Media*, pages 254–263. In [17], 1988.

[23] Bellcore Information Networking Research Laboratory. The Touring Machine System. *Communications of the ACM*, 36(1):68–77, January 1993.

[24] Keith A. Lantz. Multi-process Structuring of User Interface Software. *Computer Graphics*, 21(2):124–130, April 1987.

[25] J.C. Lauwers and K.A.Lantz. Collaboration awareness in support of collaboration transparency: requirements for the next generation of shared window systems. In *Human Factors in Computing Systems (CHI), Seattle, WA*, pages 303–311. ACM, ACM, 1990.

[26] I.M. Leslie, D.R. McAuley, and D.L. Tennenhouse. ATM Everywhere. *IEEE Network*, 7(2):40–46, March 1993.

[27] J. Liedtke, U. Bartling, U. Beyer, D. Heinrichs, R. Ruland, and G. Szalay. Two Years of Exerience with a $\mu$-Kernel-Based OS. *Operating Systems Review*, January 1991.

[28] M. Linton and C. Price. Building Distributed User Interfaces with Fresco. *The X Resource*, 5:77–87, January 1993.

[29] M. Manasse and G. Nelson. A Performance Analysis of a Multiprocessor Window System. Unpublished Manuscript, 1988.

[30] M. Mantei. Capturing the Capture Lab concepts: a case study in the design of computer supported meeting environments. In *Conference on Computer Supported Cooperative Work, Portland, OR*, pages 257–270. ACM, September 1988.

[31] M.L. Markus and T. Connoly. Why CSCW applications fail: problems in the adoption of interdependent work tools. In [1], pages 371–380.

[32] J. Menges. The X Engine Library: a C++ library for constructing X pseudo-servers. *The X Resource*, 5:129–142, 1993.

[33] B.A. Nardi and J.R. Miller. An ethnographic study of distributed problem solving in spreadsheet development. In [1], pages 197–208.

[34] T. Ohmori, K. Maeno, S. Sakata, H. Fukuoka, and K. Watabe. Distributed Cooperative Control for Sharing Applications Based on Multiparty and Multimedia Desktop Conferencing System: Mermaid. In *IEEE 12th International Conference on Distributed Computing Systems, Yokahama, 1992*, pages 538–546, 1992.

[35] R. Pascale and Jeremy Epstein. Virtual Window Systems: A New Approach to Supporting Concurrent Heterogeneous Windowing Systems. In *Usenix*, 1992.

[36] R. Rao. Implementational Reflection in Silica. Technical Report SSL-90-63, Xerox PARC, 1990.

[37] C. Shaw, M. Green, J. Liang, and Y. Sun. Decoupled simulation in virtual reality with the MR toolkit. *ACM Transactions on Information Systems*, 11(3):287–317, July 1993.

[38] R. Stults. Experimental Uses of Video to Support Design Activities. Technical Report SSL-89-19, Xerox PARC, 1989.

[39] M. Tani, M. Horita, K. Yamaashi, K. Tanikosi, and M. Futakawa. Courtyard: integrating shared overview on a large screen and per-user detail on individual screens. In *Human Factors in Computing Systems (CHI)*. ACM, ACM, 1994.

[40] Peter P. Tanner, Stephen A. MacKay, Darlene A. Stewart, and Marceli Wein. A Multitasking Switchboard Approach to User Interface Management. *Computer Graphics*, 20(4):241–248, August 1986.

[41] R. Took. The Active Medium: A Conceptual and Practical Architecture for Direct Manipulation. In D. Diaper and N. Hammond, editors, *People and Computers VI (HCI91)*, pages 249–264. Cambridge University Press, 1991.

[42] W.D. Walker, M.E. Novak, H.R. Tumblin, and G.C. Vanderheiden. Making the X window system accessible to people with disabilities. *The X Resource*, 5:213–227, 1993.

[43] R. Want, A. Hopper, V. Falc ao, and J. Gibbons. The Active Badge Location System. *ACM Transactions on Information Systems*, 10(1):91–102, January 1992.

[44] M. Weiser. Some Computer Science Issues in Ubiquitous Computing. *Communications of the ACM*, 36(7):75–84, July 1993.

# 6

# Object–Oriented Animation in the REALISM System

Ian J. Palmer, Richard L. Grimsdale

REALISM is an object–oriented animation system. It offers the user an environment whereby animation sequences may be developed using pre–defined libraries of objects and modifying their behaviour to suit a particular task. It demonstrates the application of O–O techniques to computer animation.

The classes in the system form a complex hierarchy, exploiting multiple inheritance and polymorphism to provide a rich expanse of capabilities. The two methods of influencing an object's behaviour, through rules and constraints, offer dynamic methods of control whilst retaining the mechanism within the object's structure. The separate methods for geometry dependent and independent aspects lead to a more disciplined classification of an object's behaviour.

The use of object–oriented techniques, and in particular the implementation of these in C++, in animation systems leads to certain problems. In particular the use of a 'class–instance' type language has some limitations as opposed to a 'prototype–delegation' style. This has been overcome in REALISM by objects creating replacement instances, effectively 'delegating' themselves as instances of different classes. Another problem, that of collision detection violating the encapsulation of the classes and creating heavy inter–object communications, has been solved by implementing a two–stage approach using a global table of bounding volumes as the first stage, and a direct peer-to-peer dialogue as the final stage.

The REALISM system therefore has the advantages of the traditional properties of object–oriented systems but also overcomes some of the difficulties that arise in applying O–O techniques to an animation system.

## 1  Introduction

The use of computer animation is rapidly becoming commonplace in fields as diverse as medical research and light entertainment. This explosion of applications has led to an increase in the demands placed upon the packages used to produce the animation, demands for more active objects in a scene and for more realistic behaviour of those objects. Substantial research has been carried out into the use of object–oriented techniques as an attempt to manage this expansion in complexity [4, 5, 8, 9, 10, 11, 13, 16]. This paper describes a particular system, REALISM, that addresses some of the problems caused by the use of an object–oriented approach as well as exploiting many of its advantages[1].

Firstly, the system is described showing how the use of object-oriented techniques has led to a flexible and efficient environment for developing animation. It reveals the method-

---

[1]REALISM is an acronym for 'Reusable Elements for Animation using Local Integrated Simulation Models'.

ology behind REALISM and describes the underlying structure of the software. It also summarises the two approaches to influencing object behaviour and their particular implementation. Secondly, some of the problems of applying O–O techniques to animation in general, and this implementation in particular, are discussed. It will be shown that the O–O paradigm has certain disadvantages and how these have been addressed in the REALISM system will be explained.

## 2  The REALISM System

The REALISM system is designed to allow explicit or implicit control of animated objects to enable a sequence of desired events to be visualised. To this end there is a hierarchical control scheme consisting of a script, a scene and an actor. Each of these major classes encapsulates enough data and processes to govern its own behaviour and to interact with other classes through message passing in classic O–O style. The construction of a scene, therefore, involves defining instances of these classes and creating the conditions that cause the desired events to occur. To understand this process, it is necessary to describe the system in greater detail.

### 2.1  The Class Hierarchy

The fundamental active object in an animation is an instance of an *actor*, representing objects that control their own behaviour. Actors that participate in a particular sequence are linked together in an instance of a scene. The sequence of events that defines the animation of the scene is then defined by a script object.

The *scene* class is a child of the actor class, which in addition to the control mechanisms, has a cast defining the actors involved in the scene. It also defines the number of frames per second (i.e. the temporal resolution of the scene) and is active in detecting collisions between objects within its scope.

The *script* class (again derived from the actor class), in its most basic form, is a list of events and commands that must be implemented by the scenes and actors within its influence. These events may be simple 'update all objects to time $t$' type commands, or they may be more explicit, defining positions and changes in behaviour of objects at particular times and places. This therefore allows differing methods of control from pure simulation to key-framed animation sequences.

An extract of the class hierarchy is shown in Fig. 1 (using notation from Booch [3]). From this it can be seen that all the active elements in an animation are derived from the actor class. This means that for most purposes all objects in the scene can be controlled in the same way, i.e. there is a high degree of polymorphism. This is desirable because all objects will exhibit some kind of behaviour, be subject to some constraints and have some kind of time dependency.

An example of a class that has a typical structure is the *polyhedronActor* class (as shown in Fig. 1). This has two direct parents, *polyhedron* and *geometricActor*. The parent geometricActor defines the object as having some physical shape, resulting in data members exhibiting simulated physical properties through the inclusion of a data member of type *material*. The material class itself is derived from two parents, a *surface class* defining the visual properties and a *physical* class specifying the properties of density and coefficients of restitution and friction. The polyhedron parent specifies the nature of the class geometry. Both the polyhedron and the geometricActor classes share the *geometry3D* parent (which defines operations for geometric transformations), leading to the necessity to specify them as virtual parents of the polyhedronActor classes to prevent multiple instances of the ge-

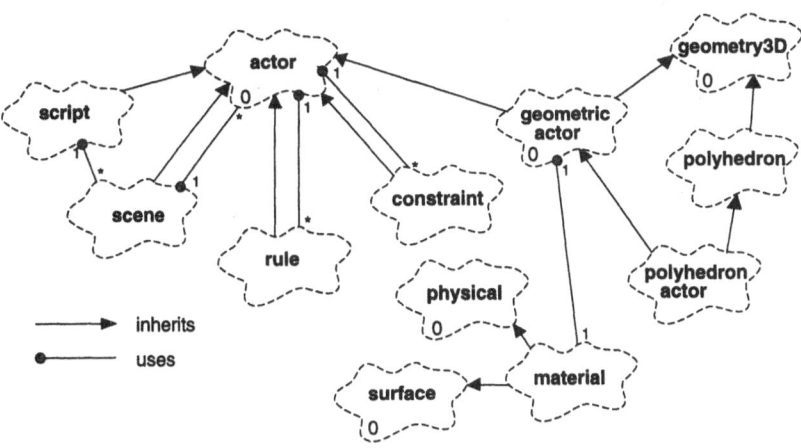

**Figure 1:** Extract from class hierarchy

ometry3D data in the child class. The behavioural information of the polyhedronActor is defined through the geometricActor class, which in turn inherits them from the actor class.

As can be seen from this small part of the class hierarchy, the family tree of the system is fairly complex. This is unfortunate but necessary in a general animation system implemented in C++. It is because the objects at the lowest level of the system require properties and procedures that allow them to be treated by part of the system as pure geometries, by another part as physical objects with mass, by a further part as geometric objects with visible surface properties and so on. This leads to the desire to keep separate these different facets of the objects structure, since it is beneficial that, for example, a renderer has knowledge only of an object's surface characteristics whilst a physical simulation process need only know of the object's physical properties. This therefore localises the data of the object in the processes that require that data, effectively distributing the description of the object throughout the system.

The REALISM system is therefore, by definition, object–oriented since the encapsulation of data and processes is its foundation. This leads to certain decisions relating to controlling the objects to achieve certain results, since these too must be contained within the object's structure.

## 2.2 Methods of Influencing Object Behaviour

Ensuring that an object has within its structure sufficient data and processes to enable it to behave correctly in any given simulated environment leads to inconceivably complex classes that would prove far too general for any given task. Hence the scheme adopted here allows refinement of an object's functional features through the use of two dynamic data structures within the actor class. This leads to two distinct implicit methods of affecting an objects behaviour.

The first is through the use of a list of rules associated with the object, each of which governs a particular aspect of the operation of the object. An example would be a rule to govern how an object reacts when a force is applied, i.e. does it accelerate, deform or fracture? The rules themselves are active objects in the system and so they themselves exhibit dynamic properties. Hence an object may initially deform under an applied force, but after a period of time it may 'solidify' and thereafter behave like a rigid body. The influence of a single rule may affect several objects. For example a rule that models a ferrous body's behaviour under the influence of a magnetic field may be applied to all relevant objects in a scene and only one copy of the rule would be created. This limits repetition of data and allows changes in multiple object behaviour to be easily and efficiently implemented.

The constraints experienced by an object are also contained in a list, in this case a list of constraint objects. These affect geometry and position dependent aspects of the object behaviour, such as fixing rotation about a certain axis or motion to within a given plane. They are again dynamic objects, so their parameters may alter throughout their lifetime. The use of constraints allows efficient modelling of potentially complex situations. As an example, consider a cylinder constrained to rotate about its major axis. To model this an appropriate constraint is created and added to the object's constraint list. If a force is then applied to the object such as to violate the constraint, for example causing the cylinder to translate away from the axis of rotation, then the violating component of the force is set to zero and takes no further part in the dynamic calculations of the object. This situation remains until the force and/or constraint is altered. This means that the constrained behaviour of the object is event driven; recalculations of dynamic state are only performed when some event causes the conditions of the object to change. The constraints are processed after the rules, and hence may override them. This is desirable in general, since typically an enforced constraint would provide a stronger behavioural condition than, for example, a 'rule' of gravity.

These two approaches allow the behaviour of an object to be specifically tailored to the environment in which it exists but is also general enough to model most kinds of behaviour. The distinction between the rules and constraints is provided to discipline the user of the system to differentiate between geometry dependent and independent processes. It should be noted that there are many cases when a particular behaviour could be implemented equally well by either a rule or a constraint, but by considering the implications of the scope and dynamic nature of the problem, usually one approach emerges as more appropriate.

## 2.3   A Typical REALISM Animation

The construction of a typical animation sequence begins with the creation of a single top–level script specifying the important events in the progress of the animation, one or more scenes defining the elements that take part in the animation and multiple actors performing the actions required to satisfy the top–level goals. A non–trivial example is shown in Fig. 2. This shows an example of a multi–level control scheme in which some of the low level 'actors' are in fact scripts and scenes defining further systems of actors.

The script will firstly define the initial conditions of the objects in the scene by setting their positions, velocities and so on. Thereafter the nature of the script will depend on the type of animation. In a pure simulation the script will merely consist of a 'for' loop of 'update to next frame' type commands. The behaviour of the actors to implement these commands is entirely defined by the actors themselves. Explicit control may be attempted within the script by an 'update object to position' type command, but even in this case an object may refuse to obey the directive. This would be because compliance will violate some behavioural condition of the object, for example causing penetration between two rigid bodies, or the object may have some intelligence and refuse to comply by using some pre–defined reasoning.

The development of animation sequences follows a process of creating instances of

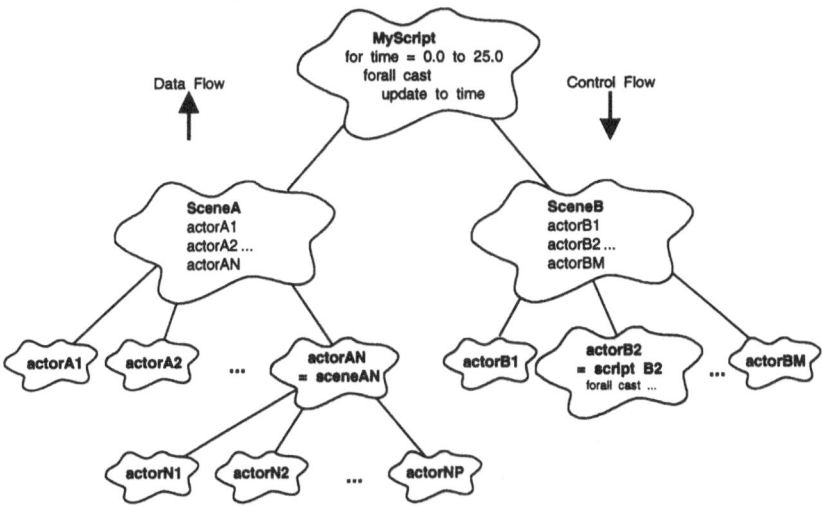

**Figure 2:** Typical environment object structure

library objects that have the desired behavioural characteristics and placing them in a particular environment. The progress is then controlled by a simple sequence of commands that can define the operations to be performed in as much detail as is required to produce the desired result. The procedure is both simple and powerful enough to allow rapid development of complex scenes.

## 2.4 The Implementation

The REALISM system has been implemented in C++ and the use of the language in its current form has certain implications. The use of templates was not possible as a solution to implementing generic features in the system as the compilers available at the start of the work did not support this feature. This results in the necessity for extensive use of pointers to objects of a common base class as a means of implementing generic methods. This is a not entirely satisfactory solution as it raises problems of other kinds, such as the casting between types of pointers, problems caused by multiple inheritance and so on. It does however offer the use of a simple form of polymorphism and with care provides the desired result.

The language, being a class–instance type scheme, offers only rigid class relationships. This is undesirable in a dynamic system such as REALISM. It is possible to circumvent this problem, however, and this will be discussed in Section 3.

The platforms used for this work have been varied and the success of porting the code to different machines has been greatly assisted by the availability of suitable C++ compilers. During its lifetime it has been ported to a PC, an Apollo workstation, a Sun SPARC machine and most recently, an Iris Indigo workstation.

The REALISM system in its current form consists of more than 16000 lines of C++ code, and contains 86 separate classes. All non–trivial objects in the system are implemented as individual classes, from vectors to polyhedra with physical properties. This has allowed a great deal of flexibility in the system with all objects tailored for their specific purpose in the animation system. Any interfaces to other code, for example a wire frame display in an X–window or the use of a ray–tracer for final rendering, are implemented by converting the class instance data to a form readable by the external code. The division therefore between the object–oriented REALISM environment and less specifically object–oriented code is maintained.

Rigidly enforced O–O style allows efficient procedures to be written for each individual aspect of the animation process without recourse to the rest of the system. It does however result in potentially large inter–object communication requirements. This is a problem that has been addressed in the system.

## 3   Some Problems of Object-Oriented Animation

The use of C++ in developing REALISM has resulted in the identification of certain problems in the implementation of object–orientation in the language and led to the development of alternative approaches to overcome these problems.

The first problem that is apparent in using a class–instance based language for animation is that in many ways the problem is best suited to a prototype–delegation style environment [16, 15]. This becomes obvious in the example of an object morphing between two geometries. This would typically require an object to change its geometric information between two distinct end states, for example between a sphere and a cube. In C++ there is no way that an object that is derived from a sphere geometry base class can 'divorce' its geometry parent and 'adopt' a new, different (in this case cubic) one. This could be overcome by having a data member of the object that described its geometry and hence changing this data member would result in a change of geometry. However, this would lose the advantages of inheritance that is so much a part of the C++ style of O–OD, and which allows a complex object derived from a simple geometry to be treated (at appropriate times) as an instance of that simple parent class. To overcome this a different approach is taken in REALISM. When a member of a scene's cast changes its geometry it creates an instance of the new geometry and assigns this new object to its own position in the cast. Finally, the new object destroys the original object that created it. This process is shown in Fig. 3. In this way any object may transform to any other object in the manner of a prototype–delegation type language, but still retain the advantages of inheritance.

Another problem with object–oriented animation is that of detecting collisions, an issue that is important for efficient animation [1, 2, 6, 7, 12, 14, 17]. To enable a collision to be detected between two objects, the geometry of each must be known. Traditionally animation systems have used some global method that processes object positions and geometry information to detect collisions. This requires that the global process interrogates each object and then calls the required procedure for the pair of geometries. Hence it must be possible to inquire an object's class, a process not explicitly implemented in C++. Realising a method to explicitly interrogate every object's class would necessitate that every object knew of the existence of every other class of object and would negate the advantage of polymorphism and encapsulation. Further to this, addition of new classes would involve the extensive modification of all existing classes. The REALISM system approaches this problem differently.

Each instance of a scene maintains a table of bounding volumes of the objects within its cast. When an object updates its position it also writes its new bounding volume representation into the scene's table. After all objects have updated, the scene scans the table for updated entries. Any that are found are then checked against all other boundaries for intrusion. If an intruding pair is discovered, then one of the objects is notified of the identity of the second object. This is achieved by the scene calling:

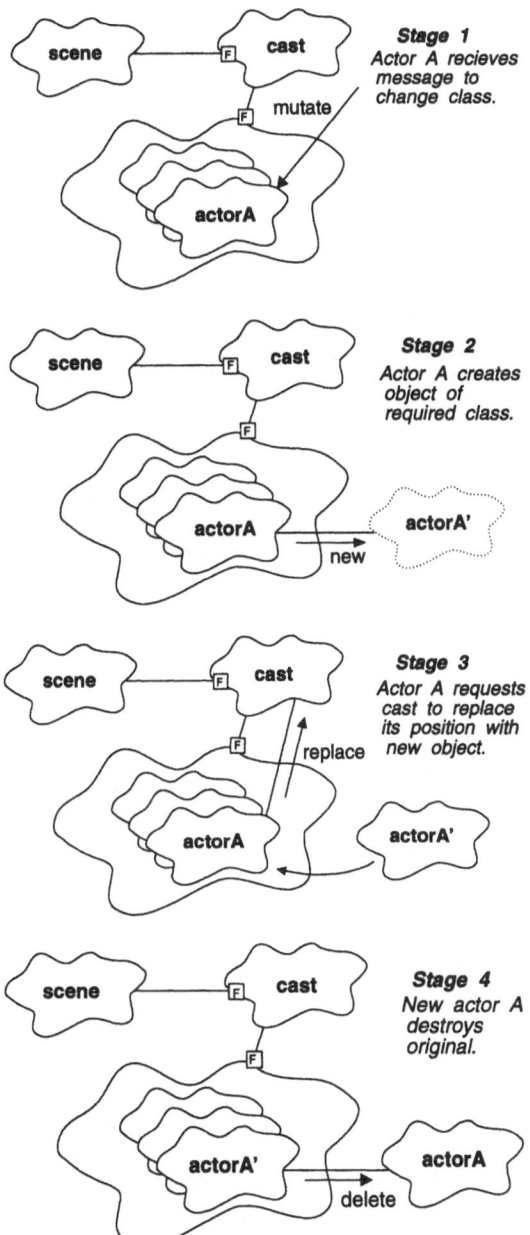

**Figure 3:** Stages in inter-class transformation

```
objectB->collision(objectA);
```

Hence, in this example, the method 'collision' of object B is called with a pointer to object A. The actual geometry of object A is not known at this stage since the type of the pointer is that of the shared base class actor, and so object B cannot perform the collision detection. As a result, object B calls a method of object A:

```
objectA->collision(this);
```

The 'this' pointer in C++ points to the current object and as a result is of the appropriate type for the class of object B. Hence object A now knows the class of object B and can perform the appropriate collision detection. This process is shown in Fig. 4.

The process, which at first appears somewhat complex, has certain advantages. It removes the necessity to implement a 'what are you' type method for every class. It also means that if new classes of geometries are added the new collision detection processes can be implemented in the new object class. For example, if a class 'torus' was added to a conventional system it would then be necessary to add to all existing classes a process to detect collisions with the new class. In this scheme, however, it is only necessary to provide procedures within the torus class to detect collisions with existing classes of objects. It should be noted, however, that this approach does not remove the necessity for recompilation of existing code when a new class is added to the system. It does prevent extensive modification of existing code and the resulting problems of maintenance and support.

The bounding volume scheme means that communication between objects is kept to a minimum, the only extensive dialogue being the final stage where the full geometric collision detection process is carried out. The necessity for one object to have full knowledge of another object's geometry does not violate encapsulation of data because the objects are peers and the request (from actor A to actor B in Fig. 4, for example) identifies the specific type of object involved.

The final interesting feature of the system is the method of displaying objects. This uses a delegation type approach together with a technique similar to that used for collision detection to identify the geometric type of objects (see Fig. 5). The first event in the sequence that results in the display of a scene at a particular time is the sending of a 'display' message to the scene. This message would generally have no parameters and is interpreted as a request to view the scene using all cameras present within its cast. The scene, of course, has no explicit 'display' operation itself, and so delegates the task to all its cast members. The 'display' messages that it multicasts, however, has the added parameter of a copy of the cast list to identify to the receiving objects the objects to display.

When the objects receive the display message, only those that are cameras will perform any operations as a result. All other classes of objects return 'false', indicating that they cannot process the message. The cameras respond by sending a 'display' message to each of the members of the cast with a pointer to themselves as the parameter. This is effectively saying 'display yourself to me' to each other object.

Visible objects (i.e. those that have a geometry and are made of a material) respond to this by sending the camera a 'view' message with parameters representing their geometry and surface characteristics. The camera can now generate a visualisation of the objects.

This process has the advantage that the scene need not know which objects in the cast are cameras, and that new types of cameras can be added without extensive alterations to the existing geometry classes. The disadvantage is that all actors in the system must

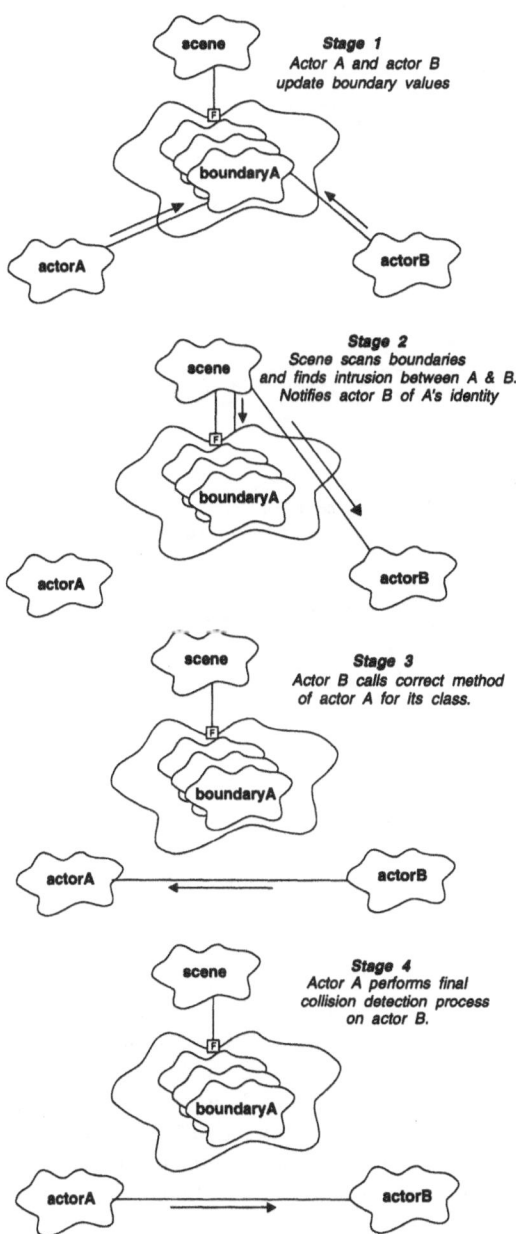

**Figure 4:** Collision detection process

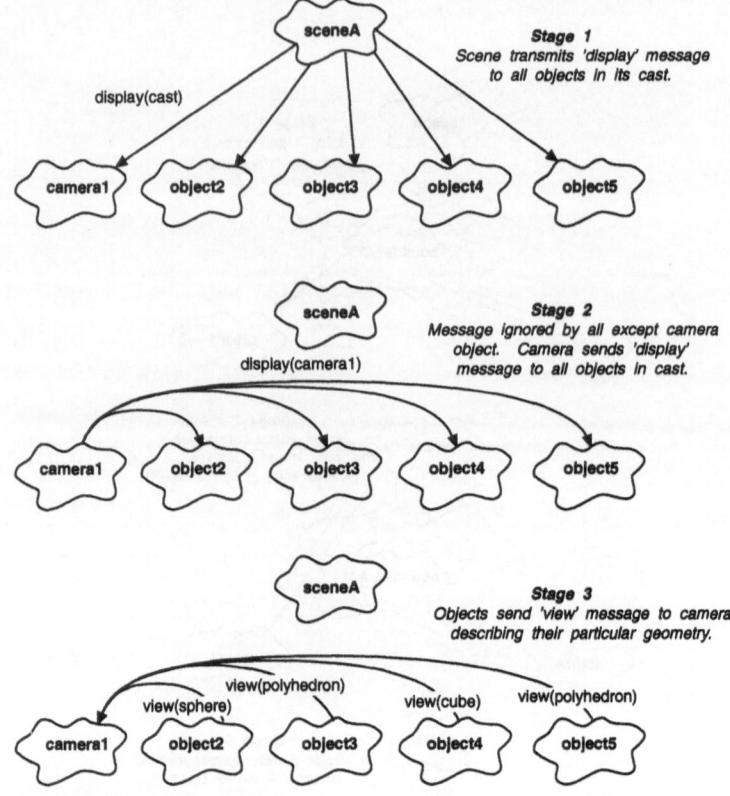

**Figure 5:** The display process

have 'display' methods, even if these are empty functions. This is supported in REALISM by the base actor class having the appropriate virtual methods, which are then inherited by all actors in the hierarchy and redefined as necessary.

## 4  Conclusions

The development of the REALISM animation system has revealed some problems specific to the application of object–oriented techniques to the field of computer animation. Some of these are particular to the use of C++ for the implementation, that of the inappropriateness of a class–instance approach, whilst others are more general, such as the requirement for detecting collisions between different types of objects breaking the object's encapsulation and requiring extensive inter–object communication. It has also revealed, however, the usual benefits argued for O–O techniques, particularly in the rapid prototyping of code and the safe nature of encapsulated data and methods. The latter is particularly attractive for animation since it allows the localisation of object behavioural procedures and parameters that is the very essence of the REALISM system.

The limitations of using C++ for the system have been identified and solutions to the important issues found. The use of 'delegation' style techniques allows inter–class transformations within the rigid class hierarchy of the C++ environment and generic display operations. Collision detection using a dual level approach and progressive definition of the detection problem limits the inter–object communication requirements, and lessens the problem of the breakdown of encapsulation between communicating objects.

The REALISM system effectively utilises the advantages of the efficiency and portability traditionally associated with C++ together with the flexibility and strict encapsulation usually associated with more classical object–oriented systems.

## References

[1] D. Baraff. Analytical Methods for Dynamic Simulation of Non–penetrating Rigid Bodies. In *Proceedings of SIGGRAPH '89*, pages 223–232. SIGGRAPH, 1989.

[2] D. Baraff. Curved Surfaces and Coherence for Non–penetrating Rigid Body Simulation. In *Proceedings of SIGGRAPH '90*, pages 19–28. SIGGRAPH, 1990.

[3] G. Booch. *Object Oriented Design with Applications.* Benjamin Cummings, Redwood City, 1991.

[4] D. Breen, P. Getto, A. Apodaca, D. Schmidt, and B. Sarachan. The Clockworks: An Object–Oriented Animation System. In *Proceedings of Eurographics 87*, pages 275–282. Eurographics, 1987.

[5] M. Chmilar and B. Wyvill. A Software Architecture for Integrated Modelling and Animation. In R.A. Earnshaw, editor, *New Advances in Computer Graphics*, pages 257–276. Springer–Verlag, 1989.

[6] J. Hahn. Realistic Animation of Rigid Bodies. In *Proceedings of SIGGRAPH '88*, pages 299–308, 1988.

[7] Ming C. Lin and John F. Canny. Efficient Collision Detection for Animation. In *Proceedings of the Third Eurographics Workshop on Animation and Simulation*, Cambridge, 1992.

[8] N. Magnenat-Thalmann and D. Thalmann. Construction and Animation of a Synthetic Actress. In *Proceedings of Eurographics '88*, pages 55–66, 1988.

[9] M. Mahieddine and J. Lafon. An Object–Oriented Approach for Modelling Animated Entities. In N. Magnenat-Thalmann and D. Thalmann, editors, *Computer Animation '90*. Springer–Verlag, 1990.

[10] R. Maiocchi and B. Pernici. Directing an animated scene with autonomous actors. In N. Magnenat-Thalmann and D. Thalmann, editors, *Computer Animation '90*, pages 41–60. Springer–Verlag, 1990.

[11] M. McKenna, S. Pieper, and D. Zeltzer. Control of a Virtual Actor: The Roach. In *Proceedings of SIGGRAPH '88*, pages 289–298, 1988.

[12] M. Moore and J. Wilhelms. Collision Detection and Response for Computer Animation. In *Proc. of SIGGRAPH '88*, pages 289–298, 1988.

[13] C. Reynolds. Computer Animation with Scripts and Actors. In *Proc. of SIGGRAPH '82*, pages 289–296, 1982.

[14] J. Tornero, G. Hamlin, and R.B. Kelley. Collision–detection based on a fast distance computation technique. In S.G. Tzafestas, editor, *Engineering Systems with Intelligence, Concepts, Tools and Applications*, pages 305–13. Kluwer Academic Publishers, Dordrecht, Netherlands, 1991.

[15] P. Wisskirchen. *Object-oriented graphics: from GKS and PHIGS to object-oriented systems*. Springer–Verlag, Berlin, 1990.

[16] R. Zeleznik, D. Brookshire Conner, M. Wloka, D. Aliaga, N. Huang, P. Hubbard, B. Knep, H. Kaufman, J. Hughes, and A. van Dam. An Object–Oriented Framework for the Integration of Interactive Animation Techniques. In *Proceedings of SIGGRAPH '91*, pages 105–112, 1991.

[17] M.J. Zyda, D.R. Pratt, W.D. Osborne, and J.G. Monahan. NPSNET: Real–time Collision Detection and Response. *Journal of Visualization and Computer Animation*, 4(1):13–24, 1993.

# 7

# Modeling Multimedia-Objects with MME

Dennis Dingeldein

This paper describes our approach to modeling multimedia with an object-oriented class hierarchy. Our model is independent from specific application domains, hardware and media types.
It abstracts from the physical data sources and sinks. The model is implemented basically as a
toolkit, called *MME (MultiMedia Extension)*, offering C++ classes to the programmer of multimedia applications and user interfaces. On top of this toolkit, some tools are realized to give
non-programmers access to the features of the toolkit. There are media-dependent classes for
modelling both media-data independent presentation (output) and interaction (input) aspects
of multimedia objects. Furthermore, there are classes that define media data-independent
relations and constraints between multimedia objects. Those relations can be spatial (layout
definitions) and temporal (animation definitions). The media-independent classes use media-
dependent classes (called *Encodings*) to access different data formats and *Connection* classes
to access media data storage. Using these classes, a multimedia application or user interface
can easily be defined by connecting media objects and application objects. The toolkit is designed to be portable.

## 1 Motivation

Multimedia offers many features to the world. It's not clear, however, how to turn those
features into benefits [2]. The conservative point of view states that hardware vendors
present the technical possibilities, but no broad application domains exist. This may be
seen from the lack of existing, convincing applications using multimedia. A more progressive point of view sees multimedia as the possibility to present information and allow
interactions in a "more human" way (i.e. better adapted to the human senses), improving
the user interface and increasing the power of the human [10]. The lack of convincing
applications is, at least partly, due to the lack of integrated and easy-to-use development
tools for multimedia applications.

Existing development tools handling multimedia usually solve only isolated problems in
specific application domains. Multimedia software at the programmers level (e.g. a toolkit)
does usually not fit to existing software tools (for example, user interface toolkits).

There is a strong focus on presentation, for example systems capable of displaying
real-time video rarely offer means to do interaction tasks using video as an input device.
Usually, this feature is missing at the modeling level, because at the low level of programming there is usually no easy access to the multimedia data directly (for example, if
the application is not programmed specifically to access single frames of an video input
stream, the user never has a chance to get any frame data). However, a model should take
such features into account.

In general, there is a lack of expressing complex relations and constraints between

graphical objects. In [13] the world of interactive systems is described as one half emphasizing graphic design (i.e. presentation), and another half emphasizing communication
(i.e. interaction). The authors of [13] describe their interest as:

*"We're interested in a system that does its own graphic design when communicating"*

This is even enforced by multimedia, because this domain adds the problem of arranging
objects temporally. So a more generalized approach to modelling multimedia objects and
relations is needed.

## 2  Goals and General Concepts

The main goals of MME are

- The object-oriented modeling of various, perhaps arbitrary, media (e.g. text, audio,
  photos, video)

- The encapsulation of (distributed) media access and control. Various media sources
  and sinks like devices (e.g. VCRs, cameras), access to window- and file-systems are
  encapsulated in the abstraction of *Media Ports*

- The modeling of *Time* as a precondition to define arbitrary temporal relations

- The modeling of *spatial and temporal relations* between media objects based on the
  time-model mentioned above. Those relations are *defined* during the design-stage
  of the application at a high level of abstraction. The *realization* of the structure is
  controlled at runtime by the toolkit

Any application using MME is basically a set of objects and relations between the
following objects:

- *Application objects* (AO). For example, a clock object or a picture source are application objects. Such objects correspond to the *model* of the *MVC-model* from
  Smalltalk, but on a finer level. Those objects can be divided in *sources, sinks* and
  *peekers*.

- *Multimedia Objects* (MO). In general, Multimedia Objects (in short Media Objects)
  manage the mapping of media sources to media sinks

- Relations between those objects above. The relations between the objects can be of
  the following types:

  - AO - AO. The relation *AO-AO* defines the semantics of the application, being
    the part of the application independent from the media objects

  - AO - MO. The relation *AO-MO* is the communication channel where changes
    in application objects are effecting the media objects (*Update-Mechanism*)

  - MO - AO. The relation *MO-AO* is the channel where interactions with the
    media objects are delivered to application objects (*Trigger-Mechanism*)

  - MO - MO. The relation *MO-MO* defines the dynamics of the application, that
    is the code of the system completly devoted to media objects and their relations

The relations can be:

- Spatial, dealing with *layout composition*

- Temporal, dealing with *synchronization*

MME Objects are in general either basic *media objects* or *complex media objects*:

- *Media objects* handle the transfer of *media data* from a set of ports (media sources) to another set of ports (media sinks). A source port is capable to generate or emit specific media data, a sink port is capable to receiving specific media data and transform it in a way that humans can understand. Often, a port can be used either as sink or as source (e.g. a VCR)

- *Complex media objects* handle the definition and maintenance of both spatial and temporal composition and relations among the media objects

This means that any MME-application is realized by executing the following steps:

- Instantiation of media objects out of the predefined set of multimedia classes offered by the toolkit

- Definition of the relations between media objects and between media objects and application objects. This includes instantiation of complex media objects to define spatial and temporal layout relations among other media objects and connection of media objects to application objects

- The optional definition of new media classes as subclasses of the predefined set of multimedia classes and instantiation of objects from those application-defined classes

- Starting the multimedia application (this means bringing the set of objects into a state where users can interact with them)

## 3  Media Objects

All objects offered by MME are composed from several sub-objects:

- A set of ports defining the different media sources *(source ports)*. Those objects are out of the class *Port* and generate media data controlled by the media object.

- A set of ports defining the different media sinks (*sink ports*). Those objects are out of the class *Port* too and are capable of receiving media data controlled by the media object.

- A *time object*. This object maintains the object's idea of time. It is capable to convert between *object-time* and *world-time* and to operate on time values submitted to the object from the application.

- A *geometry object*. For those objects having a visual representation, the actual appearance is defined in this object.

- A *transition object*. This object controls the temporal relation of the media object to another media object or to the world-time.

- An *attribute object*. Properties, e.g. the policy to generate the actual output from the source in the sink can be controlled using the attribute object

- A *behaviour object*. This object defines the interactions that a user can execute with the media object and how it reacts on that. Interactions can be of the following types:

  - *With the media object*: the goal of the user interaction is to modify aspects of the media object itself. This includes interactions like *Selection*, *Dragging* around on the screen, *Cut&Paste* etc.

  - *Through the media object*: the goal of the user interaction is to communicate using the media object as communication channel. This includes *communication with the application*, e.g. by making gestures or speaking (speech recognition) and *communication with other users*, e.g. using connected media objects as a teleconferencing tool.

## 3.1   Source and Sink Objects

The instantiation of a media object is parametrized by two sets of port objects, the *sources* and *sinks* of the media transfer. In general, a media object defines a time based function for media data and offers methods to manipulate function parameters. It depends on the media object's class if and how different media data are mapped from a set of sources to a set of sinks. Both source and sink are objects of the class *Port*. Ports can be :

- *Devices* (e.g. VCR, camera, CD player, speaker, microphone) that can be computer-controlled via a vendor-specific protocol (e.g. *RS232*-based, *SONY*s *CRTL-L*)

- *Windows* on the computers display

- *Files* (e.g. *JPEG*, *Motion JPEG* or *MPEG* for movies) or *Network Sockets*

and more. Figure 1 shows the overall structure of a media object.

## 3.2   Time Objects

Media objects maintain their own idea of *time*. This time usually deviates from the world time (real time), e.g., when a video sequence is read from a file via a computer network and the file transfer rate is too low, the number of frames played will be smaller than it should be. In this case, the object time will be smaller than the world time (the object is "in the past"). In Figure 2, the object times of several media objects are shown as time lines. The second time line shows the situation where a media object is too slow, so its object time is in the past (i.e. smaller than the world time, shown in the first time line).

If the decoding hardware is fast enough and not synchronized in any way, a video file could be posted faster than needed (more than 25 frames per second in europe), so the object time will be greater than the world time (the object is "in the future"). This can be seen in the last time line of Figure 2.

This time value is used by complex media objects that define temporal relations upon their sub objects. For example, a complex media object can prevent that a sub-object runs into the future or move it from its past to actual time.

## 3.3   Transition objects

These objects control the temporal relation of media objects to other media objects or to the world-time. In Figure 3, some possible transitions are shown. Using transition objects, a media object can be started ($T_1$) or stopped ($T_5$) as the result of a stop of another media object (or started ($T_2$) or stopped ($T_4$) as a result of the start of another media object) or as a result of the expiration of a given (world-)time value ($T_3$).

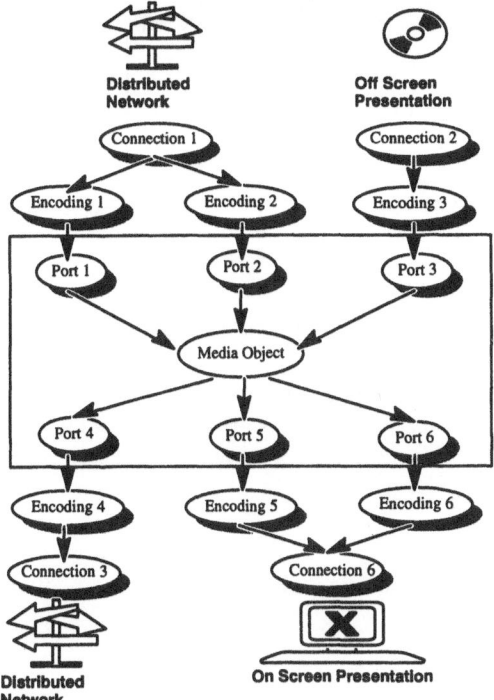

**Figure 1:** The general structure of a media object

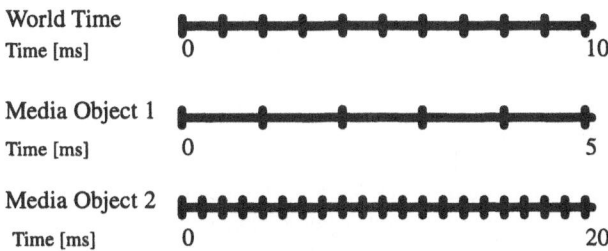

**Figure 2:** Object times of several media objects

## 3.4 Geometry and Attributes

Usually a media object has a visual representation. For example, a video is represented by itself, a sound is represented by an icon etc. The *geometry* defines e.g. the dimension and position of a media object.

The policy to generate the actual output from the sources in the sinks can be controlled using attributes. This attribute can be one of *SynchronizeToContent* and *SynchronizeTo-Time*. For example, for a video sequence in a file, the needed time is known and might be used as a time condition. If the transfer of the data from source to sink is to slow, not all frames might be displayed in order to meet the time condition. The synchronization *to content* means that all frames will be displayed, so the full object time of the object is

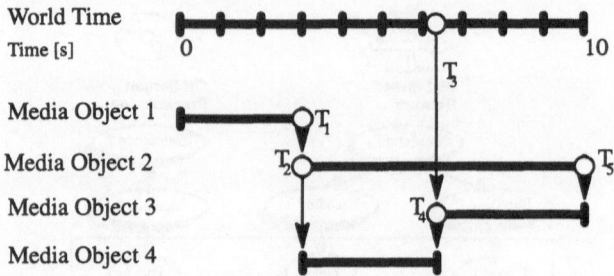

**Figure 3:** Defining temporal dependencies with transitions

used to view it, ignoring the condition. In the case of synchronization *to time*, the time allowed for the object is exactly matched, so that the remaining yet unseen parts of the video will be discarded. This models different needs of different applications.

# 4   Complex Media Objects

In every application or dialogue using multimedia, common relations are present. Those relations are

- complex *sequences* of concurrent and sequential objects

- *synchronity*

If the tool does not support those relations, the application has to realize them itself. We included those common relations by modeling them as objects out of special classes, called *Complex Media Objects* in the toolkit. Further, application-dependent relations not listed above could be implemented using the subclassing-mechanisms of C++. This would be just for convenience, because the complex media classes offered by MME are general enough to allow the definition of every possible temporal relation [12] [14].

Complex media objects control a set of media objects (*elements*). Those elements can be complex media objects again, thus offering the means to introduce multiple levels of abstraction into a definition of a multimedia dialogue. In general, the set of controlled media objects is moved in time according to the defined type of relation the complex media object realizes. Complex media objects update the object time of all elements. This includes translation in time (moving) and stopping (clipping).

Because every object has it's own idea of time, this is a non-trivial task. All activities of complex media objects are initiated by a continuously appearing event (interrupt). In the interrupt service routine, methods of media objects to recalculate their object times are invoked. Based on these object times, the complex media objects can check if elements are out of time (e.g. too fast or too slow). For such elements, the object time is rearranged to the correct value. Furthermore, complex media objects can detect if elements should be started or stopped as a function of time. In both cases, events are generated and delivered to other media objects, causing them to be started or stopped too.

In the case of user interaction, a complex object sometimes has to react by making its own state consistent. For example, when the user pauses a media object arranged in a sequence, the sequence object itself has to change into the pause state. For that reason, such state transmissions are propagated upwards in the hierarchy.

## 5  Multimedia Interactions

Most multimedia application components both have presentation and interaction aspects. The presentation aspects are described in terms of ports and time based media objects. To have a intuitive and consistent application interface, multimedia interactions are modelled with port objects and are time variant too. For example, for every still image object, it is possible to define a set of (polygonal) areas that can be picked with the mouse pointer and result in a area-specific reaction of the application (e.g. new infomation is presented). Those *Areas of Interest* can be defined upon a live video too by synchronizing the live video source port and a graphics port using a complex synchronizer object. Figure 4 shows the presentation of a live video with a single area of interest in the left and the objects used to realize both presentations and interactions for the video. The area of interest is synchronized with a surfer surfing though a large wave. The area of interest is shown for two frames and is interpolated for all frames between them.

The *Area Of Interest* interaction form the *PolygonPort* class, is a subclass of *GraphicsPort*, that realizes arbitrary time based graphical objects. The PolygonPort class adds a *callback* concept and different interpolation methods to recalculate the areas depending on the object time. Further interactions are *hotspots* (realized as circle-shaped anchors in a frame), further features include *morphing* (e.g. mapping a polygon area with n points to an area with m points)

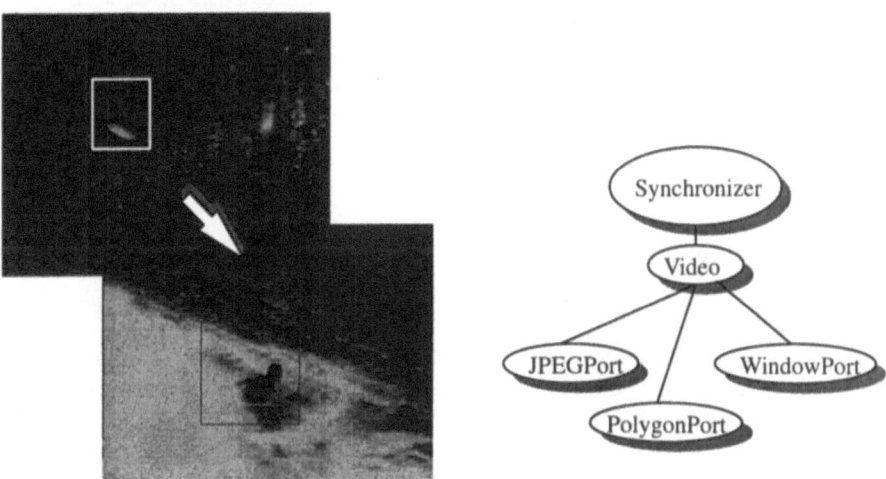

**Figure 4:** Synchronizing multimedia presentation and interactions

## 6  Architecture

Up to here, the concepts of the toolkit's application programmer's interface (*API*) were described. The following section focuses on the underlying basic concepts that form the basic building blocks to realize the API.

The toolkit is realized by the composition of several large objects. Those objects are used to encapsulate functionality that is needed by the toolkit. The structure of those objects is shown in Figure 5. Those more internal objects were used to implement all the toolkit classes described above.

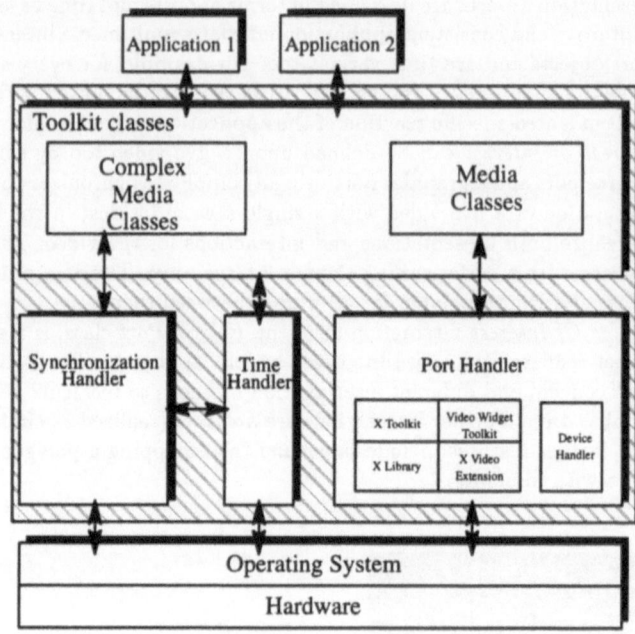

**Figure 5:** The internal objects of MME

## 6.1   The Connection to "Time"

The *time handler object* hides the mechanisms that generate and update a global time (*world time*). Media objects use this global time to calculate their own, object-specific time values (*object time*). Media objects have methods to access and modify time values and these methods always invoke the time handler. By exchanging only relative times, no synchronized clocks are needed in MME.

An interrupt-driven *synchronization handler object* is implemented on top of the UNIX operating system level. Based on the time values maintained by the time handler, complex media objects move and clip their sub-objects in time to realize for example synchronization or sequentialization.

## 6.2   The Connection to Media Devices and to the X Window System

A *port handler object* offers methods and abstractions to model various media sinks and sources. The port classes described above are implemented on top of the device handler object. Some availabe port classes are shown in Figure 6.

We introduced one further level of abstraction in the port-subclass that implements access to the window system by defining a *video widget* that follows the conventions of other X Toolkit-based widgets like buttons, scrollbars etc. For example, it can handle resize- and expose events automatically (by scaling or redrawing the video) and allows

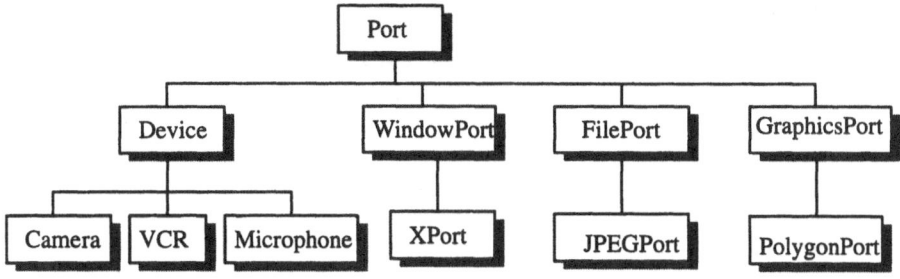

**Figure 6:** The port classes of MME

the modification of video parameters. The window port controls video using only widget methods and attributes. The widget was implemented on top of the *X Video Extension*. A more detailed description of the video widget toolkit can be found in [8].

# 7  Implementation

MME has been implemented in C++ on top of UNIX, the X Window System and a the X Video Extension. It has roughly 4500 lines of code. The object-oriented benefits like reuse and encapsulation allowed us to design and implement the toolkit in one man year. We decided to use the *X Video Extension* as a basic level, and the *GNU* C++ compiler to implement all the code. Both software products are available on almost every vendor platform. MME is developed as an extension to Theseus++ [1]. Figure 7 shows a part of the realized media class tree.

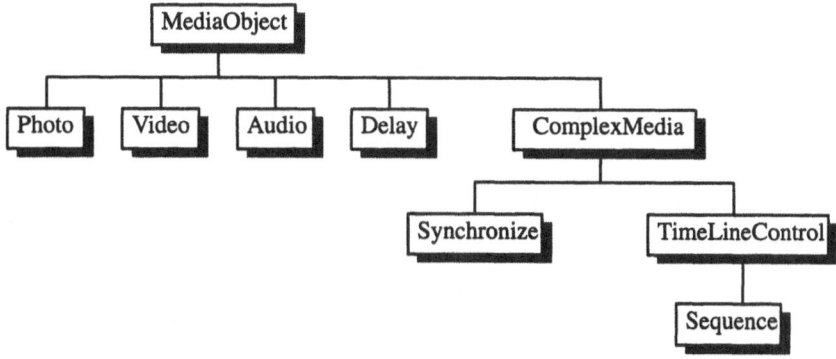

**Figure 7:** Media classes offered by MME

---

[1]THESEUS++ is developed as part of STONE, a national joint project of nine german institutes in the research and education domain. It is sponsored by the German Ministry of Research and Technology (grant no. 01IS104G/3) [7]

## 8  Related Work

There are several approaches to modelling temporal and spatial relations between multi-media presentations and interactions upon them. The approach with active objects seems to be best accepted and will make its way into upcoming standards [3] [6] [1]. Time-line based systems [5] [9] work well for small presentation systems with little interaction, because they offer no abstractions (no complex objects) and assume that the preset time schedules run as intended by an author.

The *IMA (Interactive Multimedia Association) Compatibility Projects* overall goal is to create a set of documents, called *Recommended Practice* for Multimedia Portability to realize Systems that can be used across multiple hardware and operating system platforms [4]. The architecture of MME is close to the proposed architecture of the IMA group. The *Ports* of MME correspond to the *Virtual Devices*, the *complex media classes* correspond to the *Application Synchronization Services*. The *Object Service* is integrated in our implementation language C++: MME has no *Connection Objects* yet. The *Time-* and *Synchronization Service* of the IMA architecture correspond to the *Time-* and *Synchronization handler objects* of MME. MME has no *Resource Management Service* yet.

An *Object-Oriented Framework for Multimedia Composition and Synchronisation* [11] focuses also on solving the problems of *composition* and *synchronization* of multimedia objects. The objects modeled in the framework are separated in sources, filters, sinks and *Composite Multimedia Objects*. Composite objects are created using the *Composite Timeline Diagram (CTD)*, a kind of storyboard tool. The CTD allows to locate objects in a composite object using temporal transformation. Those transformations can be *Translating*, *Scaling* and *Inverting*. Every object in a complex object has its own *channel* (timeline) in the CTD. The notion of *transition points* and *intervals* are introduced. The framework allows to define different kinds of synchronization by using attributes. The Framework does not integrate interactions with multimedia in its port abstractions.

## 9  Future Developments

Compared to the IMA architectural reference, the *Resource Management Service (RMS)* is missing in MME. In the near future, we will add this feature to MME. Resource Management establishes security in working with remote media devices. Our idea is to encapsulate the RMS into a single object, realized as a server process and to integrate the allocation and deallocation mechanisms for devices into the port handler.

The further development of the toolkit includes the following topics:

- Completion of an already started *multi media interface builder*, allowing the creation of multimedia interfaces in a direct manipulation style.

- Adding a general mechanism to media objects that allows the definition of arbitrary complex interaction with and the behaviour of media objects. At the moment, all the interactions are fixed (i.e. burned in as class-specific code). We call this mechanism *Supertranslations*.

- Defining an interface to upcoming standards for a subset of the functionality of MME, for example an interface to *MHEG*

## Acknowledgements

My thanks go to the collegues who helped me developing MME. Among them are Frank Ströbel, Hubert Wombacher and Jens Glathe, who implemented important and sometimes tricky parts of the basic code [14]. I would like also to thank Simon Gibbs for giving useful hints for the final version of the paper.

## References

[1] ISO/IEC JTC 1/SC 24/WG 1. *Presentation Environment for Multi-Media Objects (PREMO)*. ISO/IEC JTC 1/SC 24/WG 1, Gut Ising, Germany, 1992.

[2] J.L. Alty and M. Can Bergan. Multimedia Interfaces be of Benefit to Process Control rather than just provide New Features? In *Proceedings of $2^{nd}$ Eurographics Workshop on Multimedia, Darmstadt*. Eurographics, 1992.

[3] F. Arbab and I. Herman et al. An Object Model for Multimedia Programming. *Computer Graphics Forum (Eurographics Conference Issue)*, 12(3), 1993.

[4] IMA Interactive Multimedia Association. *Request for Technology: Multimedia System Services*. IMA, Interactive Multimedia Association, Annapolis, 1992.

[5] Rui Pedro Casteleiro and Fernando Vasconcelos et al. An Object Oriented Architecture for interactive Animation and Simulation. In *Multimedia-Systems, Interaction and Applications. Proceedings of $1^{st}$ Eurographics Workshop on Multimedia, Stockholm*. Eurographics, 1991.

[6] Francoise Colaitis and Francis Kretz. Coded representation of multimedia and hypermedia information objects: Towards the MHEG standard. *Image Communication*, pages 113–119, 4 1992.

[7] Dennis Dingeldein and Gregor Lux. THESEUS++ - A High Level User Interface Toolkit for Graphical Applications. *Computers & Graphics*, 17(2):147–154, 1993.

[8] Dennis Dingeldein and Frank Stroebel. Implementing a Video Widget. Paper available via WWW (http://zgdv.igd.fhg.de/), 7 1993.

[9] George D. Drapeau and Howard Greenfield. *MAEstro - A Distributed Multimedia Authoring Environment*. (Paper is part of the MAEstro-Distribution).

[10] Martin Gale. Human aspects of interactive multimedia communication. *Interacting with Computers*, 2(2):157–189, 1990.

[11] S. Gibbs and L. Dami et al. An Object-Oriented Framework for Multimedia Composition and Synchronization. In *Proceedings of $1^{nd}$ Eurographics Workshop on Multimedia, Stockholm*. Eurographics, 1991.

[12] P. Hoepner. The Presentation of Multimedia Objects - ODA Extensions. In *Proceedings of $1^{st}$ Eurographics Workshop on Multimedia, Stockholm*. Eurographics, 1991.

[13] John Lee and Irene Neilson. Interpreting Graphical Expressions. In *Proceedings of $2^{nd}$ Eurographics Workshop on Multimedia, Darmstadt*. Eurographics, 1992.

[14] Frank Stroebel. Konzeption und Entwurf eines objektorientierten Baukastens für multimediale Objekte wie Standbild, Video und Ton. Master's thesis, TH Darmstadt, FB Informatik, FG Graphisch-Interaktive Systeme, Darmstadt, 1993.

# Part II

# Programming Paradigms for Graphics

# 8

# Mixed Programming Paradigms in Computer Graphics

Parris K. Egbert, Travis L. Hilton

Due to the intrinsic object-based nature of computer graphics, the object-oriented paradigm seems to fit naturally as a tool for designing and using a graphics system. However, several attributes of computer graphics systems do not fit the object-oriented paradigm well. This paper discusses the nature of computer graphics systems, how the object-oriented paradigm meshes with these systems, and cases where other paradigms fit graphics in a more natural manner.

## 1 Introduction

Since the inception of computer graphics in the 1960's, graphics systems have been built in an "object-based" fashion, i.e., pieces of the system have been thought of as objects. Since computer graphics is the notion of generating computer images of real or imaginary scenes, the components of the scene can naturally be thought of as separate objects. The Sketchpad system designed by Ivan Sutherland [30] contained the notion of 2D objects such as lines and arcs being separate entities or objects. This is a natural way of thinking, and thus has continued throughout succeeding generations of computer graphics systems.

More recent systems have capitalized on this even further and have extended the object concepts such that the systems have been designed to be object-oriented, rather than object-based. The availability of object-oriented programming languages, as well as their widespread acceptance, has sparked much interest in applying the principles of object-orientation to computer graphics.

Although there are many benefits to be realized by using the object-oriented paradigm, there are several pieces of computer graphics systems and system functionality that do not fit this paradigm well. Although the object-oriented paradigm provides many highly desirable characteristics in computer graphics, there are other occasions where it is undesirable, if not impossible, to apply it effectively. This paper discusses the concept of object-orientation as it applies to computer graphics and discusses how a mixed programming paradigm approach to computer graphics may be more appropriate than a pure object-oriented model.

The remainder of the paper is organized as follows: section 2 discusses the concept of object-orientation in depth and how object-orientation can be applied to computer graphics systems. Section 3 discusses current graphics systems and how they have incorporated the object-oriented paradigm. Section 4 discusses functionality in computer graphics systems that suggest a mixed paradigm approach to graphics. Finally, section 5 provides conclusions.

## 2  The Object-Oriented Paradigm

Although the notion of object-orientation has permeated virtually all areas of Computer Science, there still remains much discrepancy in the definition of terms used. Wegner provides a classification that has become commonly accepted, and we restate it here as a basis for discussion [31]. According to the definitions given by Wegner, a system that supports objects as a feature of that system is termed object-based. An object-oriented system is one that supports objects, provides classing capabilities, and allows the notion of inheritance in the definition of classes. In addition to these criteria set forth by Wegner, it has become widely accepted that this definition of object-orientation lacks an additional criteria - that of supporting the late binding of methods to messages [26].

There is a continuum along which all object-oriented systems must fall. At one extreme of the continuum, every entity in the system is thought of as being an object. Objects are completely separate and distinct from other entities in the system. Each object is responsible for maintaining its internal state information, and is not allowed to share any of that information with other objects. Objects may send messages to other objects, but they cannot get information about those objects or learn of the object's attributes. This preserves object-orientation in its purest sense and keeps objects completely separate from other objects. This also provides a high degree of abstraction and generality since objects know nothing about the internal structure and composition of other objects. At the other extreme, system entities are thought of as distinct objects, but other objects may interact with them in any fashion desired. Thus, an object's internal state information and attributes may be queried, used, and altered by other objects in the system. This provides for more flexibility in the system, but destroys many of the benefits of the object-oriented paradigm. Most systems that claim to be object-oriented fall somewhere between these two extremes, usually closer to the former end than the latter. Typical objects in an object-oriented system maintain their own state information and do not allow other objects to alter that data. Other objects can often determine information about an object and about that object's internal data by sending a message to the object requesting that data be sent to the original object (the ubiquitous "get" message). This breaks the pure object-oriented nature of the system (since objects are no longer completely independent of one another), but the benefits of greater flexibility and simplicity are usually thought to outweigh the benefits of paradigm purity.

From the time the object-oriented paradigm gained wide acceptance in the Computer Science community, practically all systems that have fallen anywhere in the above mentioned spectrum have been termed object-oriented. For the purposes of this paper, we will take more of a "purist" point of view and discuss object-oriented graphics from the point of strictest adherence to principles of the object-oriented paradigm.

## 3  Object-Oriented Graphics

There has been a substantial amount of research into combining computer graphics with object-orientation. This section describes a sampling of this work and discusses how these systems fit the object-oriented paradigm. This section provides the basis for Section 4, in which we abstract ideas from these systems and from computer graphics in general to discuss shortcomings of object-orientation in graphics.

One of the earliest systems that attempted to combine object-orientation and graphics was the system built by Green and Philp [13]. Their system used the EDL programming language to implement basic 2D graphics capabilities. Graphics entities in the system were treated as distinct objects and were sent messages to accomplish transformations, image generation, and geometric alterations. This system falls short in many of the qualities of a pure object-oriented system, but it showed that there was merit in performing graphics in an object-oriented fashion.

About the same time this system was being developed, the Star system from Xerox was also being created [19]. This system incorporated object-oriented ideas into a combined text/graphics editor. The programming language Mesa was used in this project, with subclassing enhancements provided through the Trait Mechanism. As with the system of Green and Philp, this system lacked many object-oriented characteristics, but was instrumental in sparking interest in object-oriented graphics.

When it became apparent that the field of computer graphics would benefit from the object-oriented paradigm, work was begun at encapsulating graphics standards with object-oriented constructs. In 1984 Lubinski and Hutzel [22] presented an extension to the then proposed graphics standard GKS which allowed some of the features of GKS to be handled in an object-oriented fashion. Their work focused on formalizing the notion of objects as it specifically related to GKS. Thus, GKS components such as modeling primitives, views and workstations were defined as objects with the hope that user code would be minimized and simplified. However, an object-oriented system must be developed with object-orientation as the underlying methodology. Simply adding object-oriented constructs on top of an existing system may provide some desired characteristics, but will probably not allow full realization of object-oriented benefits.

HOOPS [18] is another system that was designed using concepts from a graphics standard, in this case PHIGS rather than GKS. In the case of HOOPS, however, object-orientation was given precedence over adhering to the specification of the standard. Thus, HOOPS incorporates several concepts present in PHIGS, but is designed more to take advantage of the object-oriented paradigm. Thus, this system comes closer to being a true object-oriented system.

Wisskirchen has developed an object-oriented graphics system entitled GEO++ [33] which incorporates many of the attributes of PHIGS into an object oriented environment. As a follow-on to this work, he has also been active in generating a new object-oriented graphics standard [16]. The goal of this work is to provide a standard framework for object-oriented computer graphics. As the above systems demonstrate, there has been a large interest in standardizing the notion of object-oriented graphics.

Another topic that has received a large amount of interest in object-oriented graphics is that of animation. In 1984 Lorensen published work he had conducted on an object-oriented animation system [20]. He further developed this system in later years and describes subsequent research in [21]. This work spawned a great deal of interest in object-oriented animation systems, and during the next few years several systems of this nature were developed.

The Clockworks system developed by Breen, et. al. [4, 9] is one of the more notable of these. This system performs animation by creating objects which act as directors. These objects maintain a list of scripted messages. At the appropriate times, the messages are passed to their intended graphical objects. When a graphical object receives a message from a director object, it performs the action specified by the script, thus producing the animation. Graphical objects are modeled using polygons, superquadrics, splines, and surfaces. Various animation techniques such as keyframing, inbetweening and goal-directed animation are all facilitated in this system. Each of the animation techniques eventually gets translated into a script so that animation can be understood by the objects in a unified fashion. This system provides a powerful mechanism for performing animation in an object-oriented environment. The developers of this system have done a good job of using object-oriented principles in the design and implementation of the system.

Another notable object-oriented animation system is the system was developed by researchers at Brown University [34]. In this system, an object is defined by a list of messages. These messages may specify object geometry, transformations, properties, etc. and have the notion of time inherent in them. Animation is performed by executing those messages dependent on time. The resulting object is the original object that has had alterations performed on it by the messages it received. In this fashion, animation is treated uniformly between objects. The underlying object components must each deal with time variance appropriately, but from the object's perspective the animation is uniform across objects. This system does not use the traditional object-oriented features of subclassing and inheritance, but uses delegation [32] instead. Their reasoning for this is that the dynamic nature of objects in the system make subclassing too restrictive. The designers of the system felt that by using delegation, they gained a broader degree of freedom in the way objects were created and handled.

The area of user interfaces has also received a large amount of attention regarding object-oriented implementation and usage. A system of this nature is the George Washington User Interface Management System [27]. This object-oriented user interface management system (UIMS) was designed as a tool to assist in the rapid generation of graphical user interfaces. Information is passed down from the application through various levels of the system. From the information passed to it, the system generates the user interface. By altering the objects at the various layers, new interfaces can be created and tested.

The GROW system, described by Barth [2] is an object-oriented system designed for building graphical interfaces to programs. The main tenant of this system is that graphical interfaces can aid in the use and understanding of application programs, but have traditionally been too cumbersome to construct in the past. This system is an attempt to simplify the process of building graphical interfaces so that their benefits can be realized in a broader set of applications than currently use them.

Hubner and de Lancastre describe an interaction model for user interfaces based on the object-oriented paradigm [15]. The goal of their work was to enhance user interface management systems by making them more extensible, flexible and easy to use. They do this by encapsulating graphics interaction techniques into Interaction classes. A user interface is then created by instantiating Interaction Objects and arranging them appropriately. This system seems to do a good job at making simple interaction tasks easily definable and usable, but is still difficult to use for very complex tasks.

The Inventor Toolkit from Silicon Graphics [29] is an example of an object-oriented system designed as a tool for the creation and manipulation of 3D objects. The main thrust of this system is to provide interaction tools for the application to have at its disposal and to allow simple interaction with 3D objects. The system provides a variety of object classes for components such as object shapes, object properties, and lights. The system also provides a mechanism for handling events.

Dore [17] is a commercially available object oriented graphics system that attempts to abstract the graphics process to a higher level, thus making graphics simpler to use by naive users. Dore provides a set of modeling primitives that includes polygons, meshes and surfaces, and two rendering techniques - a fast, low quality renderer and a slower, high quality renderer. Many object-oriented characteristics have been left out of Dore, such as inheritance, classing and polymorphism, and thus the system does not take full advantage of the object-oriented paradigm.

The GRAMS system [6, 8, 7] provides a framework for application modeling. GRAMS was designed to provide the system support necessary to allow modeling at a level convenient to the application. Thus, the user creates objects such as tables, chairs, or trees rather than having to deal with polygons or other primitive objects. This frees the user from many of the low-level details and allows them to concentrate on their application rather than the graphics system.

As evidenced by this section, there has been much work expended toward object-oriented graphics. The systems discussed above incorporate object-oriented concepts into their design and have been classified as object-oriented graphics systems. However, none of them adhere strictly to pure object-orientation. These systems fall at various positions along the object-oriented continuum discussed earlier, but none of them meet the goal of pure object-orientation. This suggests that there are concepts or pieces of computer graphics systems that don't fit the object-oriented paradigm exactly. Thus, it appears to be advantageous to take a mixed paradigm approach to computer graphics. Many benefits can be realized by using the object-oriented paradigm, but when this paradigm fails or is difficult to use, other paradigms may be more suitable.

The following section describes pieces of computer graphics systems that do not fit the object-oriented paradigm well. We contend that breaking the pure object-oriented paradigm has merits in these (and possibly other) cases.

## 4  Mixed Paradigm Graphics

In order to provide an efficient, extensible general computer graphics development and user friendly environment it is necessary to alter the pure object-oriented approach for its design. Components for such a system should include a module for rendering, a module for user interaction, an animation/modeling driver, and models or objects. Due to the nature of rendering and time dependent modeling like animation and physically based modeling, the pure object oriented approach must be broken.

### 4.1  Rendering

There have been several algorithms designed for the rendering of computer graphics models. Three of these algorithms are ray tracing, radiosity, and basic shading algorithms. These algorithms can be used separately or in combination with one another in the rendering process. In each of these cases, problems arise when we attempt to adhere strictly to the object-oriented paradigm. These problems, as well as possible solutions to them, are addressed in the following sections.

#### Ray Tracing

In ray tracing, rays simulating light rays are traced backwards from the eye to lights in the scene [10]. Resulting pixel intensities are generated with illuminance equations based on material properties of objects, light intensities, and object occlusion. With this technique illuminance, reflections, and shadows can be generated to produce realistic looking scenes.

The pure object oriented design requires that objects cannot know the internal data of other objects. Only messages can be passed back and forth between objects to provide inter-object communication. Even though a ray trace renderer can be designed in an object oriented fashion, illuminance equations for objects in the scene require the knowledge of the surface properties and light attributes in the scene. This implies that internal data for lights and objects must be accessible by the entity that is computing the lighting equations.

In a basic ray tracer the following objects can be designed for generality of the system and for modularization. A camera object can be used to provide viewing parameters and initiate image generation by generating rays. Ray objects traverse the scene generating a resulting pixel intensity based on recursive calculations of illumination equations at each recursion level. Each object in the scene can encapsulate geometry generation, compute ray-object intersection detection, and store surface material properties. As the ray traces a scene it recursively accumulates a resulting pixel intensity based on illuminance equations at each ray-object intersection. Since these equations are highly dependent on all objects involved in the equation, it is more appropriate to treat the ray object as a function that applies itself to a group of objects. The objects in the scene become the domain of the pixel intensity calculation function of the ray, whereas the actual pixel intensities comprise the range. This range might be a red, green, blue color band triplet, a set of wavelengths describing a color, or may contain other information about pixel intensities.

### Radiosity

Radiosity [11] is another approach used to generate realistic looking images of models. This technique in its most basic form differs from ray tracing in that it takes into account diffuse object interaction but does not handle specularities. This technique has become very popular in the image synthesis world and provides aesthetically pleasing images. It can also be designed in an object oriented manner, but still must break the pure object oriented paradigm of hiding all object data in order to resolve pixel intensities.

In a basic radiosity renderer, pixel intensities of an image of a model are calculated based of the radiosity of patches of objects. The radiosity renderer can be designed with environment, camera and application objects. This algorithm differs from ray tracing in that the environment object must initiate the calculation of form factors for each patch in the scene. The form factors represent the effect of each of the patches radiosities upon each other. Once the form factors are calculated the pixel intensities for an image of the scene can be generated. Generation of the form factors, however, conflicts with the pure object-oriented paradigm.

Form factor calculation is highly dependent on the radiosities and form factors of all the other patches in the scene. These radiosities and form factors are encapsulated data of each patch of the object and therefore should not be visible to other objects according to pure object orientation. Therefore, we must again break this paradigm by treating the generation of form factors as a function. The domain of this function is the radiosities and form factors of all the other patches in the scene, and its range is a form factor. A form factor calculation could be a child object of a patch, and it should have access to form factor and radiosity encapsulated data of all other patches in the scene.

### Shading Models

Shading Model algorithms like Gouraud [12] or Phong [25] shading use normal or intensity information of the vertices of a polygon to calculate pixel intensities across the polygon. This generates a smooth shaded effect across the polygon. Even though shading model algorithms do not produce as high quality images as do ray tracing and radiosity, they are of considerable interest since they lend themselves to straightforward implementation in hardware. For this reason most moderately priced hardware graphics engines that generate images in real-time use shading model algorithms [5, 14]. Radiosity and ray tracing can be done with massively parallel super computers in real time, but not on currently available midrange workstations.

It is possible to implement shading of objects in an object oriented manner. A basic shading rendering system can contain the application objects and a graphics engine object. The graphics engine object may be tied directly to the hardware and contains the state of the rendering hardware. It may know how to render primitives from polygons to NURBS surfaces depending on its complexity. The conflict with pure object orientation arises when the application object tries to send the graphics engine these primitives. Sending encapsulated data from the application object to the graphics engine object violates data hiding.

### Appropriate Design for Rendering

In ray tracing and radiosity, part of rendering should be treated as a function. The domain of the function should be other objects in ray tracing and other object's radiosities and form factors for radiosity. We can, however, still use an object oriented design to allow for inheritance and specialization of objects and rendering techniques. This allows the user to extend the rendering module of the graphics system.

In shading model techniques a graphics engine class is necessary to encapsulate the state of the hardware or software polygon shading engine. The objects in the scene, however, must be allowed to send geometric primitives to the shading engine in a rendering pipeline.

## 4.2  Time Dependent Graphics

Time dependent graphics systems use rendering techniques such as those described above. In addition, these systems alter modeling environments over time. Animation systems and physically based modeling systems fit into this category. Animation techniques tend to fit the pure object oriented paradigm very nicely whereas the physically based modeling techniques tend to break the paradigm due to object dependencies.

### Animation

Animation is the process of moving and modifying objects in an environment over time. In traditional computer graphics the user specifies paths of these objects through techniques like scripting or B-splines. At each time step in an animation the object's location and orientation changes to that specified in the script file or by the B-spline equation. Each object is responsible for its own encapsulated data modification and readjusts object location, orientation and other parameters during each time slice. An animation system need only add an object that tells all the objects in the scene what the new time is. Since all of the objects can hide their own data from all other objects and only message passing is required to keep the animation running, animation as a higher level technique satisfies the requirements of pure object orientation. Since each time step requires rendering, however, all the rendering dependencies for a single frame still exist.

### Physically Based Modeling

Physically based modeling in computer graphics attempts to generate realistic motion, collisions, and responses over time from objects in an environment. Through use of the physical properties of objects such as mass, velocity, acceleration, and momentum, impressive realistic object interaction and motion can be achieved. There has been considerable interest in recent years in this area and examples can be found in [1, 3, 23].

A basic physically based modeling environment can be designed in an object oriented fashion. A set of abstract classes representing the simple objects can be designed to provide basic functionality of objects such as user interaction, motion dynamics, collision detection and collision resolution. An environment object can be designed to periodically tell objects to move to a given time, detect collisions and resolve collisions.

Conflicts with pure object orientation arise during collision detection and collision resolution. One method for detecting collisions was devised by Snyder [28] in which a set of differential equations are used to solve for collision times and locations for implicit surfaces. Other systems have solved for collisions by moving a discrete time and then checking for intersections between all objects in the scene [24]. Both of these methods are highly dependent on the encapsulated data from other objects in the scene. Once the collisions are detected, forces that keep objects from intersecting must be applied. The calculation of these forces depends on the momentum of all objects involved. The resolution of these forces to provide dynamics for each object may also depend on data from other objects. Since internal data from objects must be visible to all other objects the pure object oriented paradigm is broken.

### Appropriate Design for Time Dependent Graphics

With time dependent graphics like physically based modeling it is again necessary to use functions that apply operations to a scene database. Functions that detect and resolve collisions, apply forces, and resolve forces should use the objects' internal attributes and data as their domain and supply collision locations, resulting forces, and resulting dynamics as a range. These functions should be methods on objects that govern the entire scene database.

## 4.3  Efficiency

In graphics systems there is always a desire for efficiency. However, in some cases algorithms can be applied which improve efficiency but violate pure object-orientation. One example of this is the GRAMS system [6, 7]. One of the features of GRAMS is that it supports multiple renderers and can be extended to include others. Each renderer will have particular characteristics associated with it. One characteristic is the set of primitives supported by the renderer. A simple renderer may support only primitives such as polygons, points, and lines, while more sophisticated renders may support higher level objects such as NURBS surfaces and conic sections. When an application object represented by a NURBS surface tries to send its data to the simple renderer, it must break the NURBS into small polygons for rendering. The GRAMS system provides a mechanism that allows the renderer to tell the application objects the kind of primitives it can render most efficiently. In the above example, the more sophisticated renderer would tell the application object that it is capable of rendering NURBS surfaces. Having this information, the system would send the NURBS surface directly to the renderer rather than tessellating into polygons first. Since the renderer can efficiently render NURBS surfaces, and since the system doesn't have to tessellate the NURBS into polygons, considerable savings are achieved. This ability of the renderers to tell other objects about their internal functionality is a violation of pure object orientation, but this communication capability is necessary for efficient rendering. Sharing of internal data provides a means for other objects to make intelligent decisions that result in efficiency, but at the same time violates pure object orientation.

## 5  Conclusions

The integration of computer graphics and the object-oriented paradigm has received a large amount of attention. There have been many graphics systems designed to take advantage of object-oriented qualities such as inheritance, classing, and polymorphism. However, none of these systems adhere strictly to pure object-orientation. This suggests that there may be particular characteristics about computer graphics that do not fit the object-oriented paradigm naturally. We have shown what some of these characteristics are and how they break pure object-orientation. For most of these characteristics, adhering strictly to the object-oriented paradigm is too limiting and does not provide the flexibility desired. Thus, we advocate a mixed paradigm approach to computer graphics. Because of the positive attributes inherent in object-orientation, this paradigm should be followed as long as it does not impose severe restrictions on the graphics system. When this does happen, the system designer should be given the flexibility to move from strict object-orientation to a more suitable paradigm. This mixed approach provides the benefits of object-orientation but eliminates the undue restrictions inherently placed on graphics systems by strict adherence to the object-oriented paradigm. We feel that the flexibility gained outweighs the benefits of paradigm purity.

## References

[1] Alan H. Barr. Global and Local Deformations of Solid Primitives. In *Computer Graphics (SIGGRAPH '84 Conference Proceedings), 18(3)*, pages 21–31, July 1984.

[2] Paul S. Barth. An Object-Oriented Approach to Graphical Interfaces. In *ACM Transactions on Graphics, 5(2)*, pages 142–172, April 1986.

[3] Ronen Barzel and Alan H. Barr. A Modeling System Based On Dynamic Constraints. In *Computer Graphics (SIGGRAPH '88 Conference Proceedings), 22(4)*, pages 179–188, August 1988.

[4] David E. Breen, Phillip H. Getto, Anthony A. Apodaca, Daniel G. Schmidt, and Brion D. Sarachan. The Clockworks: An Object-Oriented Computer Animation System. In *Eurographics '87*, 1987.

[5] Michael F. Deering and Scott R. Nelson. Leo: A System for Cost Effective 3D Shaded Graphics. In *Proceedings of SIGGRAPH 93. In Computer Graphics Proceedings, Annual Conference Series, Anaheim, California*, pages 101–108, 1993.

[6] Parris K. Egbert. *An Object-Oriented Approach to Graphical Application Support.* PhD thesis, Department of Computer Science, University of Illinois at Urbana-Champaign, June 1992.

[7] Parris K. Egbert and William J. Kubitz. Application Graphics Modeling Support Through Object-Orientation. In *IEEE Computer 25(10)*, pages 84–91, October 1992.

[8] Parris K. Egbert and William J. Kubitz. The Graphical Application Support System. In S. Cunningham, N. Knolle Craighill, and J. Brown, editors, *Computer Graphics Using Object-Oriented Programming*, pages 137–164. J. Wiley and Sons, New York, 1992.

[9] Phillip Getto and David Breen. An Object-Oriented Architecture for a Computer Animation System. In *Visual Computer 6(2)*, pages 79–92, March 1990.

[10] A.S. Glassner, editor. *An Introduction to Ray Tracing.* Academic Press, London, 1991.

[11] Cindy M. Goral, Kenneth E. Torrance, Donald P. Greenberg, and Bennett Battaile. Modelling the Interaction of Light Between Diffuse Surfaces. In *Computer Graphics (SIGGRAPH '84 Conference Proceedings), 18(3)*, pages 212–222, July 1984.

[12] Henri Gouraud. Continuous Shading of Curved Surfaces. In *IEEE Transactions on Computers, 20(6)*, pages 623–628, June 1971.

[13] M. Green and P. Philp. The Use of Object Oriented Languages in Graphics Programming. In *Graphics Interface '82*, pages 354–353, 1982.

[14] Chandlee B. Harrell and Farhad Fouladi. Graphics Rendering Architecture for a High Performance Desktop Workstation. In *Proceedings of SIGGRAPH 93 InComputer Graphics Proceedings, Annual Conference Series, Anaheim California*, pages 93–100, 1993.

[15] Wolfgang Hubner and Manuel de Lancastre. Towards an Object-Oriented Interaction Model for Graphics User Interfaces. In *Computer Graphics Forum 8(3)*, pages 207–217, September 1989.

[16] K. Kansy and P. Wisskirchen. The new graphics standard – object-oriented. In Edwin Blake and Peter Wisskirchen, editors, *Advances in Object-Oriented Graphics I (Proceedings of the Eurographics Workshop on Object-Oriented Graphics, 1990)*, EurographicSeminars Series, pages 199–215. Springer-Verlag, 1991.

[17] M. Kaplan. The Design of the Dore Graphics System. In Edwin Blake and Peter Wisskirchen, editors, *Advances in Object-Oriented Graphics I (Proceedings of the Eurographics Workshop on Object-Oriented Graphics, 1990)*, EurographicSeminars Series, pages 177 – 198. Springer-Verlag, 1991.

[18] B.D. Kliewer. HOOPS: Powerful Portable 3D Graphics. In *BYTE, 14(7)*, pages 193–194, 1989.

[19] Daniel E. Lipkie, Steven R. Evans, John K. Newlin, and Robert L. Weissman. Star Graphics: An Object-Oriented Implementation. In *Computer Graphics (Proceedings of SIGGRAPH '82), 16(3)*, pages 115–124, July 1982.

[20] William E. Lorensen. An Object-Oriented Design of a Graphics Animation System. In *Fifth GE Software Engineering Conference*, 1984.

[21] William E. Lorensen and Boris Yamrom. Object-Oriented Computer Animation. In *Proceedings of IEEE NAECON, IEEE, New York, 2*, pages 588–595, 1989.

[22] Thomas Lubinski and Ingeborg Hutzel. An Object-Oriented Graphical Kernel System. In *Computer Graphics World*, pages 69–75, July 1984.

[23] Dimitri Metaxas and Demetri Terzopoulos. Dynamic Deformation of Solid Primitives with Constraints. In *Computer Graphics (SIGGRAPH '92 Conference Proceedings), 26(2)*, pages 309–312, July 1992.

[24] Matthew Moore and Jane Wilhelms. Collision Detection and Response for Computer Animation. In *Computer Graphics (Proceedings of SIGGRAPH '88) 22(4)*, pages 289–298, 1988.

[25] Bui Tuong Phong. *Illumination for Computer-Generated Images*. PhD thesis, University of Utah, July 1973.

[26] Gregory Scott Rogers. *Visual Programming Using Graphics, Relations,and Classes*. PhD thesis, Department of Computer Science, University of Illinois at Urbana-Champaign, October 1990.

[27] J.L. Sibert, W.D. Hurley, and T.W. Bleser. An Object-Oriented User Interface Management System. In *Computer Graphics (SIGGRAPH '86 Conference Proceedings), 20(4)*, pages 259–268, August 1986.

[28] John M. Snyder, Adam R. Woodbury, Kurt Fleischer, Bena Currin, and Alan H. Barr. Interval Methods for Multi-Point Collisions between Time-Dependent Curved Surfaces. In *Proceedings of SIGGRAPH 93. InComputer Graphics Proceedings, Annual Conference Series, Anaheim, California*, pages 321–334, 1993.

[29] Paul S. Strauss and Rikk Carey. An Object-Oriented 3D Graphics Toolkit. In *Computer Graphics (SIGGRAPH '92 Conference Proceedings), 26(2)*, pages 341–349, July 1992.

[30] Ivan E. Sutherland. *Sketchpad, A Man-Machine Graphical Communication System.* PhD thesis, Department of Electrical Engineering, Massachusetts Institute of Technology, January 1963.

[31] Peter Wegner. Dimensions of Object-Based Language Design. In *Proceedings of OOPSLA '87, ACM*, pages 168–182, October 1987.

[32] Peter Wegner. The Object-Oriented Classification Paradigm. In P. W. a. B. Shriver, editor, *Research Directions in Object-Oriented Programming.* The MIT Press, 1987.

[33] Peter Wisskirchen. GEO++ - a System for Both Modelling and Display. In *Eurographics '89 Conference Proceedings*, pages 403–414, September 1989.

[34] R.C. Zeleznik et al. An object-oriented framework for the integration of interactive animation techniques. In *SIGGRAPH '91 Proceedings, Computer Graphics Vol. 25, no. 4*, pages 105–112, 1991.

# 9

# Talktalk

## Peter Bouwman, Hans de Bruin

Recent developments in graphical user interface technology show an increase in complexity, with multiple input and output devices and a freedom for the end-user to be engaged in multiple dialogues simultaneously. Although existing models and programming languages come a long way, they lack the expressive power to describe such complex systems elegantly. We have extended Smalltalk with concurrency, interaction (access and output) protocols, and dialogues for easy specification of concurrent object-oriented (interactive) systems, supporting both delegation and inheritance.

## 1 Introduction

The graphical user interfaces pioneered in Smalltalk environments have demonstrated the effectiveness of object-orientedness for building interactive systems. Interface technology is rapidly evolving, introducing new types of interfaces, such as multi-media. We are faced with constructing complex concurrent interactive systems, involving a multitude of input and output devices and in which the end-user can be engaged in multiple dialogues simultaneously.

In this paper we present Talktalk, a general purpose concurrent object-oriented programming language (OOL), especially suited for implementing concurrent event-driven interactive (graphical) systems. Talktalk, based on concepts found in the OOL Procol [8], and extended to specify refinable dialogues, is superposed on the programming language Smalltalk [4]. In Talktalk, objects are active, autonomous concurrent entities, they can communicate via synchronous as well as asynchronous message passing.

An important concept in Procol is the protocol. Using an augmented regular expression syntax, a protocol describes the legal (message-) access pattern to the object, helping to assure the object's state integrity by only allowing method activation in a specific sequence. Besides input protocols, Talktalk supports output protocols, describing the output behavior of the object. The input/output protocols serve as a high level, executable, formal specification of the dialogue between objects. By coupling an object's output protocol declaratively to an other object's input protocol, an asynchronous communication link is automatically established at run-time. Synchronization of objects is established by the protocols.

Talktalk evolved from the need for a concurrent, interpreted language in the research project DIGIS (Direct Interactive Generation of Interactive Systems) [3]. DIGIS is a User Interface Design Environment for non-programmers, in which all aspects of UI design can be specified with Direct Manipulation techniques. For user interface design, an interpreted environment like Smalltalk, is most appropriate: user interfaces still under construction can be read in and tested immediately after creation, thereby avoiding the traditional time consuming edit-compile-run cycle. While Smalltalk supports concurrency to some extent by providing Processes and semaphores for synchronization, safely designing and implementing large concurrent systems is very difficult and error-prone. We chose Smalltalk as host language nonetheless because of an important pragmatic reason. Smalltalk is a widely accepted *interpreted* object-oriented language, with a versatile and mature set of reusable objects. A small and efficient compiler translates a Talktalk program into native Smalltalk code. Talktalk programs can therefore be easily used in existing Smalltalk environments. Talktalk is now used as the implementation language for DIGIS.

## 2  Talktalk Basic Concepts

The programming language Talktalk derives many of its concepts from the OOL Procol. In this section we discuss the concepts which were taken from Procol. Procol is a concurrent object-oriented language with protocols, delegation, persistence and constraints. Objects execute in parallel except when engaged in communication. The main features of Procol have been incorporated in Talktalk: concurrency, protocols and delegation. The computational model of Procol is based on many concurrent objects acting as servers. The access to an object is protected by a protocol describing the legal interaction patterns with the object. Procol uses delegation as an alternative for inheritance. Both concepts are valuable, inheritance has an edge over delegation when it comes to specify specialized behavior, delegation is an important concept in modeling and implementing dynamic concurrent systems. Because these concepts don't necessarily preclude each other, Talktalk supports inheritance as well as delegation.

### 2.1  Protocols and Message Passing

Protocols for an object are specified using augmented regular expressions over object methods. A protocol expression is constructed with 6 operators: interleave ($\|$), selection ($+$), sequence ($;$), (bounded) repetition ($*$ or $[m,n]$), and guard ($[\varphi]$) (in increasing precedence). The semantics of protocol expressions are summarized in Table 1, where E and F are arbitrary sub-expressions over object methods.

**Table 1:** Semantics of protocol expressions

| Operator | Name | Meaning |
|---|---|---|
| E $\|$ F | *composition* | E and F may occur interleaved |
| E $+$ F | *selection* | E or F is selected |
| E ; F | *sequence* | E is followed by F |
| E $*$ | *repetition* | Zero or more times E |
| E $[m,n]$ | *bounded repetition* | $m \ldots n$ times E |
| $[\varphi]$ E | *guard* | E only if $\varphi$ is true |

For example, a bounded buffer object with guarded protocol protection can be specified as follows:

```
Class BoundedBuffer : Object
    | notFull notEmpty list maxSize |
protocol [
    input [
        ( [notFull]put: + [notEmpty]get ) *
    ]
]
methods [
    new
            list ← List new.
            maxSize ← 100.
            notFull ← true.
            notEmpty ← false.
    |
    put: aVal
            list addLast: aVal.
            notEmpty ← true.
            notFull ← list size < maxSize.
    |
    get
            | tmp |
            tmp ← list first.
            list removeFirst.
            notFull ← true.
            notEmpty ← list size > 0.
            ^ tmp.
]
```

Here, the only difference with native Smalltalk code is the addition of a protocol section. Two protocol methods are defined in this example: put: and get. The protocol takes care that no object can be retrieved from an empty buffer and no object can be stored in a full buffer. The protocol manages the access to an object, at most one action may be active at any one time: the one-at-a-time principle. After a method is completed, the guards are evaluated and the new set of acceptable messages is determined.

There are three important benefits of protocols and the protection they provide. Firstly, the objects are simpler to design and implement since interactions with an object are guaranteed to occur according to the well-defined interaction patterns specified in the protocol. Secondly, protocols partly obviate the need for intra-object synchronization, e.g., the protocol excludes the possibility of retrieving an object from an empty BoundedBuffer. Thirdly, a protocol documents the functionality provided by an object, and also, when and how to use these services.

### Synchronous Message Passing

Synchronous message passing in Talktalk has the same syntax and procedure-call semantics of Smalltalk. An object sending a synchronous message to an other object is blocked until the receiving object has entirely processed the message. The synchronization between two objects engaged in synchronous message exchange is depicted in Figure 1. Putting a value into an instance of type BoundedBuffer using a synchronous message can be done as follows:

buffer put: aValue.

Getting a value from a buffer is done as follows:

aValue ← buffer get.

### Asynchronous Message Passing

Besides sending synchronous messages, objects can also send asynchronous messages. Objects receiving an asynchronous message immediately return a *Future* object [6]. As soon as the Future object has been returned, the sending object continues. The Future

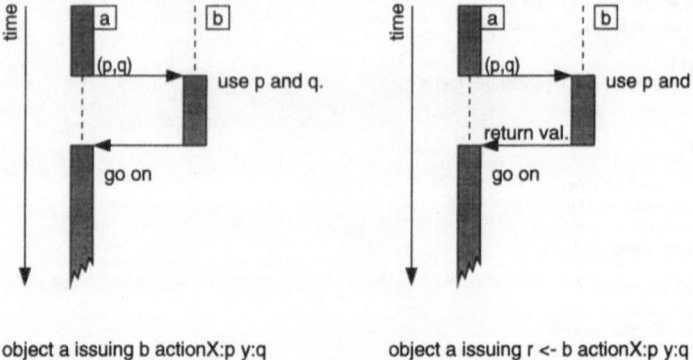

object a issuing b actionX:p y:q        object a issuing r <- b actionX:p y:q

**Figure 1:** Synchronous message passing in Talktalk

object is used to hold a possible result value from the receiving object when it has finished its computation. The sending object can get this result value from the future object by sending it the **value** message. If this value is available the Future object will return that value, otherwise it will block the sending object until the result value has been stored in the Future object by the original receiving object. To prevent blocking on the request for the result value, the Future object can at any time be queried whether the result is already there, by sending the **isReady** message. If the sending object does not need a return value, the Future object is ignored. Synchronization between two objects engaged in an asynchronous message exchange is depicted in Figure 2. In 2.a, object a sends the

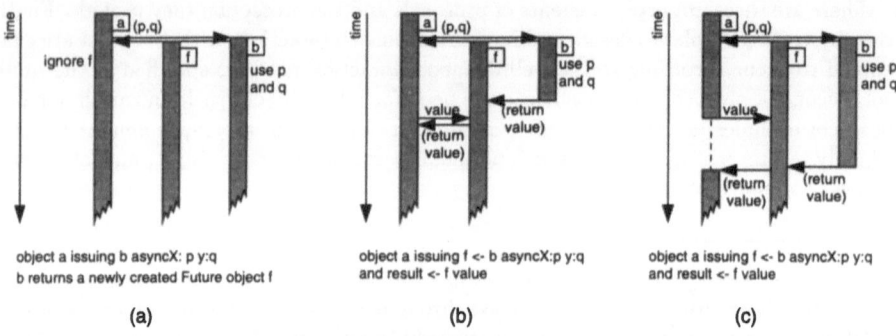

object a issuing b asyncX: p y:q          object a issuing f <- b asyncX:p y:q        object a issuing f <- b asyncX:p y:q
b returns a newly created Future object f    and result <- f value                      and result <- f value

(a)                                  (b)                                  (c)

**Figure 2:** Asynchronous message passing in Talktalk

asynchronous message x:y: to object b, with arguments p and q. Since the message is asynchronous, object b returns a Future object. Object b does not return a usable value, so the Future object is ignored by object a. In Figures 2.b and 2.c, object b *does* return a usable value. In 2.b, object a requests the result value from the Future object after object b has finished its computation and stored the value in the Future object. In 2.c, object a requests the result before b has finished, and will therefore block until the result is available.

Syntactically, an asynchronous message is sent by prefixing the message with **async** and capitalizing the first letter of the original message. The Talktalk compiler automatically generates the asynchronous counterparts of all messages of an object. An example asynchronous message without a return value is:

buffer asyncPut: aValue.

An example asynchronous message with a return value is:

future ← buffer asyncGet.

The future object returned will hold the value of the computation. If it is ready, the result value can be obtained by requesting its value (synchronously):

```
(future isReady)
    ifTrue:   [ result ← future value.]
    ifFalse:  [ "do something else" ].
```

## 2.2  Delegation

A client uses the services of an object by means of sending messages to and requesting results from this object. An object is free to delegate a partial or an entire method to an other object, using the delegate primitive. After a computation has been delegated to and accepted by an other object, the delegating object is ready to accept a new message. A delegate may in its turn decide to delegate an action to yet an other object, and so on. If a delegate returns a result, the result is directly sent to the original client. Delegation is transparent from the viewpoint of the client, as though the result has been obtained from the original first server. (See Figure 3).

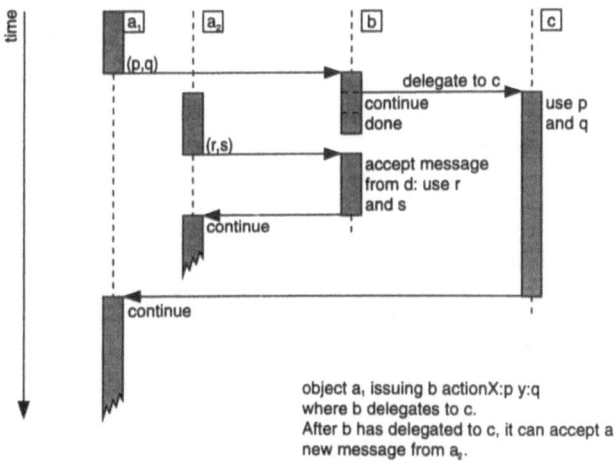

object a₁ issuing b actionX:p y:q
where b delegates to c.
After b has delegated to c, it can accept a
new message from a₂.

**Figure 3:** Synchronization of the delegate statement

An object can delegate to another object by sending the **delegate:to:with:** message to **self**. Referring to the scenario in Figure 3, object b can for example delegate to object c by issuing:

self delegate:#xx:yy: to:c with:p with:q

In this case, the message **xx:yy:** will be sent to object c, with arguments p and q, after which object b executes any remaining statements in method **actionX:y:**.

## 2.3  Inheritance

Besides delegation, Talktalk supports single inheritance. All methods in a *base* class can be freely used, or overruled, in a *derived* class. In contrast to most object-oriented languages with inheritance, attributes are *not* accessible in derived classes, abiding to strict information hiding principles. Access to attributes in base classes must be made explicit by providing methods for reading and setting attributes.

# 3  Additional Talktalk Concepts

In the previous section we have discussed the basic concepts of Talktalk. In this section we extend this set with two important new concepts: output-protocols, and Dialogue blocks.

## 3.1  Output Protocols

The programming language Procol encourages a client-server model of computation. A system based on the client-server model consists of a collection of cooperating objects, taking interchangeable roles as clients and servers. Objects communicate with each other by means of message exchange. An object is passive until activated by a service request from another object, the requesting object is called the client, the receiver of the message called the server. Objects can take the role of server and as client at the same time: a server can make use of other servers, and in that case behaves as a client with respect to these servers. An object is free to delegate the request for the service to yet another object (see section. 2.2). Using this model in a graphical interactive system, end-user interaction is handled by servers. A typical scenario is as follows: a client object, wanting end-user's input at some point in its activity, creates a server object. The server object handles the end-user's input and reports back to the client. This schema results in a user interface which is 'internally controlled', the end-user must follow the instructions of the interactive system. Although it is possible to use a client-server model for designing an interactive system in which the end-user is in control, this is not an easy task.

For the implementation of highly interactive systems, such as direct manipulation user interfaces, an event-driven multi-agent approach is more appropriate. In such systems, the end-user is in control, and has many degrees of freedom, that is, the end-user has the choice of activating more than one interface object, or is engaged in multiple dialogue threads simultaneously. Event-driven multi-agent models are organized as a collection of agents which react to external stimuli and in their turn produce new stimuli. The striking difference between the client-server model and the multi-agent model is that in a client-server model a client explicitly requests a server for a service, while in a multi-agent model a server notifies a client that it has performed a service. Client-server and multi-agent models can be mixed, an agent may explicitly request a service from an other agent (see Figure 4).

Access to an object is protected by a protocol. Clients may not enter the object unscrupulously, but must do that in the particular order described in the protocol. With that, in a client-server model, the protocol describes the possible services the server can provide. In the event-driven situation, the initiating role has been moved to the server-agents which need not be activated by a client-agent. As a result, the input protocol only partially describes the functionality provided by an object. What is missing is a description of the output behavior. This is captured in the *output* protocol. The output protocol is described in the same way as the input protocol is described, using the same operators. However, terms in the output protocol are not methods as is the case in

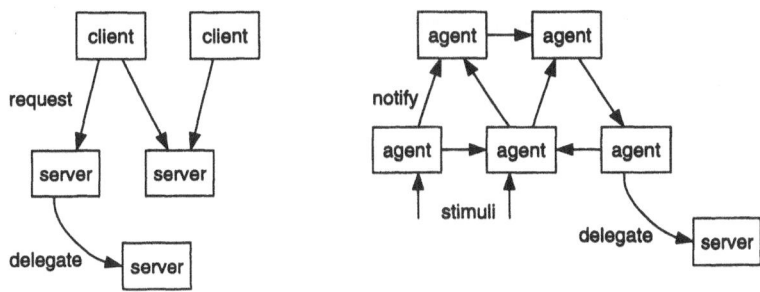

**Figure 4:** Visualization of the client-server model versus the multi-agent model

input-protocols, but symbolic event-names. Output messages are generated by the newly introduced bang-bang ( ! ! ) statement. An output message generated using the bang-bang operator is asynchronously multicast to all objects that have declared their interest in that message.

As an example, the output protocol of a Button object can be specified as follows:

( (arm ; (disarm ; arm)* ; activate[0,1] ; disarm) )*

This output protocol states that a button must first be armed before it can be activated, and eventually an armed button is disarmed. A button being activated by the end-user will emit the output message **activate** by issuing:

!!activate.

The output protocol is a guarantee that the output messages will be generated in a particular order. Describing which output messages will be generated is only interesting if the generation of an output message will result in a method activation of client-agents. Method activation of an object is always controlled by the input protocol of the object. There is therefore a relationship between the output messages of a server-agent, i.e., the services provided by the agent, and the input protocol of a client-agent. This relationship between agents can most of the time be determined at the time the agents are being identified. A declarative approach for describing the relationship between the output of an agent and the methods of an other agent is therefore most appropriate. In Talktalk, the declaration of the relationship is included in the input protocol of client-agents, and serves as a *formal executable specification*. An agent expresses its interest in a service of an other agent by mapping the agent and the required service onto the right method. The method will be executed automatically after the server has sent the notification of the completion of the service, and the protocol of the receiver is willing to accept this notification. The client-agent, which knows of the existence of the server-agents, but not the other way round, maps the output of the servers onto its own methods:

server.outputMessage → method

The declarative approach has a number of advantages over the programmatical approach:

- it is a formal specification. It has a mathematical basis, and particular properties of interactions can be proven;

- no programming is required for establishing input/output protocol links;

- the relationship between the serving agent and the client is localized in one section, and not scattered around in the programming code;

- the specification is easy to read, and therefore easy to maintain.

An example application of linking an output protocol to an input protocol is using the output messages of buttons in a dialogue box. Below an example dialogue box is shown. The dialogue box pops up with a prompt and two buttons, one to reply positively to the prompt, the other one to reply negatively. This dialogue box is initialized by sending it the message `prompt:yesText:noText:` with the appropriate arguments.

```
Class YesNoBox : Object
    | window text yesButton noButton |
protocol [
    input [
        prompt:yesText:noText: ;
        ( yesButton.activate → yesReply + noButton.activate → noReply )
    ]
    output [ yes + no ]
]
methods [
    prompt: tStr yesText: b1Str noText: b2Str
        text          ← Text new; display: tStr.
        yesButton     ← Button new; display: b1Str.
        noButton      ← Button new; display: b2Str.
        window        ← PopUpWindow new; add: text; add: yesButton; add: noButton.
        window popUp.
    |
    yesReply
        window popDown.
        !! yes.
    |
    noReply
        window popDown.
        !! no.
]
```

The input protocol of this YesNoBox declaratively maps the activation message of the buttons onto methods `yesReply` and `noReply`. These links are established dynamically at run-time, that is, the link is established as soon as the object referenced by the variable in the protocol comes into existence. The mappings in the protocol can change dynamically, dependent on the context, that is, dependent on the object that a protocol variable references. If such a variable in the protocol happens to get a new value, the old link is first removed, and a new link between the new object and the method onto which it should be mapped, is established.

## 3.2  Dialogue Blocks

The Dialogue block which is presented in this section evolved from the wish of having a sub-protocol with each method. A method in an agent is usually described in terms of services provided by other agents. In an event-driven environment, these services will be implemented as notification messages which, due to the concurrent nature of agents, are generated in an unpredictable order. As shown in section 2, a protocol is well suited to order the potentially unordered stream of incoming messages. It is therefore natural to define a method of an agent in terms of a sub-protocol over sub-methods. Applying the argument recursively implies that these sub-methods are also defined in terms of a sub-sub-protocol over sub-sub-methods. The recursion stops when a method is defined solely in terms of primitive operations: making state changes, i.e., making assignments to variables, creating agents and generating output messages. Each sub-method defined using a sub-protocol has local variables and local methods, resulting in a block-structured language as visualized in Figure 5. Although sub-protocols are a natural way for describing methods in an event-driven environment, the resulting language would suffer from an important

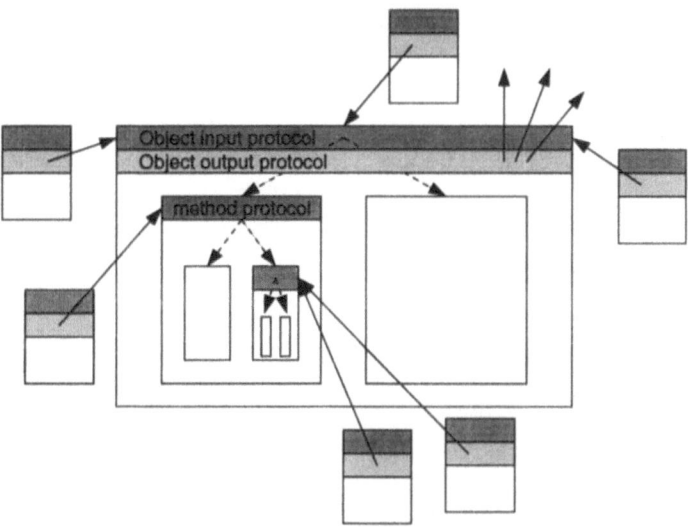

**Figure 5:** Using a hierachy of protocols is a natural way for describing methods

drawback if it were designed the way described: there is hardly any resemblance with the
base language Smalltalk anymore. A solution has been found in a generalization of the
recursive sub-protocol concept: the *Dialogue block*. The Dialogue block is modeled after
the Smalltalk block. Like a Smalltalk block, a Dialogue block contains deferred statements.
These deferred statements will be executed in the context in which the block was created,
after sending the Dialogue block the **value** message with optional parameters. Because
the Dialogue block is modeled after the Smalltalk block, it is possible to transfer a sub-
dialogue from one object to an other by passing a Dialogue block containing the dialogue.
A Dialogue block contains optional **init** and **exit** sections. The **init** section is executed
after sending the **value** message to the Dialogue block. Completion of the Dialogue is
indicated by the bang (!) statement, followed by an expression for the return value of
the dialogue block. After encountering this bang-operator, the method currently active
is completed, the **exit** section is executed, and the result of the return expression is
returned. A larger example demonstrating the usage of sub-protocols is given in section 4.
The example below is used for clarification of the Dialogue block principles.

```
 1    Class FileManager : Object
 2        | files |
 3    protocol [
 4        input [
 5            (
 6                   .. delete: + deleteAll: + ..
 7            ) *
 8        ]
 9    ]
10    methods [
11        delete: aFile
12            "delete aFile"
13    |
14        deleteAll: confirmationBlock
15            files do: [:aFile |
16                    (confirmationBlock value: aFile) ifTrue: [
17                        self delete: aFile.
18                    ]
19            ]
20    ]
```

```
21
22  Class Desktop : Object
23      | myFileManager |
24  protocol [
25      (
26          ..
27          deleteAllWithoutConfirmation +
28          deleteAllWithConfirmation +
29          ..
30      ) *
31  ]
32  methods [
33      new
34          myFileManager ←FileManager new.
35  |
36      deleteAllWithoutConfirmation
37          myFileManager deleteAll: [:aFile | true ].
38  |
39      deleteAllWithConfirmation
40          myFileManager deleteAll:
41              Dialogue [:aFile |
42                  | yesNoBox |
43                  init [
44                      yesNoBox ←YesNoBox new;
45                          prompt: ('Delete: ', aFile name)
46                          yesText: 'Yes'
47                          noText: 'No'.
48                  ]
49                  protocol [
50                      ( yesNoBox.yes → yes + yesNoBox.no → no ) *
51                  ]
52                  methods [
53                      yes
54                          ! true.
55                  |
56                      no
57                          ! false.
58                  ]
59              ]
60  ]
```

There is no semantic difference between 'ordinary' Smalltalk blocks and Dialogue blocks, from the standpoint of the object that sends the **value** message to it (as in line 16). The **deleteAll:** method in line 14 expects a block as argument which takes a file as input parameter and returns a boolean, indicating whether the file should be deleted or not. In the method **deleteAllWithoutConfirmation** (lines 36-37), the **Desktop** passes an ordinary Smalltalk block to the the fileManager, which always evaluates to **true**. In the method **deleteAllWithConfirmation** it passes a Dialogue block (lines 41-59), which asks the end-user for a confirmation to delete a file. The **fileManager** does not know (and need not know) whether the passed argument is a Smalltalk block or a Dialogue block.

The input-output behavior of an object is described in the protocol section of the object. The protocol in a Dialogue block is only used for the implementation of an method, it has no relationship with the protocol of the object in which it is defined. Therefore, Dialogue blocks have no output protocol.

Dialogue blocks can be used for defining a method with a sub-protocol. Instead of having a protocol defining each method, the Dialogue block contains the sub-protocol and sub-methods, and indeed, if necessary, a purely multi-agent system can be programmed using only sub-protocols. But this is only a possibility, and not a strict requirement. Using sub-protocols only where needed, client-server models and multi-agent models can both be described, and combined (see Figure 6).

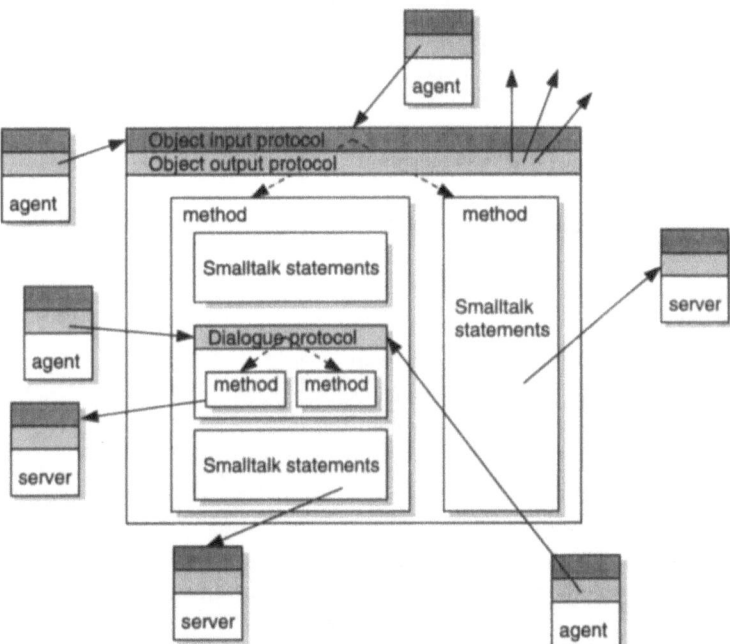

**Figure 6:** Dialogue blocks allow a combination of multi-agent and client-server architectures

## 4 Example

In this section we give a more elaborate example of the usage of input and output protocols and Dialogues. The Talktalk code for this example is given in Figure 14. Consider a hard-disk maintenance tool, which can be activated to display the current free disk space, undelete a file, format the hard-disk and so on. The hard-disk maintenance tool, the HDUMaintainer is the intermediary between the hard-disk and the end-user. It accepts and translates messages originating from both sides (see Figure 7). We will focus on

**Figure 7:** The HDU-maintainer is the intermediair between hard-disk and end-user

the process of formatting the hard-disk. The end-user requests a specific service from the HDUMaintainer by clicking on the associated button. The graphical interface of the HDUMaintainer can be visualized as shown in Figure 8. The graphical interface of the HDUMaintainer consists of a panel and a number of buttons, one for each possible hard-disk maintenance operation. Each button serves as an agent, the HDUMaintainer specifies its interest in their activation by naming them in its input-protocol:

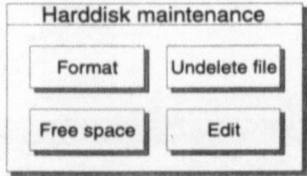

**Figure 8:** Graphical interface of the HDU-maintainer

```
protocol [
    input [
        (
            formatButton.activate        → format      +
            undeleteButton.activate      → undelete    +
            freeSpaceButton.activate     → freeSpace   +
            editButton.activate          → edit
        ) *
    ]
]
```

If the end-user presses the **formatButton** the method **format** will be performed. This method pops up the dialogue-box shown in Figure 9 for a confirmation of the irreversible action it is about to perform. Activating the **yesButton** will start the method **doFormat**,

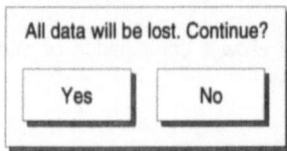

**Figure 9:** Pop-up dialogue box for confirmation of the format operation

which will start the format of the hard-disk by sending the message **format** to the controller.

The (simplified) protocol of the hard-disk controller is specified as follows:

```
protocol [
    input [
        format ; (pause ; continue) * ; pause[0,1] ; stop
    ]
    output [
        (busy: + panic)* ; done
    ]
]
```

The input protocol of this hard-disk controller states that the format process may be paused and continued any number of times, and that the format process must be stopped explicitly, either with or without a preceding pause. The output protocol states that the controller continually sends **busy:** notifications to indicate its progress, and it can send **panic** notifications, indicating some error, and that it informs about its completion with a **done** notification. Tracing the format-process is visualized by a slider showing the percentage of the hard-disk that has been formatted so far, as shown in Figure 10. The progress of the format process is monitored by mapping the **busy:** notifications that the controller continually sends to the **update:** method:

$$hdu.busy: → update:$$

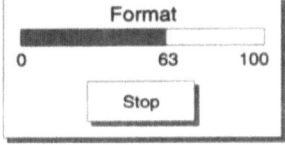

**Figure 10:** Graphical interface of the format operation in progress

The end-user can interrupt the format process at any time by pressing the stopButton. Because stopping in the middle of a format process is in general not a reasonable thing to do, a dialogue box is popped up, see Figure 11. The format method can also be inter-

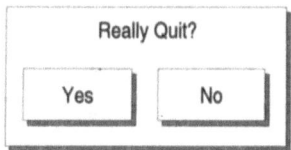

**Figure 11:** Dialogue box after the end-user has pressed the stop-button

rupted by the controller, for example in case that a bad sector could not be formatted. On occurrence of this event, the end-user may want to stop the format process, a possibility given by yet another dialogue (Figure 12). All these messages can be generated

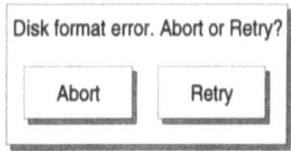

**Figure 12:** Dialogue box after occurrence of a disk format error

asynchronously by the controller as well as the end-user. The example shows that dialogue block protocols can be used for managing this complexity. The protocol of the doFormat method maps them onto the right local methods (shown below). A schematic overview is given in Figure 13.

```
hdu.busy:            → update:   +
hdu.panic            → panic     +
stopButton.activate  → stop
```

# 5   Discussion

Talktalk is a general purpose programming language. It incorporates input and output protocols for describing object functionality and its Dialogue block concept enables a programmer to construct complex dialogues in a very natural way, allowing for the client-server approach as well as the multi-agent approach. In the literature several models for dialogue control can be found, the most prominent ones being grammars, state transition

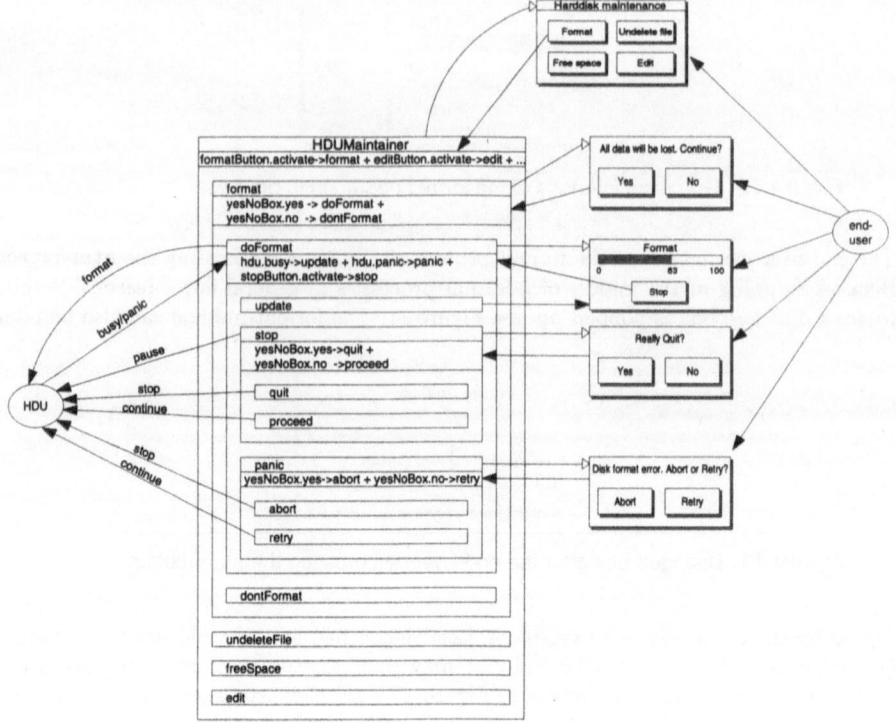

**Figure 13:** Schematic overview of the hard-disk maintainer program

networks and event response systems. Supporters of a specific model have always been able to find deficiencies in the other models. Items addressed are then related to descriptive power, e.g. the possibility to describe interleaving, sequencing, and so on. Grammars perform poorly for describing interleaving, state transition networks become saturated with nodes for more complex systems, while sequencing is hard to specify in Event Response Systems [5]. To address shortcomings, models can be adapted, or extended, to overcome the alleged deficiencies. Grammars, for instance have been extended with a permutation construct to allow interleaving. State transition networks have been extended with the possibility to encapsulate regularity, rather than enumerate it [2]. Although the models tend to grow towards each other, as far as descriptive power is concerned, and therefore become theoretically equivalent, they individually perform better in different application areas.

For our purpose, we chose the protocol model for describing dialogue control in interactive systems with concurrent active objects. Protocols have at least the same descriptive power as grammars and event response systems. As with all models, the protocol model has been subject to change too. It can be traced back to path-expression for process synchronization in operating system theories [1]. The protocols for object access in Talktalk originate from [8, 7], and have evolved over time. Addition of sub-protocols adds a substantial amount of expressive power, comparable to the addition of sub-networks in state transition networks.

```
Class HDUController : Object
protocol [
  input [
    format ; (pause ; continue) * ; pause[0,1] ; stop
  ]
  output [
    (busy: + panic)* ; done
  ]
]
methods [
  ..
]

Class HDUMaintainer: Object
  | formatButton "and other interaction tools"
    hduController |
Protocol [
  input [ ..
    formatButton.activate → format +
        ..
  ]
]
methods [
  new
      hduController ←HDUController new.
      formatButton ←Button new; text: 'Format'.
  |
  format
      "check that user really wants to lose all
        his data "
      Dialogue [
        | yesNoBox |
        protocol [
          yesNoBox.yes→ doFormat +
          yesNoBox.no→ dontFormat
        ]
        init [
          yesNoBox ← YesNoBox new;
          prompt: 'All data will be lost. Continue?'
          yesText: 'yes' noText: 'no'.
        ]
        methods [
          doFormat
            Dialogue [:hdu |
              | display stopButton |
              protocol [
                (
                  hdu.busy:   → update: +
                  hdu.panic   → panic +
                  stopButton.activate→ stop
                ) * ;
                hdu.done →done
              ]
              init [
                "set up display: slider for
                  percentage of work done,
                  and a button with: 'stop' "
                display popUp.
                hdu format.
              ]
              exit [ display popDown ]
```

```
            methods [
              update: percentage
                display show: percentage.
              |
              stop
                hdu pause.
                Dialogue [
                  | yesNoBox |
                  protocol [
                    yesNoBox.yes→ quit +
                    yesNoBox.no → proceed
                  ]
                  init [
                    yesNoBox ←YesNoBox new;
                    prompt: 'Really quit?'
                    yesText: 'yes' noText: 'no'.
                  ]
                  methods [
                    quit
                      hdu stop.
                    |
                    proceed
                      hdu continue.
                  ]
                ] value.
              |
              panic
                Dialogue [
                  | abortRetryBox |
                  protocol [
                    abortRetryBox.yes → abort +
                    abortRetryBox.no → retry
                  ]
                  init [
                    abortRetryBox ←
                    YesNoBox new;
                    prompt:
                     'Disk error. Abort or Retry?'
                    yesText: 'abort'
                    noText: 'retry'.
                  ]
                  methods [
                    abort
                      hdu stop.
                    |
                    retry
                      hdu continue.
                  ]
                ] value.
              |
              done
                ! #ready.
            ]
          ] value: hduController.
          ! #done.
        |
        dontFormat
          ! #done.
      ]
    ] value.
  ]
```

**Figure 14:** HDUMaintainer code

The server specification in interaction terms in an input protocol allows for describing communication links declaratively, rather than programmatically, resulting in code which is easier to to write, to read, and therefore easier to maintain. But above all, Talktalk is a *pragmatic* approach. It has been superposed on Smalltalk, enabling a Talktalk programmer to directly take advantage of its mature set of classes and programming environment.

A number of theoretical issues has not been mentioned in this paper, partly because they fall outside the scope of this paper, partly because research is still being conducted on them. In the near future more research is planned in the following areas:

- The clear separation of the syntax of the interaction patterns described by the protocol of objects and Dialogue blocks, and the semantics described by the methods can possibly be used to prove certain properties of interactions. For instance, can it be shown, by looking at the protocols of `HDUMaintainer` and `HDUController`, (preferably by a machine) that a hard-disk is only formatted when the end-user has clicked both the `formatButton` and the `yesButton`?

- Are (sub-)protocols and their relationships easy to visualize? This is of particular interest in environments like DIGIS, in which User Interface designers manipulate scenarios and dialogues. A visual representation would benefit the designer's understanding of the structure of the dialogue.

Talktalk has been successfully used in the research project DIGIS, a highly interactive User Interface Design Environment. While it is too early to draw definitive conclusions, we are convinced that Talktalk can be applied in a broader context.

## References

[1] R. H. Campbell and R. H. Habermann. The Specification of Process Synchronization by Path Expressions. In *Lecture Notes in Computer Science 16*, pages 89–102. Springer-Verlag, Berlin, 1974.

[2] Gilbert Cockton. Designing Abstractions for Communication Control. In Michael Harrison and Harold Thimbleby, editors, *Formal Methods in Human-Computer Interaction*, number 2 in Cambridge Series on Human-Computer Interaction, chapter 8, pages 233–271. Cambridge University Press, Cambridge, England, 1990.

[3] Hans de Bruin, Peter Bouwman, and Jan van den Bos. DIGIS; a Graphical User Interface Design Environment for Non-Programmers. In Roger Hubbold and Robert Juan, editors, *Computer Graphics Forum, Conference Issue*, volume 12–3, pages 13–24, Oxford, England, June 6–10, 1993. Proceedings Eurographics '93, Barcelona, NCC Blackwell.

[4] Adele Goldberg and David Robson. *SMALLTALK-80; the Language and its Implementation*. Addison-Wesley, Reading, Massachusetts, 1983.

[5] Ralph D. Hill. Event Response Systems: a Technique for Specifying Multi-Threaded Dialogues. In *Proceedings SIGCHI+GI'87: Human Factors in Computing Systems*, pages 241–248. ACM, April 5–9 1987.

[6] Henry Lieberman. Concurrent Object-Oriented Programming in Act 1. In Akinori Yonezawa and Mario Tokoro, editors, *Object-Oriented Concurrent Programming*, pages 9–36. MIT Press, Cambridge, Massachusetts, 1987.

[7] Jan van den Bos. Abstract Interaction Tools; a Language for User Interface Management Systems. *ACM-TOPLAS (Transactions on Programming Languages and Systems)*, 10(2):215–247, April 1988.

[8] Jan van den Bos and Chris Laffra. PROCOL; a Concurrent Object Language with Protocols, Delegation and Persistence. *Acta Informatica*, 28:511–538, September 1991.

# 10

# OOCS – Constraints in an Object Oriented Environment

Quinton Hoole, Edwin Blake

Object orientation is a suitable abstraction for computer graphics, but significant problems exist in specifying relationships *between* objects, since relationships are not easily encapsulated *within* the objects concerned. *Constraints*, where the relationships between objects are maintained by the system, are an especially useful abstraction. Many existing constraint systems are forced to violate encapsulation and hence lose significant benefits of object orientation. This is because constraints are typically expressed by the programmer in terms of internal instance variables, which are then manipulated by the constraint solver to satisfy the constraints.

We present a solution which incorporates constraints while maintaining the benefits of object orientation. Constraints are expressed in terms of responses to messages, and are hence independent of the internal implementation of the objects. In addition, the solver uses the interfaces provided by objects to propagate changes, rather than writing directly to instance variables.

Some previous approaches were forced to sacrifice the power of the constraint solver while others are subject to certain restrictions. Examples are given in this paper. We present a solution which does compromise encapsulation (this is unavoidable), but the violation is done in a controlled and localized manner.

Solutions to the constraint set are arrived at by the constraint solver in consultation with constrained objects. Solutions are propagated back to objects strictly via their interfaces.

## 1   Introduction

The inherent complexity of computer graphics is very well addressed by the abstraction of object orientation. The advantages offered by object orientation in this field include:

- The complexity of the problem is easily partitioned into more manageable components ('objects').

- Strict information hiding and definite interface specification allow for relatively easy modification of existing code without detriment to the overall correctness of the system.

- Software re-use is encouraged through inheritance and 'part-whole' hierarchies.

These benefits exact a price. Some problems are well known, such as the difficulties experienced with multiple inheritance and the learning curve associated with having many predefined (but reusable!) classes.

The difficulty of expressing relationships between objects is a problem that is less widely recognized. Simply put, a relationship between two objects cannot be cleanly associated with one and not the other object, and hence does not lend itself to elegant encapsulation within either one of the objects. An early example of this is the difficulty in expressing the coercion of one type of number to another in Smalltalk.

The problem is particularly apparent in graphics and animation. The specific problem of *constraints* will be covered in the remainder of this paper.

## 2 Constraints

It is often advantageous to be able to enforce logical relationships between objects. These *constraints* can be maintained implicitly by adding segments of code to object definitions to ensure the maintenance of the constraints. It is however far more elegant to be able to define constraints external to the objects, and to express and maintain them explicitly by means of a constraint solver. Constraints specified declaratively in this manner offer a very intuitive way of describing the relationships between objects and remove the burden of ensuring that the constraints are maintained from the programmer [13]. Owing to these obvious benefits, several constraint-object integrations have been proposed. These include Thinglab [4], Kaleidoscope [9, 10], ALIEN [6], Garnet [16], Equate [22], PROCOL [13], GICS [17], [21] and others.

Two aspects of constraints may be distinguished [15]:

- the *declarative* aspect, expressing the nature of the constraint, and

- the *procedural* aspect, specifying the actions to be taken to ensure that the constraint is satisfied.

In most constraint systems the procedural aspect is determined by the constraint solver, and the programmer may focus upon the declarative aspect (ThingLab [5, 11], GICS [17], [21], [23]), [13], [24] and many more).

It is preferable, in an object oriented environment, for user-defined objects to assist in providing the procedural components of constraints imposed upon them [22]. This enables constraints to be declared on high level, user defined objects, and not just primitive object types provided by the language. It avoids situations where the solver imposes a solution on an object which knows the solution to be unsuitable. In addition the object is usually able to provide more intelligent procedural components than the solver, because it has more knowledge of its internal functioning than the solver.

The job of the constraint solver is thus to provide a transformation from a state which is inconsistent with the constraints, to one which *is* consistent with them. Approaches to this problem are diverse; prominent examples include:

- *local propagation*, in which changes local to objects are propagated to their global environment. Such a change of state may violate some constraint, in which case the *procedural aspect* of that constraint would be triggered by the constraint solver. This action may change the local states of one or more objects and these changes will again be *propagated* to the environment, possibly triggering further constraint actions. This is by far the most common technique, owing to its simplicity and speed. It cannot however handle cyclic constraints or partial information (e.g greater-than) constraints. Obviously this approach may lead to infinite looping as noted in [15, 17, 24], although most systems detect this and report an error. Prominent examples of local propagation systems include Alien [6], Garnet [16], Thinglab [4], GICS [17] and the Model-View-Controller mechanism of Smalltalk [12]

- *global reasoning*, in which all constraints and related variables in the system are considered in attempting to arrive at an optimal solution. This approach is more complicated to implement, but can provide solutions to constraint situations where local propagation solvers fail. Also, iteration within solution code can often be avoided, resulting in more efficient solutions. Examples of systems which employ this approach include Kaleidoscope [9, 10], Bertrand [15] and Equate [22]. As mentioned, this approach implicitly violates the information hiding principle of object oriented programming, because the solver requires a global name space within which to work. A solution to this problem is given in this paper.

Although computer programs for constraint solving have existed for over thirty years [20], the problems mentioned above have hindered the effective incorporation of constraints into object oriented systems. These problems, some solutions, and an implementation of OOCS, our object oriented constraint solver, will be discussed in more detail in the remainder of this paper.

In Section 3 we look more closely at the source of the difficulties in marrying constraints and object orientation. Section 4 gives an overview of our proposed solution to the problems, with a detailed example given in Section 5. We then compare our approach with others in the field in Section 6. We finish with a final example and conclusion in Sections 7 and 8.

## 3   What is the Problem?

"Encapsulation is the process of hiding all of the details of an object that do not contribute to its essential characteristics. In practise one hides the representation of an object, as well as the implementation of its methods." [3].

This information hiding has a direct impact upon the semantics of operations on objects. These must necessarily be independent of the representation of the object and the implementation of its methods.

Powerful and efficient constraint solvers (global solvers) however require a global name space to reason about and propagate changes to. In addition, to express useful constraints in existing constraint systems, the programmer typically needs access to, and places constraints on, state variables (or parts) of constrained objects. This again points to a global name space.

Conversely, the primary benefits to be derived from object orientation, including ease of code re-use, code maintenance and debugging, stem from strict information hiding. Hence there is apparently a contradiction between powerful constraint systems and object oriented programming. It is a well known fact that it is possible to mimic objects with state in a pure declarative language by using the concept of infinite streams, with lasy evaluation, but to quote Abelson and Sussman:

"Streams with delayed evaluation can be a powerful modelling tool, providing many of the benefits of local state and assignment. Morover they avoid the theoretical tangles that must acompany the introduction of assignment into a programming language... The absence of assignment [in functional languages] means that the programmer need not be concerned with synchronisation errors caused by values being evaluated in the wrong order. On the other hand, it is an open question whether all need for assignment can be reasonably bypassed using delayed evaluation. One particularly troublesome area arises when we wish to design interactive systems, especially ones that model interactions between independent entities" [1].

One should distinguish whether it is the *programmer* or the *system* which violates encapsulation, and to what extent this occurs. Freeman-Benson for example argues in [10] that it is not necessary for the constraint system to adhere to encapsualtion principles, for the same reason that optimising compilers are allowed to perform such optimisations as direct access to instance variables, and inlining of methods. Equate [22] however focusses on preventing the constraint system from directly writing to instance variables. The advantages and disadvantages of these two approaches are discussed in Section 5.2.

Clearly, the mere *appearance* of information hiding can be maintained if we make all objects part of some grand manager object that owns all of them. Equally clearly this violates the spirit and looses the benefits of object orientation in the same way as a global name space. This is simply another manifestation of the general problem of dealing with relationships as expressed in part-whole hierarchies (which express "is-part-of" relationships between objects). These are difficult to implement satisfactorily without compromising the goal of information hiding ([18], [2]).

# 4   A Solution

The solution we adopt is to maintain encapsulation from the application programmer's perspective, while allowing the constraint solver to view the global state of the system. In this way the programmer keeps the benefits of object oriented programming, while the solver is able to arrive at globally acceptable, efficient solutions. Assuming that the solver does not contain bugs[1], the effects of programming errors will be localized to the objects in which those errors occur. Errors in constraint specification may not be as easy to track however.

In our Object Oriented Constraint System (OOCS), this philosophy is implemented as follows: The constraint solver accepts as input a set of constraints, and produces as output a set of object-oriented solution programs (i.e. sequences of message passes). The execution of any one of these programs is guaranteed to place the system in a state which complies with the constraints. To achieve this goal, the solver interacts with constrained objects in two ways. Firstly each object supplies a set of *solution program segments* (or steps) for each constraint which has been imposed upon it. The object guarantees that execution of any one of these segments will leave the object in a state which satisfies the constraint.

Secondly, each object provides a so-called *read-set* and *write-set* for each message that it accepts. The read-set corresponds with all variable slots read as a result of that message send. The write-set contains all variables written during the message send. In order to maintain encapsulation, read-sets and write-sets are only available to the constraint solver, and not the application programmer.

With the above information regarding the internal implementation of constrained objects, the constraint solver is able to determine which solution program segments might interfere with the effects of each other. Based upon this, it is able to propose various alternative solution programs, which are those permutations of the solution steps where no step undoes the effects of any previous step. The application programmer may then choose any one of these as the current solution to the existing constraint set, and execute it. As suggested in [22], this choice of solution may be governed by the execution time of

---

[1]The solver should be viewed as being part of the operating system rather than part of the application program.

the solutions (as approximated by their complexity), or by some other comparator.

This approach contrasts with the vast majority of constraint systems (with the exception of Equate [22]), which produce a set of variable assignments. In Kaleidoscope, Garnet and Alien for example, the solver writes directly to instance variables, making it difficult for the programmer to track all state changes to the object during debugging, as not all access is via the object interface. Discussion of the perceived merits of this approach may be found in [16].

It may be argued that our solver violates encapsulation in that it knows exactly which instance variables are read and written by each method. However the original objectives of the principle are maintained, because application code still adheres to encapsulation. The application programmer never has access to the internal representation of encapsulated objects. This means that he/she cannot write code which depends upon object implementation. Also, because solutions are propagated back to objects strictly via their interfaces, the programmer is never able to directly access objects' internal states, even by imposing external constraints.

## 5  An Example

Consider the case presented in [24] which is depicted in Figure 1. A line line1 with

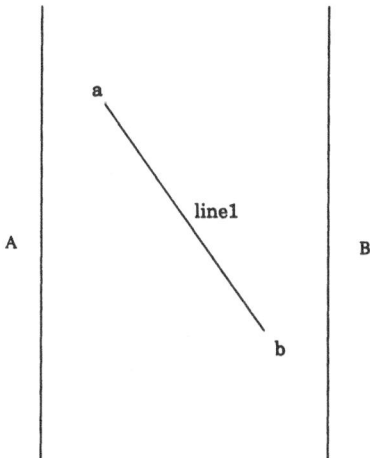

**Figure 1:** A Compound Constraint: line1 is of fixed length 5, and is constrained such that its endpoints lie on the vertical lines A and B. The perpendicular distance between A and B is less than 5.

endpoints a and b and fixed length 5, between two vertical lines A and B, is constrained such that a lies on A and b lies on B. Hence the following constraints are specified:

1. Constrain line1 such that the $x$-coordinate of endpoint a equals the $x$-coordinate of vertical line A.

2. Constrain line1 such that the $x$-coordinate of endpoint b equals the $x$-coordinate of vertical line B.

3. Constrain A such that it remains vertical.

4. Constrain B such that it remains vertical.

5. Constrain line1 such that it's length remains equal to 5.

We now expect to be able to move the vertical lines A and B, as well as the fixed length line line1, and the system should ensure that all of the constraints are satisfied. For example, if A moved closer to B, we might expect line1 to rotate anti-clockwise to maintain the constraints on its endpoints. We will now use this example to outline the differences between our object oriented constraint solver and some other systems which either use local propagation, with associated disadvantages discussed in Section 2 or use global solvers but violate encapsulation in doing so, thus losing its benefits. Examples of the former include Alien, Garnet, Thinglab, GICS [17] and the Smalltalk Model-View-Controller mechanism. The latter is exemplified by Kaleidoscope [9, 10].

## 5.1  Constraint Declaration

The first difference is in how constraints are declared. Many solvers require constraints to be expressed in terms of variables. The constraint set given on page 147 would thus be specified as:

**C1.** line1.a.x = A.x

**C2.** line1.b.x = B.x

**C3.** A.a.x = A.b.x

**C4.** B.a.x = B.b.x

**C5.** line1.length = 5

This approach has several weaknesses, the primary one being that the expression of the constraints is tied to the *internal* implementation details of the objects being constrained, although the constraints are expressed *externally* to the objects. The main benefits of object oriented programming result from the fact that all code which depends upon internal representation of an object is encapsulated within the object. In the above example, the application programmer making use of the line class, relies on it having instance variables length, a and b. The points a and b are in turn relied upon to have an instance variable x. The programmer thus clearly loses the well-known benefits of information hiding[2].

In OOCS, constraints are declared through the message interfaces of the constrained objects. The example constraints are expressed (in Smalltalk) as:

**C1.** line1 leftConstraint: [A x].

**C2.** line1 rightConstraint: [B x].

**C3.** A angleConstraint: 0.

**C4.** B angleConstraint: 0.

**C5.** line1 lengthConstraint: 5.

---

[2]You will also note that the part-whole hierarchy has been effectively flattened. Discussion of this issue is beyond the scope of this paper, but refer to [2] and [10] for further details.

The difference is subtle but important. Note that [A x] is not a direct reference to the x instance variable of object A, but rather a message x being sent to A, which responds acccordingly. These constraint expressions are thus *independent of objects' internal state variables.* For example lines may be represented as an origin point and direction vector, or simply as two end points. Either way the line object will respond correctly to the x message. The short constraint program above is independent of these details. This contrasts with the first approach shown.

## 5.2  Constraint Solution

The second important difference between OOCS and most other object-constraint systems is in how solutions are found. A simple local constraint solver would consider constraints in sequence and attempt to validate them. line1 might first be translated to the left in order to validate constraint 1 and then translated to the right in order validate constraint 2. As both [24] and [17] have observed and as can be seen by inspection of the simple example above, this process would continue *ad infinitum,* resulting in oscillation of the line. It is hence not a satisfactory solution to the problem. Systems which use this approach are listed in Section 2. Of course a process of global reasoning, which considers the constraint set as a whole, could easily avoid the looping by deciding to rotate the line. Such a solution would clearly be preferable in this case.

OOCS approaches this problem by determining which solution steps interfere with each other. The looping above could have been averted had the solver been intelligent enough to predict that the above two solution steps would interfere with each other as witnessed.

Hence we require some partial ordering on solution steps based upon which steps interfere with the accomplishments of others. One simple approach is to inspect the variables read and written by each solution step. We refer to these sets of variables as the **read-set** and **write-set** of the solution step respectively. This idea is borrowed from Equate [22]. Owing to the fact that the write-sets of the above two solution steps intersect, it is prudent to assume that the one step (e.g translation to the right) undoes some of the achievements of the other (translation to the left). A solution program which executes these two steps should thus be avoided.

Based upon the above discussion, line1 therefore proposes two alternative solution steps to constraint 1

**S1.1** translate line1 horizontally, or

**S1.2** rotate line1 about b

and similarly for constraint 2

**S2.1** translate line1 horizontally, or

**S2.2** rotate line1 about a

To ensure that A remains vertical, it suggests the following alternatives:

**S3.1** rotate A about a, or

**S3.2** rotate A about b, or

**S3.3** translate a in the x dimension, or

**S3.4** translate b in the x dimension.

To ensure that B remains vertical, analogous solution steps S4.1–S4.4 are suggested.
To ensure that line1 has length 5 any one of the following steps may be used:

**S5.1** extend line1, keeping a fixed, or

**S5.2** extend line1, keeping b fixed, or

By arranging these solution steps into a directed graph representing the partial ordering mentioned above, and traversing a suitable path through it, the OOCS solver is able to decide that the following is a feasible solution program[3].

**S3.1** rotate A about A.a (such that A is vertical).

**S3.1** rotate B about B.a (such that B is vertical).

**S5.1** extend line1 (to length 5), keeping a fixed.

**S1.2** rotate line1 about line1.b (such that a lies on A)

**S2.2** rotate line1 about line1.a (such that b lies on B)

As mentioned in Section 4, this is a true object-oriented solution, rather than a set of variable assignments, as produced by Kaleidoscope, Garnet and most other constraint-object systems. While these may solve the constraints at hand, blindly assigning values to variables violates encapsulation principles and can result in important side effects being by-passed, a simple example being the redrawing of a moved line.

In contrast, OOCS produces object oriented programs as solutions. These solution programs comprise messages to objects, which hence only interact via their strictly defined interfaces. The well-known benefits of such proper object oriented practise include more predictable behaviour in constrained objects and easier programming error detection and correction.

A different solution proposed in [16] is to impose further constraints to ensure that the necessary side effects are triggered, but this implies that the programmer is required to make a complete paradigm change from imperative object-oriented to declarative constraints. We share the opinion of Freeman-Benson [10] that the programmer should be free to use which ever paradigm suites his or her needs, and not be forced completely from one to the other. Ironically however, Kaleidoscope does not feature true assignment, but rather mimics it by using a model of infinite streams as described in section 3 and detailed in [1]

## 6  Related Work

Several object-oriented approaches to constraints have been investigated in recent literature. Of these, the approaches adopted in Equate [22] and Kaleidoscope [9, 10] are the most similar to our OOCS system. As mentioned however, Kaleidoscope solutions are simply sets of assignments to instance variables, whereas OOCS produces solution programs, composed of a sequence of object-oriented message sends, in a similar manner to Equate. Also, Equate models assignment using infinite streams, thereby dispensing with true imperative assignment.

Garnet [16] differs rather dramatically from OOCS in that it promotes breaking object encapsulation completely by constraining instance variables directly. This author feels

---

[3]There are many feasible solutions, but only one is given for simplicity of the discussion.

that the arguments used in favour of this approach are simply the arguments in favour of declarative programming as opposed to imperative programming. Our aim has been to integrate the two paradigms, rather than replace one by the other.

Alien [6] also attempts to integrate objects and constraints, but uses a prototype-delegation model in preference to a class-instance model. The approach to encapsulation is similar to OOCS in that constraints are not placed on instance variables, but rather on so-called "slots". Slots can also be read from and written to, much like variables. To maintain encapsulation, any access to a slot triggers a method in the owner object, which is thus able to provide controlled access to it's internal state.

GICS [17] uses a simple local propagation method to maintain encapsulation, with the associated disadvantages discussed in Section 2. As such it is a good example of pushing the local propagation approach to the limit, and achieving strict encapsulation of objects. The Appendix contains an example formulation of the constraint set discussed in Section 5 to illustate this point.

## 7  A Final Example

Let us consider another example constraint set (used in [22]) as handled by the OOCS system: a geometric figure editor in which rectangles are represented by objects called *boxes*. The editor could use a constraint solver to find arrangements of figures that meet certain conditions (cf. window layout in a window manager).

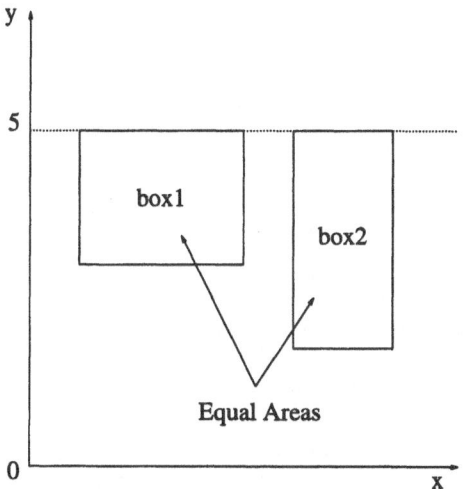

**Figure 2:** A Geometrical Editor using Constraints

Figure 2 shows two boxes with two constraints imposed upon them:

1. the areas of the boxes should be equal

2. their tops should co-incide with the line $y = 5$

These constraints are expressed in OOCS as follows:

```
C1.     box1 areaConstraint: [box2 area].
```

```
C2.    box1 topConstraint: 5.
C3.    box2 topConstraint: 5.
```

The box class provides the following solution program segments for each constraint[4]:

```
S1.1.  box1 width: (box2 area/box1 area/box1 height).
S1.2.  box1 height: (box2 area/box1 area/box1 width).

S2.1   box1 moveTopTo: 5.

S3.1   box2 moveTopTo: 5.
```

Either of solution steps S1.1 or S1.2 are sufficient to ensure that constraint C1 holds. S2.1 and S3.1 ensure that C2 and C3 hold respectively.

In this example **Box** objects are represented internally by four integers $x$, $y$, $w$ and $h$, where $x$ and $y$ are the co-ordinates of the top left corner of the box, and $w$ and $h$ are the width and height respectively. The read-sets and write-sets of the above solution steps are thus:

```
S1.1.  read-set  = {box2.w, box2.h, box1.w, box1.h}
       write-set = {box1.w}
S1.2.  read-set  = {box2.w, box2.h, box1.w, box1.h}
       write-set = {box1.h}

S2.1   read-set  = {}
       write-set = {box1.y}

S3.1   read-set  = {}
       write-set = {box2.y}
```

OOCS hence deduces two possible solution programs, corresponding to the sequences $(S1.1, S2.1, S3.1)$ and $(S1.2, S2.1, S3.1)$. Both are permissible as the read and write sets of all steps in each solution program are disjoint.

# 8  Conclusion

The need for a workable marriage of object-orientation with the declarative paradigm has been highlighted by much of the current research in these fields. Several of the difficulties documented in this book stem directly from the inability to cleanly express declarative relationships between objects. Temporal relationships between video streams are one example discussed in [7] and Egbert notes in [8] the need for combining a state-base paradigm with a declarative one. Once again in [19], the need for incorporating functional notions is emphasized.

Despite the difficulties in expressing inter-object relationships, as exemplified by the complications experienced with integrating objects and constraints, it *is* possible to marry the two paradigms without losing the principal benefits of either. Because relationships do not encapsulate cleanly within the related objects, we can at best achieve a controlled violation of encapsulation while maintaining the objectives of information hiding by another mechanism. The only alternative would have been to separate the declarative expression

---

[4]Smalltalk syntax is used here.

of constraints completely from the imperative object oriented language, but the goal of this research project was to see how far one could go in integration of the two paradigms.

The OOCS constraint system presented here attains this goal by allowing the constraint solver, which is assumed to be an error-free component of the operating system, limited access to the internal state of objects, while maintaining strict encapsulation from the programmer's perspective. This ensures, amongst others, that programmer errors are contained and more easily located. Controlled access to global state by the solver facilitates global reasoning, so the solver is able find solutions where local propagation methods fail, while the encapsulation benefits associated with local propagation solvers are maintained.

## 8.1  Extensions

The current implementation of OOCS in Smalltalk is our first attempt at integrating the two powerful programming paradigms of object orientation and constraints. Various improvements are envisaged.

### Constraint Message Explosion

Currently, each class wishing to allow external constraints to be imposed upon it is required to implement one method for each constraint. For example, a class `Rectangle` wishing to allow constraints to be imposed on each of its corners would respond to each of the following four messages

1. `TopLeftConstraint: aPoint`

2. `TopRightConstraint: aPoint`

3. `BottomLeftConstraint: aPoint`

4. `BottomRightConstraint: aPoint`

with an instance of class `Constraint` which contains alternative solution steps that class `Rectangle` has proposed. These constraints are then passed to the solver which produces a solution as described in previous sections.

If class `Rectangle` then wished to support constraints on the midpoints of its sides, four further messages would require similar responses:

1. `TopMidConstraint: aPoint`

2. `BottomMidConstraint: aPoint`

3. `LeftMidConstraint: aPoint`

4. `RightMidConstraint: aPoint`

This places a burden on the implementor of the constrainable class. It also restricts the user of the class to those constraints which were deemed necessary by the class implementor.

One obvious (but disastrous) alternative is to add redundant instance variables to objects, and impose constraints on these variables. For example, we might add variables `TopMidpoint`, `BottomMidpoint`, `LeftMidpoint` and `RightMidpoint` to the class `Rectangle`, with constraints that each each point lies in the middle of the appropriate side. We could then impose further constraints such as:

```
rectangle.TopMidPoint = aPoint
```

This quite clearly defeats the entire aim of the exercise and is very definitely not a viable solution. Not only have we lost all encapsulation by directly accessing internal instance variables when imposing external constraints. To make matters worse, storage requirements of each **Rectangle** object have been increased by adding redundant variables. In addition, the number of constraints in the system has unnecessarily increased, with an associated performance penalty.

A better solution is used by, amongst others, Kaleidoscope [10] and Alien [6], where *virtual variables* (or *slots* in Alien) are used. These are not actually stored, but are rather calculated upon request. The difference may appear subtle; the important point is that access to these slots is strictly through object interfaces. We are currently adding the feature of virtual variables to OOCS.

### Missed Solutions

As mentioned in Section 4, OOCS decides which permutations of solution program segments are permissible based upon partial ordering of these segments with respect to read-sets and write-sets. The simple approach we adopt is as follws: if step 'a' writes to any location that is either read from or written to by step 'b' then it is possible for 'a' to interfere with 'b', and is hence necessary for 'a' to precede 'b' in a partial ordering of solution steps. It is possible for this approach to falsely discard valid solutions as described below. This can result in OOCS failing to find a solution when one does in fact exist. We hope to improve the comparator used for partial ordering of solution steps to minimize this shortcoming.

An ideal partial order of solutions has at the bottom those steps which can be called without interfering with any others. At the top are those steps that must be called first because calling them later will invalidate all other solutions. The method currently used by OOCS to determine whether two steps interfere, it is not ideal, and more sophisticated methods are being investigated. What is required is a mechanism that can order proposed solution programs depending on their ability to interfere with one another.

Clearly if step 'b' does not write to variables which were used in program 'a' then 'b' cannot interfere with 'a'. But even if 'b' does write to the variables of 'a', but within an acceptable range, then the partial ordering can be preserved. Inferring these relations is a problem requiring further research. The first approach could be to have various guidelines for coding constraint methods, but eventually one might try to apply the ability to infer properties of the declarative constraint specifications and try to make more intelligent decisions on the "who interferes with whom" partial order.

# Appendix: A Local Propagation Example

Let us compare our OOCS system with GICS system presented in [17]. GICS is not the most recent work by that author, but is a good example of how local constraint solving can be used to maintain encapsulation, and also illustrates some of the problems which can arise when such local solving is pushed to its limits. To make the comparison more concrete, we will briefly show how the constraint program illustrated in Figure 1 might be formulated and solved by GICS.

Briefly, the GICS programming model comprises *graphics entities* (GE's) which are simple graphics output primitives such as line segments and circles. These are then combined via *external constraints* to form more complex and useful *graphics objects* (GO's). GE's may themselves also have *internal constraints*, which they handle privately. To simplify the discussion only constrained line segment GE's will be discussed. Examples include line segments with the following internal constraints:

- fixed length

- fixed angle

- fixed angle and length

- one fixed endpoint ('pendulum')

An object class exists for each one of these GE strains. Each GE line object accepts two desired endpoints $P$ and $Q$ as input, and in response, solves its internal constraint(s) and produces, as output, the points $P'$ and $Q'$ which it was able to adopt (as illustrated in Figure 3).

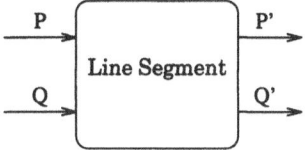

**Figure 3:** An example line segment GE with inputs $P$ and $Q$, and outputs $P'$ and $Q'$

Hence for an unconstrained line segment $P' = P$ and $Q' = Q$, whereas for a line segment of fixed length $a$, the equations might be $P' = P$ and $Q' = P' + a(Q - P)/|PQ|$. In other words, the line $PQ$ is simply scaled to length $a$ to produce line $PQ'$ which passes through $Q$.

In explaining how constraints between objects are handled in GICS, so called *schematic diagrams* are used. In these diagrams, input and output points are linked as shown in Figure 4.

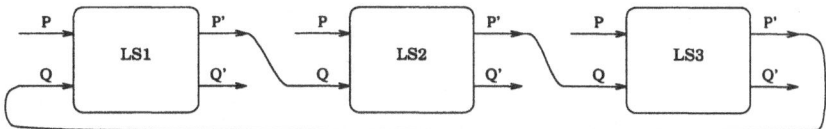

**Figure 4:** The schematic diagram for three line segments, constrained to form a triangle.

There is a trivial transformation from a schematic diagram to the solution code for a set of constraints. Values are simply fed from one GE to the next in the chain. A loop in the schematic diagram produces a loop in the solution code. Iteration through such loops continues until values converge to a stable state. To formulate the constraint illustrated in Figure 1 we will need the following GE's:

- *point on a line*, which accepts three input points $P, Q$ and $R$ and returns the point $R'$ on line $PQ$ which is closest to the point $R$.

- *fixed angle $\alpha$ line segment*, which accepts two proposed endpoints $P$ and $Q$, and outputs $P' = P$ and the point $Q'$ on the line through $P$ at angle $\alpha$ and closest to $Q$. In this example we set $\alpha$ such that the line $P'Q'$ is vertical.

- *fixed length line segment,* as described above.

These may then be composed as shown in the schematic diagram in Figure 5.

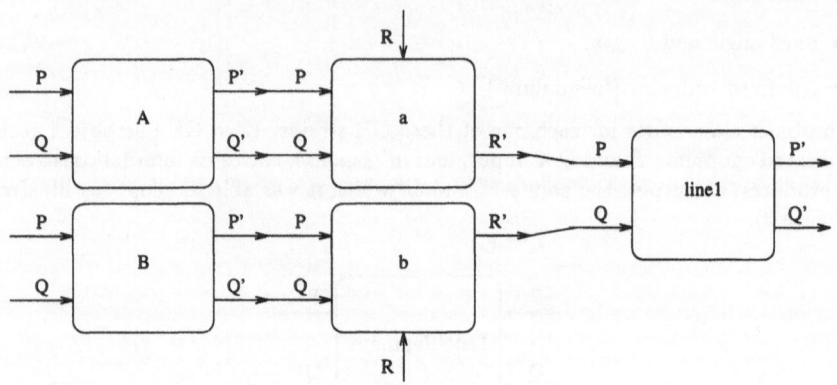

**Figure 5:** Schematic diagram representing the constraints in Figure 1.

A and B are fixed angle lines, a and b are 'point on line' GE's, and line1 is a fixed length line. Inputs which are not connected to outputs of a GE take their values from the current state of the model, or may be input via an external source, such as a mouse pointer.

The code derived from this first attempt schematic diagram does not in fact solve the given constraints. The reason for this is that solving of the length constraint on the fixed length line is performed locally by the constrained object, which does not have information relating to global constraints. It hence arbitrarily decides to scale the line in a particular direction, while this may in fact not be the best solution to the problem.

All is not lost however. By inserting a loop and a function call into the schematic diagram for each end of the fixed length line segment, it is possible to cause the resulting code to converge to a feasible solution.

Is this a satisfactory solution to the problem? First, potentially inefficient iteration has been introduced. More importantly though, the user composing the GE's into a useful model has been forced to express constraints in such a way as to suggest an iterative solution. Thus the declarative semantics of the constraints are compromised.

In addition, the user based his/her solution on knowledge of the way in which the various GE's in the loop solve their internal constraints. This implies that encapsulation of the GE objects has been broken. The primary aim of integrating declarative constraints with imperative object oriented programming is to combine the well-known benefits of both paradigms. The above constraint program seems to lose some of the benefits of both encapsulation and declarative programming.

On the other hand GE's are relatively easily created in GICS, while writing constrainable classes in OOCS is a considerable programming task (as discussed further in Section 8.1). In general, local propagation solvers like GICS place less burden on the programmer than OOCS, but local solution mechanisms can prove to be restrictive in many cases. While it may in certain cases be possible to work around these restrictions, the solutions are often unsatisfactory.

# References

[1] Harold Abelson and Gerald Jay Sussman. *Structure and Interpretation of Computer Programs*. The MIT Electrical Engineering and Computer Science Series. MIT Press, 1985.

[2] Edwin Blake. On Including Part Hierarchies in Object Oriented Languages with an Implementation in Smalltalk. In *European Conference on Object Orientated Programming*, 1987.

[3] G Booch. *Object Oriented Design with Applications*. Benjamin/Cummings, 1991.

[4] Alan H. Borning. The Programming Language Aspects of Thinglab. *ACM Transactions on Programming Languages and Systems*, 4(3):353–387, October 1981.

[5] Alan H. Borning, Robert Duisberg, Bjorn Freeman-Benson, Axel Kramer, and Michael Woolf. Constraint Hierarchies. In Norman Meyrowitz, editor, *OOPSLA '87*, OOPSLA, pages 48–60. ACM, ACM Press, October 1987.

[6] Eric Cournarie and Michel Beaudouin-Lafon. ALIEN: A Prototype-based Constraint System. In [14].

[7] Dennis Dingeldein. Modelling multimedia objects with MME. Chap. 7 of this book.

[8] Paris K. Egbert and Travis L. Hilton. *Mixed paradigm graphics*. Chap. 8 of this book.

[9] Bjorn N. Freeman-Benson. Kaleidoscope: Mixing Objects, Constraints and Imperative Programming. In Norman Meyrowitz, editor, *OOPSLA '90*, pages 77–88, Ottawa, Canada, October 1989. Object Oriented Programming: Systems, Languages and Applications, ACM Press.

[10] Bjorn N. Freeman-Benson. Integrating Constraints with an Object-Oriented Language. In *ECOOP '92 European Conference on Object-Oriented Programming*, pages 268–286. Springer-Verlag, Berlin, June 1992. This paper is all about Kaleidoscope '91.

[11] Bjorn N. Freeman-Benson, John Maloney, and Alan Borning. An Incremental Constraint Solver. *Communications of the ACM*, 33(1):54–63, January 1990.

[12] Adele Goldberg. *Smalltalk-80: the Language and its Implementation*. Addison-Wesley series in Computer Science. Addison-Wesley, May 1983.

[13] Chris Laffra. *PROCOL: A Concurrent Object Language with Protocols, Delegation, Persistence, and Constraints*. PhD thesis, Erasmus University, Rotterdam, May 1992.

[14] Chris Laffra, Edwin Blake, Vicky de Mey, and Xavier Pintado, editors. *Object-Oriented Programming for Graphics*. Springer-Verlag, 1995.

[15] W. Leler. *Constraint Programming Languages: Their Specification and Generation*. Addison Wesley Series in Computer Science. Addison-Wesley, 1988.

[16] Brad A. Myers, Dario A. Guise, and Brad van der Zanden. Declarative Programming in a Prototype-Instance System: Object-Oriented Programming Without Writing Methods. In Andreas Paepcke, editor, *OOPSLA '92 Conference on Object-Oriented Systems, Languages and Applications*, volume 27 of *ACM Sigplan Notices*, pages 184–200, Vancouver, British Columbia, Canada, October 1992. ACM, ACM Press.

[17] John R. Rankin. A Graphics Object Oriented Constraint Solver. In C. Laffra et al., editor, *Object-Oriented Programming for Graphics*, pages 71–91. Springer-Verlag, 1994.

[18] James Rumbaugh. Controlling Propagation of Operations Using Attributes on Relations. In Norman Meyrowitz, editor, *OOPSLA*, pages 285–296. ACM Press, November 1988.

[19] Greg Schechter, Conal Elliot, Ricky Yeung, and Salim Abi-Ezzi. *Functional 3D Graphics in C++ - with an Object-Oriented Multiple Dispatching Implementation*. Chap. 12 of this book.

[20] Ivan E Sutherland. Sketchpad: A Man Machine Graphical Communication System. In *Proceedings of the AFIPS Spring Joint Computer Conference*, pages 329–346, May 1963.

[21] Remco C. Veltkamp. A Quantum Approach to Geometric Constraint Satisfaction. In [14].

[22] Michael R. Wilk. Equate: An Object-Oriented Constraint Solver. In Andreas Paepcke, editor, *OOPSLA*, pages 286–298. ACM Press, October 1991.

[23] Andrew Witkin, Kurt Fleischer, and Alan Barr. Energy Constraints on Parameterized Models. In *Computer Graphics*, pages 225–2297, Anaheim, California, July 1987. ACM SIGGRAPH.

[24] R. Zeleznik et al. An Object Oriented Framework for the Integration of Interactive Animation Techniques. *ACM Computer Graphics (SIGGRAPH 91)*, 25(4):105–112, July 1991.

# 11

# Event-based.constraints: coordinate.satisfaction -> object.state [1]

Remco C. Veltkamp, Edwin H. Blake

This paper is about systems support for interactive computer graphics. The aim is to integrate the two major approaches to dealing with complexity in the design and implementation of such systems, namely, constraints and object-oriented programming.

The use of constraints in managing the complexity of designing interactive graphics systems and the use of object-oriented methods for describing simulations and systems of concrete objects have been two natural methods for building large complex graphics systems. This widely acknowledged way of dealing with the complexities of modelling and interface design has had disappointingly little practical impact.

We have identified a major cause for the lack of progress in combining constraints and object-oriented methods. We believe that a proper solution to the problem requires a radical separation of the constraint system and the normal object-oriented framework. In this paper we propose a way of dealing with these problems by means of two orthogonal communication strategies for objects: events and messages.

## 1 Introduction

The use of constraints in managing the complexity of designing interactive graphics systems and graphical user interfaces dates back to the earliest days of interactive graphics — consider Sutherland's Sketchpad from the early sixties [15]. Object-oriented methods with their usefulness for describing simulations and systems of concrete objects have been a natural method for building large complex graphics systems. The great benefits of class inheritance in user interface design is well recognized and is finding increasing commercial application.

The desirability of combining object-oriented methods and constraints has a similar venerable and distinguished lineage — a major system from the late seventies was Borning's ThingLab [5] which was written in Smalltalk. On the whole, and rather surprisingly, this widely acknowledged way of dealing with the complexities of modelling and interface design has had disappointingly little practical impact.

If one plans to use object-oriented methods to manage complexity in building interactive computer graphics systems, and if one also wants to provide constraints as a tool to manage the complexity of analysis, design, and interaction, then constraints and objects must be combined in a harmonious and coordinated whole. However, the integration of

---

[1] The syntax used in the title is explained in Section 6.

constraints and objects leads to conflicts in programming methodologies [10], and we believe that this is one of the major causes of the lack of application of constraints and their low profile within the mainstream object-oriented approach (another major problem is the difficulty in providing powerful and general constraint solving methods).

We distinguish two incompatibilities between constraints and object-oriented concepts:

- a constraint solver looks at, and sets, the constrained objects' internal data, which conflicts with the data encapsulation concept in the object-oriented paradigm;

- object-oriented programming is imperative, while constraint programming is declarative.

## 2  Constraints and Data Encapsulation

To illustrate the problem, let us look at an example, say from a geometric figure editor. Suppose we have a circle C with data fields x, y and r representing the centre and radius, an axis parallel rectangle R with data fields l, r, b, and t representing the left, right, bottom, and top sides (see Figure 1). Suppose further that we have the constraints that the objects touch each other and have equal area.

We could express our constraints as follows:

```
touching:    C.x+C.r=R.l
areas equal: π×C.r×C.r = (R.t-R.b)×(R.r-R.l)
```

A constraint solver may come with the following solution (see Figure 2):

```
C.x=5, C.r=1
R.l=6, R.r=7
R.b=0, R.t=π
```

Encapsulation is first violated by the constraint expressions, and then by expressing the solution. To avoid this problem, approaches based on message passing have been proposed. In [12], the methods of an object that may violate constraints are guarded by so-called propagators. The propagators send messages to other objects to maintain the constraints. This technique is similar to the pre- and postcondition facilities in Go [8] [6]. This approach is limited to constraint maintenance (i.e. truth maintenance, as opposed to starting with an inconsistent situation that is then resolved).

A more powerful technique is presented in [17]. The constraint solver produces a set of programs that solve constraints which are stated in the form of equations in terms of

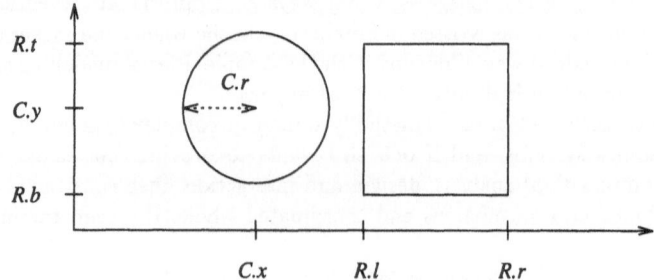

**Figure 1:** The circle and the rectangle must touch and must have equal area

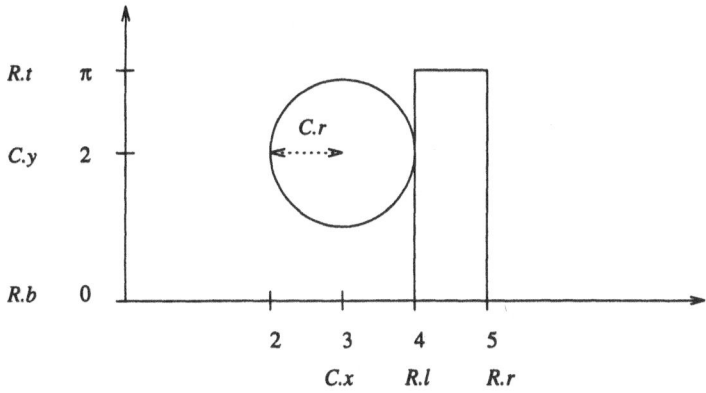

**Figure 2:** The circle and the rectangle touch and have equal area

messages to the objects. It translates a declarative constraint into procedural solutions in terms of messages back to objects. This amounts to the constraint system maintaining a view on the states of the objects. The constraint solver is then able to reason about the current state of the objects and propose procedures to fulfill the constraints.

For the above example, typical constraint equations would be:

```
left(R)=right(C)
area(C)=area(R)
```

And a possible solution is:

```
scale(C,distance(R)/radius)
scale(R,area(C)/area)
```

The problem here is that the second method destroys the first constraint, which must be repaired. Doing so destroys the second constraint, etc. The real problem is the local character of the solution. More powerful solution are necessarily global in nature. The danger is that all objects need methods to get and set their internal data. This however, allows every other object to get and set these values, which is clearly against the object-oriented philosophy.

One way to restrict this, is to have an object allow value setting only when its internal constraints remain satisfied (see [14]). A constraint could be made internal by constructing a 'container object', which contains the constraint and the operant objects, but this does not solve the basic problem. In particular, the state of active objects cannot be changed without their explicit cooperation. (Active objects, or actors, conceptually have their own processor and behave autonomously, which is typical in animation and simulation.) Another approach is to limit access to private data to constraint-objects or the constraint solver-objects only. For example C++ provides the 'friend' declaration to grant functions access to the private part of objects. This is also comparable to the approach taken by [7], where special variables (slots) are accessible by constraints only. One can argue that encapsulation is still violated (and specifically that the C++ friend construct is not intended to allow changing the state of an object). Alternatively one can see constraints more as a means to manipulate information in an orderly and restricted way, than that they violate the data encapsulation principle [16], i.e. they provide controlled violation [4].

## 3  Relations in the Object-Oriented Paradigm

It should be pointed out that the problem of integrating constraints in the object-oriented paradigm is a sub-class of the problem of expressing relations in general in object-oriented programming. Constraints are functional relations that restrict the values which variables in an object can assume. One simple way of avoiding the encapsulation problems associated with constraints would be to include the constrained objects as part of some larger container object. It should be obvious by now that this is no real solution [3].

However, we would expect that a good approach to combining constraints and objects would provide interesting and useful pointers to dealing with problems of aggregation, parts and wholes, and inter-object relationships in general. This in turn has clear connections with object-oriented database research.

## 4  Imperative Versus Declarative

Object-oriented languages are imperative, and thus use a notion of state, particularly represented by objects. On the other hand, pure constraint languages are declarative, and thus specify one single timeless state: the solution to the specified problem. Both paradigms can be combined as in [9], where an imperative assignment to a variable sets a value at one moment in time, and a declarative constraint dictates a value from that moment on.

However, active objects, or actors, behave totally independently and do not by themselves need to have a notion of some sort of global time. This holds in particular in simulation and animation applications if objects are modelled as concurrent autonomous entities. One aspect of time, however, is the synchronization of objects, such as the constraint that actions of objects take place in intervals that must overlap, or have an explicit ordering. Another type of constraints on time is for modelling object behaviour during the life time of the object.

One important issue involved with constraints and time is that if the solution depends on the order in which constraints are solved, then some of the declarative semantics is destroyed.

## 5  Combining Objects and Constraints

The justification for combining objects and constraints derives from the fact that it addresses the problems of complexity in large interactive graphical systems which arises on two fronts. The first is the complexity inherent in specifying the behaviour of animations and interactions with many components or objects. Constraints allow the declarative modelling of the behaviour of such systems. The second front is the complexity due to the fact that we are dealing with large software systems. Sound software engineering principles, such as data encapsulation, are needed to cope with large complex software systems.

It appears that all constraint systems in an object-oriented environment infringe the data encapsulation principle to some extent. The debugging of the constraint *satisfaction* routines, which have global effects, is the responsibility of the system programmer who provides the whole interactive graphical programming environment. At least the responsibility for integrity is shifted from the constraint user to the constraint system implementor. A problem that remains is the difficulty of debugging a constraint *specification*, due to the global effects of constraints. However, these global effects should be contained within a declarative constraint programming environment where the well known techniques of declarative software engineering are applicable (e.g., provability, executable specifications).

The time complexity of constraint satisfaction depends on both the domain and the kind of constraints. For example, linear constraints over real numbers can be solved in polynomial time, discrete constraint satisfaction problems are NP-complete, a single polynomial constraint of degree higher than four does not even have an analytical solution, and the complexity for integer polynomials of degree greater than two is still unknown. An interesting conjecture is that in the absence of global information of some kind, "interesting" constraint resolution will require exponential time [personal communication, Wilk]. It might be interesting to prove the NP completeness of an identified class of constraint resolution methods under the assumption of strict data encapsulation.

Concluding, powerful constraint solvers are global in nature and are hard to integrate with objects. Wilk's solution [17] is too complex to be really useful, and the global view on the object states does not reduce resolution complexity. Rankin's approach [14] does not allow powerful constraint solvers. The integration of Freeman-Benson [9, 10] has been taken about as far as it can in terms of efficiency. By contrast, we believe that it is worthwhile to explore a solution that keeps the paradigms distinct and does not compromise the benefits which they severally confer.

## 6    Event-Based Constraint Handling

We believe that a proper solution to the problem requires a radical separation of the constraint system and the normal object-oriented framework. In this paper we propose a way of dealing with these problems by means of orthogonal communication strategies for objects. These are events and data streams on one hand, and messages on the other hand.

*Events* are globally broadcast communications which can be received selectively. When they are received, events cause a pre-emptive invocation of routines (interrupts). Events can be generated by state changes in objects. A *stream* is a connection between an output and an input port of processes, for example objects. Coordinators determine how these objects are interconnected by streams and how their interaction pattern changes during the execution life of the system. *Messages* are the normal communications between objects in the object-oriented sense.

For the modelling of the interaction pattern we use the Manifold model of coordination [2]. The focus of this model is on the coordination of processes and on their communication, not on the computations performed by some of the processes. These processes are considered as black boxes whose behaviour is abstracted to their input and output. The communication is supported by two mechanisms: data-flow streams and event broadcasting. The data-flow streams form a network of streams, linking input and output ports of the processes and carrying the units exchanged between them. The event broadcasting mechanism provides control on the dynamical modification of the data-flow network.

Atomic processes are external for Manifold, and atomic in the sense that they are considered as black boxes of which no internal feature or behaviour is known. At the level of Manifold, they cannot be decomposed further than their input and output channels. An atomic process can:

- raise an event,

- take a unit from a stream connected to an input port,

- put a unit out to the streams connected to an output port.

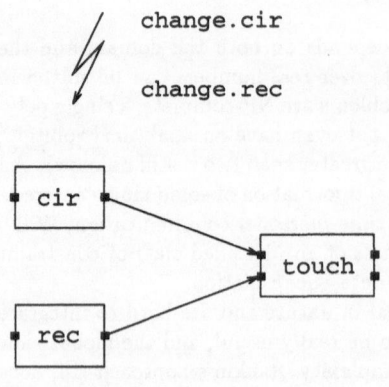

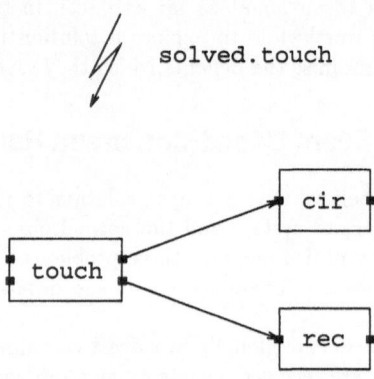

**Figure 3:** Data-flow networks controlled by coordinator `touch_coord`, triggered by the events

Streams carry units from the output port to the input port. There is no assumption about the contents of units, this is left to computations in atomic processes. A 'coordinator' is a process that sets up and breaks down streams between processes, i.e. a data-flow network. When an event is raised the previous network is dismantled and the new network is set up.

In the syntax of Manifold, `ev.obj` denotes the event `ev` raised by object `obj`, and `obj1.out -> obj2.in` denotes the linking of output port `out` of `obj1` to the input port `in` of `obj2` by a stream. `(a,b)` is the parallel composition of `a` and `b`, where `a` and `b` are processes or streams. The full syntax is described in [1]. (This syntax is also used in the title.)

A possible coordinator for a global solution of the above example may partially look as follows:

```
touch_coord(cir,rec,touch)
process cir, rec, touch.
{ event wait.
```

```
start:              do wait.

change.cir:         (cir->touch.in1, rec->touch.in2).
change.rec:         (cir->touch.in1, rec->touch.in2).
satisfied.touch:    do wait.
solved.touch:       (touch.out1->cir,touch.out2->rec).

wait:               (cir,rec).
}
```

Event **change** from either `cir` or `rec` causes the creation of a communication network from the constraint operands to the constraint (see Figure 3). In this example the constraint touch itself does the satisfaction. If it finds a solution, it raises the event `solved.touch`. Then the coordinator creates streams from the constraint to the operand objects. The coordinator only creates the communication network, all the atomic processes are responsible for actually doing something.

## 7  Object and Constraint Models

We want a change of a variable to lead to the checking of the validity of constraints on the variable. A possible approach is to have a central data base with values of the object member variables, and a data manager. Satellites processes could then subscribe to events such as changing variables. When an event occurs, the data manager notifies all satellites that subscribed to that event. The concept of such a central data manager is hard to combine with object-oriented concepts such as data encapsulation.

In Manifold, all the objects conceptually are active objects. This means that every object has its own virtual processor with its own thread of control (as mentioned in section 2). When the value of an object's variable is changed, we let it raise the event **change**.

We are currently exploring two alternative approaches to modelling constraints. In the first approach, the constraints are solved and maintained in Manifold. In this way the application objects and the constraints are completely orthogonal. The communication between the objects and the constraint side is via data streams set up under Manifold control.

In the second approach, constraints are modeled as objects, just like the application objects. In this scheme, each constraint object `cstr` has an associated shadow coordinator `cstr_coord` (like `touch_coord` in the example above). The coordinator can listen to an event **change** for each of the constraint operands. The constraint coordinator can then decide to perform global or local satisfaction.

If the constraints are ordinary objects, the application programmer could create new constraint classes and new operand classes. The system should automatically generate the event raising behaviour of the objects, input and output ports for communication with Manifold, and the shadow coordinators for constraint objects. The programmer has to provide methods to write data into the output port and to read from the input port that are consistent with those at the other side of the stream, i.e. the stream between a constraint and an operand. This defines an interface between the two. In this way, the state of an object can be completely read and set, but the exact implementation of the object remains hidden. Note however that this state can only be read and set from the Manifold side, not by the other application objects.

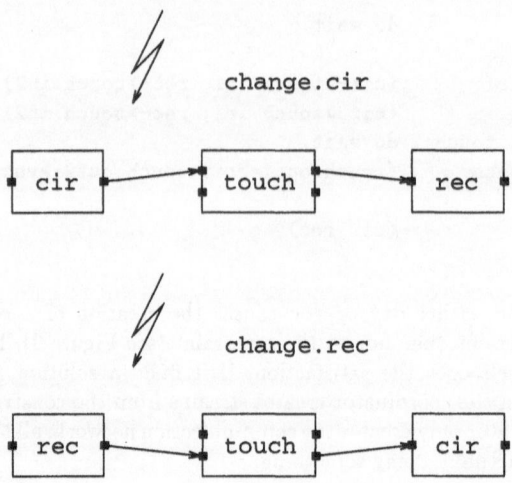

**Figure 4:** Local propagation networks controlled by `local_touch_coord`

## 8 Implications

We are currently exploring the implications of these two alternatives in terms of functionality, style, and ease of use. One of the implications of the separation of objects and constraints management is that several satisfaction techniques can easily be used in one system. Indeed it may be profitable to use a class of algorithms that can be used to eliminate local (node, arc, and path) inconsistencies [13] before any attempt is made to construct a complete solution. Another possibility is the combination of propagation of degrees of freedom and propagation of known states (also just called local propagation). Propagating degrees of freedom amounts to discarding all parts of the constraint network that can be satisfied easily and solving the rest by some other method. Propagation of degrees of freedom identifies a part in the network with enough degrees of freedom so that it can be changed to satisfy all its constraints. That part and all the constraints that apply to it are then removed from the network. Deletion of these constraints may give another part enough degrees of freedom so as to satisfy all its constraints. This continues until no more degrees of freedom can be propagated. The part of the network that is left is then satisfied by some global method. The result can now be propagated towards the discarded parts, which are successively satisfied (propagation of known states).

Local propagation is easily coordinated. In our example this could be done in the following way (see Figure 4):

```
local_touch_coord(cir,rec,touch)
process cir, rec, touch.
{ event wait.

    start:              do wait.

    change.cir:         (cir->touch.in1, touch.out2->rec).
    change.rec:         (rec->touch.in2, touch.out1->cir).
    satisfied.touch:    do wait.
```

```
   wait:               (cir,rec).
}
```

A change of one of the constraint operands results in the raising of an event. This causes `local_touch_coord` to create streams from the altered object to the constraint, and from the constraint to the other object. The constraint is responsible for finding a new solution for the other object.

Some situations allow an even simpler coordination. For example after a local distortion of the constraint, e.g. by a method 'translate' of `cir`. For such methods that make constraints fail, corresponding events (e.g. `translate.cir`) may trigger local propagation similar to the approach in [12]:

```
   translate.cir: (cir.out -> rec.in).
```

The above examples are by no means complete, but give a flavour of the type of solution we propose. In our approach we retain strict encapsulation for all modelling of concrete objects. Relationships between objects which cannot logically be ascribed to the internal actions of a container object are expressed in terms of constraints. These constraints may be global but the referential transparency of functional relationships allows one to reason about them and prove their correctness. The proofs of correctness will of course only apply provided the objects, which are regarded as atomic objects from the point of view of constraints, act according to specifications. All modelling of objects with states and behaviour is done in the normal object-oriented framework. In this framework correctness depends (as it always did) on correct program design, using concepts such as modularity and hierarchical decomposition.

One of our next research goals is to model the satisfaction of meta-constraints and higher-order constraints. The strict separation between coordination and functionality of constraint satisfaction provides a way to handle constraints on the satisfaction mechanism (meta-constraints), and constraints on constraints (higher-order constraints).

## 9 Conclusions

This paper proposes a relevant and important contribution to systems support for interactive computer graphics. This contribution, the combination of constraints and object-oriented methods, has been much heralded but has yet to arrive. We believe that we have identified a major cause for this lack of progress.

The problem is to combine two important approaches to software engineering: object-oriented and declarative programming, in casu constraint programming. The two naturally come together in computer graphics when the behaviour of active objects is partly modelled through constraints. Several approaches to integrate constraints and objects have been taken, see section 5. We have proposed a solution that keeps the object-oriented and constraint programming paradigms distinct and does not compromise the benefits which they severally confer.

The results of our research will lead to better design, analysis, and implementation of interactive graphics systems. The abstraction developed will have immediate application in graphical simulation and visualization as well as graphical user interface management systems. More generally a way of expressing relations between objects, within a robust software engineering based approach, is urgently needed in multimedia applications and other complex interactive graphical applications.

This paper describes a research project in progress. We are currently elaborating and implementing the alternative object and constraint models with the event-based mechanism. Our next research goal is to model the satisfaction of meta-constraints and second-order constraints. This enhances the power of constraint resolution, which alleviates a second reason for the lack of impact of constraints in the object-oriented approach: the lack of powerful and general satisfaction techniques.

The example of the touch-constraint on the rectangle and the circle has been implemented in C++ and Manifold. A complete demo program is available for ftp in the directory ftp.cwi.nl:/pub/remco/EventBasedConstraints.

## Acknowledgements

We like to thank Richard Kelleners for programming the Manifold demo. This research has been supported in part by NWO (Dutch Organization for Scientific Research) under Grants NF-51/62-514, SION-612-322-212, and SION-612-31-001.

## References

[1] F. Arbab. Specification of Manifold. Technical Report CS–9220, CWI, Amsterdam, The Netherlands, 1992.

[2] F. Arbab, I. Herman, and P. Spilling. An Overview of Manifold and its Implementation. *Concurrency: Practice and Experience*, 5(1):23 – 70, February 1993.

[3] E. H. Blake and S. Cook. On Including Part Hierarchies in Object-Oriented Languages, with an Implementation in Smalltalk. In *Proc. ECOOP'87*, volume 276 of *Lect. Notes Comp. Sci.*, pages 41–50. Springer-Verlag, Berlin, 1987.

[4] Edwin H. Blake and Quinton Hoole. Expressing Relationships Between Objects: Problems and Solutions. In *Proceedings of the Third Eurographics Workshop on Object-Oriented Graphics*, Champery, Switzerland, 1992.

[5] Alan Borning. The Programming Language Aspects of ThingLab, a Constraint-Oriented Simulation Laboratory. *ACM Transactions on Programming Languages and Systems*, 3(4):353 – 387, October 1981.

[6] Bull – Imaging and Office Solutions. *GoPATH 1.2.0 — A Path To Object Oriented Graphics, a public domain environment for graphical and interactive application development*, 1993.

[7] Eric Cournarie and Michel Beaudouin-Lafon. Alien: a Prototype-Based Constraint System. In [11].

[8] Jacques Davy. Go, A Graphical and Interactive C++ Toolkit for Application Data Presentation and Editing. In *Proceedings 5th Annual Technical Conference on the X Window System*, 1991.

[9] Bjorn N. Freeman-Benson. Kaleidoscope: Mixing Objects, Constraints, and Imperative Programming. *(ECOOP/OOPSLA '90 Proceedings) SIGPLAN Notices*, 25(10):77 – 88, October 1990.

[10] Bjorn N. Freeman-Benson and Alan Borning. Integrating Constraints with an Object-Oriented Language. In O. Lehrmann Madsen, editor, *Proceedings ECOOP'92 – European Conference on Object-Oriented Programming, Utrecht, 1992*, Lecture Notes in Computer Science 615, pages 268 – 286. Springer-Verlag, 1992.

[11] Chris Laffra, Edwin Blake, Vicky de Mey, and Xavier Pintado, editors. *Object-Oriented Programming for Graphics*. Springer-Verlag, 1995.

[12] Chris Laffra and Jan van den Bos. Propagators and Concurrent Constraints. *OOPS Messenger*, 2(2):68 – 72, April 1991.

[13] Alan K. Mackworth. Consistency in Networks of Relations. *Artificial Intelligence*, 8:99 – 118, 1977.

[14] John R. Rankin. A Graphics Object Oriented Constraint Solver. In [11].

[15] Ivan E. Sutherland. Sketchpad: A Man-Machine Graphical Communication System. In *Proceedings of the Spring Joint Computer Conference, Detroit, Michigan, May 21-23 1963*, pages 329 – 345. AFIPS Press, 1963.

[16] Remco C. Veltkamp. A Quantum Approach to Geometric Constraint Satisfaction. In [11].

[17] Michael Wilk. Equate: an Object-Oriented Constraint Solver. In *Proceedings OOPSLA '91*, pages 286 – 298, 1991.

# 12

# Functional 3D Graphics in C++ – with an Object-Oriented, Multiple Dispatching Implementation [1]

Greg Schechter, Conal Elliott, Ricky Yeung, Salim Abi-Ezzi

Constructing interactive, animated 3D graphics applications has been notoriously difficult for well over twenty years. Even though significant advances in the state- of-the-art have been made, this situation persists. The system described here simplifies the programmatic construction of geometry in ways that we have not seen elsewhere, and does so within the framework of an accepted production language, C++. It has been our experience that the resulting programs are quite succinct and comprehensible, and execute efficiently. The programmer is presented with a simple, general interface that is both declarative and conforms to the functional programming paradigm. Pursuing a functional interface for developing interactive 3D applications is a novel concept that, in our experience, has been successful in providing a simple, powerful interface and a relatively straightforward implementation. The implementation of the system is highly object-oriented, relying heavily upon multiple dispatching. The system itself is extensible and adding new geometric primitives and operations is straightforward. Entirely new media types, such as sound and image, may be (and have been) added to the system.

## 1 Introduction

This paper has two primary goals. The first is to describe the programmer's interface to the geometry-specific layer of the TBAG system, and communicate the level of expressiveness that can be achieved by using this interface. The second is to describe an efficient implementation of the interface that also allows for straightforward extensibility of the system.

TBAG is a general framework for creating interactive, time-varying integrated media applications, and is discussed in detail in [4]. The geometry layer is a C++ interface for constructing and processing geometry "values". This interface conforms to the functional programming paradigm [5] and is very simple, yet general and powerful. It has been our experience that programs written with this interface are more succinct, comprehensible, and amenable to aggressive optimization techniques when compared with programs written using any other system we have seen.

[1] This work was done at SunSoft, Inc.,2250 Garcia Av., Mountain View, CA 94025 USA. Greg Schechter, Conal Elliot, and Ricky Yeung are currently at Microsoft Corporation, One Microsoft Way, Redmond, WA 98052-6399 USA

Our interface has an efficient, highly object-oriented implementation. Furthermore, the system[2] is highly extensible in the sense that it is straightforward to add new geometric primitives and attributes as well as new operations to be performed on geometry values. The system may be, and has been, further extended to support additional media types, such as sound and image.

While TBAG provides sophisticated support for modeling interaction and time, for network distribution, and for the construction of collaborative applications, detailed discussion of these aspects is beyond the scope of this paper. The reader is encouraged to consult [4] for more information on the aspects of TBAG not discussed here.

We believe that our approach of providing one programming paradigm (namely, the functional paradigm) to best meet the needs of the community using the interface, and another programming paradigm (the object-oriented paradigm) to best meet the needs of the extenders and implementers of the system is rare, and possibly unique, in the world of 3D graphics systems. In what is perhaps a somewhat heretical position to take within the object-oriented graphics community, we shall attempt to show why we feel that the functional approach is more appropriate for the user of the interface we provide, and how a functional interface can be provided while still retaining an efficient object-oriented approach for extension and implementation.

## 2  Related Work

Easing the construction of interactive 3D applications has been a primary goal of a number of commercial and research systems. Traditional display list systems such as PHIGS [7], HOOPS [15], and Doré [10] have existed for up to ten years and are available on a wide range of computers and operating systems. The design of these systems was largely driven by the capabilities of the graphics hardware that existed at the time. Thus, these systems are not known for their expressiveness or their simplicity.

More recent advances in object-oriented graphics systems have produced Mirage [14], Inven tor [11], GEO++ [16], and GROOP [9]. These systems go a long way towards simplifying the conceptual model presented to the programmer. However, we don't believe that they afford as simple a representation of geometry as our system does, nor do they allow the same opportunities for aggressive optimization.

[1] describes a functional approach to specifying discrete frames of an animation, but doesn't address the issue of constructing geometry. The Fugue system [3], takes a functional approach to describing computer-generated music similar to our functional approach used for describing geometry, but invents its own language in the process. We know of no other system that provides a functional interface for geometry construction, let alone one that is targeted at building interactive applications using an accepted production language such as C++.

Inventor supports a multiple dispatching facility similar to the one described in Section 6.3. These facilities were developed independently and achieved similar results (although the facility presented here can be used in arbitrary places, unlike Inventor's).

---

[2]In this chapter, when we refer to the *system*, the *interface*, or the *implementation*, we mean the geometry-specific layer of the TBAG framework. When we are referring to TBAG itself, we explicitly say *TBAG*.

Mirage and DIVER [6] provide for a declarative specification of lights, similar in result, if not in form, to that described in Section 7.1.

## 3   Programmer's Interface to the TBAG Geometry Layer

The geometry layer is accessed through a functional programming interface that defines a number of abstract data types, constant values of these types, functions for creating values of these types ("construction functions"), and functions for combining values of these types into new values ("combination functions"). Note that there are no mechanisms provided to alter these values once they have been constructed. This principle of immutability results in many of the simplifications we have achieved, without sacrificing flexibility or efficiency. As mentioned in the introduction, we know of no other functional interface for constructing 3D geometry, let alone an interface in as commonly accepted a language as C++.

### 3.1   Types and Their Meanings

Values of type Geometry simply represent three-dimensional geometry. Some of the operations in our system allow Geometry values to be rendered into a frame buffer, to be intersected with a ray (in order to perform picking), to have their bounding box calculated, to have their shadow geometry created, etc.

When a value of type Attributer is applied to a Geometry value, a new Geometry value is created attributed with the Attributer. For example, if we attribute a cube geometry with the Attributer edges_on, the resulting geometry will be a solid cube with visible edges. The attribution operation is further discussed in Section 3.4.

Values of type Transform represent a geometrical transformation that can be applied to Geometry values to create a transformed geometry value. Unlike most systems, ours does not require Transforms to have a 4x4 matrix representation – in fact, the internal representation is completely hid den from the programmer. This allows our system to be extended to include new types of transformations, such as deformations, that cannot be represented as a 4x4 matrix.

In addition to Geometry, Attributer, and Transform, the system also provides types such as Color, Point, Vector, Axis, Quaternion, etc. From the point of view of the application programmer, types do not have a subclassing or inheritance relationship with other types. This is unlike most object-oriented graphics systems, and the reason for this will be explained in Section 4.3.

### 3.2   Constant Values

Following are some declarations of constant values of various types. (TBAG is fully accessible through C++, and all of the examples in this paper are given in C++.)[3]:

```
extern Geometry&  cube;
extern Geometry&  sphere;
extern Geometry&  line_segment;
extern Color&  red;
extern Attributer&  invisible;
extern Transform&  identity_trans;
```

---

[3]The geometry interface is also completely accessible through standard C, with the exception of the overload operators + and *, for which other functions may be substituted.

```
extern Point&  origin;
extern Vector&  x_vector;
```

Note that C++ references (denoted by the ampersand) are used for most of the values. We find this preferable to using pointers. (Additionally, pointer values cannot be used with overloaded operators in C++ – a facility we make considerable use of.)

New values are created either by using a construction function or a combination function, as described below.

## 3.3  Construction Functions

Here are C++ declarations for a few construction functions:

```
// Color creation
extern Color& rgb_color(float r, float g, float b);
extern Color& hsv_color(float hue, float saturation, float value);

// Vector creation
extern Vector& rect_vector(float x, float y, float z);
extern Vector& spherical_vector(float theta, float phi, float rho);

// Axis creation
extern Axis& axis_along_vector(Vector& vec);

// Transform creation
extern
  Transform& xlt(float x, float y, float z); // translation
extern
  Transform& scale(float x, float y, float z); // non-uniform scale
extern
  Transform& rot(Axis& axis, float angle); // rotation
extern
  Transform& rot_from_quat(Quaternion& quat); // rotation

// Attributer creation
extern
  Attributer& front_color(Color& col); // front coloring Attributer

// modeling transform Attributer
extern Attributer& model_xform(Transform& xf);

// Geometry creation
extern Geometry& stroke_text(char *text, Point& position,
  Vector& horizontal_vec,
  Vector& vertical_vec);
extern Geometry& regular_polygon(int num_sides);
```

Note that there are often multiple ways to construct values of a given type. For instance, a Color may be created by specifying either RGB values or HSV values, a Vector may be created by specifying either Cartesian coordinates or spherical coordinates, etc. The internal representation of the values is completely hidden from the programmer.

### 3.4  Combination Functions

The geometry layer of TBAG derives much of its expressiveness from the way in which values may be combined to create new values. The two primary combination functions provide *aggregation* and *attribution*:

```
extern Geometry& operator+(Geometry& geo1, Geometry& geo2);
extern Geometry& operator*(Geometry& geo, Attributer& attr);
```

The "+" operator allows two Geometries to be combined into a new Geometry, and the "*" operator allows an Attributer to be applied to a Geometry and result in a new Geometry. Some examples:

```
// combination of cube, line segment, and cone
cube + line_segment + cone

cube * front_color(red) // a red cube
cube * model_xform(xlt(1,1,1)) // a translated cube

// a translated red cube
cube * front_color(red) * model_xform(xlt(1,1,1))

// a translated, rotated red cube
cube * front_color(red) * model_xform(xlt(1,1,1))
* model_xform(rot(y_axis, pi/4))
```

Since attributing Geometry with a color or with a modeling transformation is such a common operation, we provide additional overloadings for "*" that allow a Color[4] or a Transform to be specified directly, rather than forcing them to be turned into Attributer's. This allows the last example to be rewritten as a more manageable:

```
cube * red * xlt(1,1,1) * rot(y_axis, pi/4)
```

Notice how these operations may be chained, and they compose as one would expect.

## 4  Design Principles Underlying the Interface

The above section described the interface to our system, without discussing any of the issues that influenced our design choices. Here we discuss these issues, and attempt to convey why we think the functional approach to specifying geometry is more concise, comprehensible, and amenable to optimization than other approaches we have seen, while retaining the useful flexibility that other systems possess.

---

[4]In fact, the overloading of * on applying a color to a Geometry results in setting a front color, back color, line color, and text color.

## 4.1  Immutability of Values

One of the most important aspects of our system is that operations on values always construct new values, rather than altering existing values. Thus, `cube*red` does not change the color of cube to red, rather it creates a new geometry that represents a red cube. This is a key feature of the functional programming paradigm – values are constructed, not altered.

We say that our values are *immutable* in that, once constructed, there is no way to alter them. Thus, unlike most object-oriented graphics systems, these values are not "objects" in the traditional sense – they do not have mutable state nor do they have the corresponding methods to alter that mutable state. While at first this may seem like a debilitating restriction, we shall see in 5 why this is not the case. In fact, we shall see how this approach allows programs to be more succinct, more comprehensible, more amenable to both multithreading and aggressive optimization techniques, and provide straightforward support for network distribution. This approach may also introduce major concerns about efficiency. We shall show how our implementation overcomes these concerns.

## 4.2  Simplicity and Efficiency for Multithreaded Applications

Many multithreaded or re-entrant software systems become considerably more complex when they start having to deal with issues of mutual exclusion and locking around critical code sections in order to maintain a consistent shared state. In addition to the complexity of adding code to ensure consistency, such code also tends to decrease the level of concurrency achievable in such systems, since all other threads are locked out while one thread is in a critical section of code.

The functional approach of producing immutable values considerably simplifies the writing of multithreaded code that manipulate such values. Since the values are immutable, any number of threads can simultaneously access the same value without any fear of inconsistency or corruption. As a result, very high levels of concurrency may be achieved.

## 4.3  To Subtype or Not to Subtype?

We mentioned earlier that the programmer is not exposed to any subtyping or inheritance relationships between the types available in the system. Subtyping of an interface, when used properly, has the effect of extending the set of methods (protocol) available. From the point of view of the TBAG application programmer, subtyping is not useful, because all of our values are immutable (so they needn't have methods that alter their properties), and because they are all capable of responding to the base protocol defined by the abstract type itself. Moreover, introducing subtypes encourages the introduction of functions and methods that can only operate on values of that subtype, thus making the interface less general. Our approach of not exposing subtyping increases the amount of information hiding or encapsulation in the system, bringing along the accompanying well-known benefits of information hiding.

Clearly, however, subtyping is a useful tool to be taken advantage of when it comes to extending a system. It is desirable to re-use as much interface and implementation as is possible. So how do we provide this advantage and still not expose subtyping to the programmer? The answer lies in our insistence on a strong separation between the needs of the application programmer and the needs of the system extender. We believe that with any successful system, while extensibility has to be straightforward, it is not as important as usability for the user who is not interested in extending the system. Thus, a system should not complicate the programmer's model for the sake of the extender. A successful system will have a large community of users, the majority of whom do not extend the system, while a minority do extend the system.

To be consistent with this separation, we do not expose the programmer to any subtyping or inheritance relationships, but the system extender does have access to this information, and can do his or her own further subclassing when appropriate, thus re-using both interface and implementation.

## 4.4  Leveraging of Programming Language Facilities

As a design principle, we leave support for generally useful facilities to the host programming language wherever possible, thus distilling geometry support into as simple a form as possible, while allowing great flexibility and ease of expression. Consider creating a rectangular block with a ball on top of it, and having this geometry parameterized by the color of the ball and the transformation that gets applied to the entire geometry. Rather than introducing a new mechanism into our system that allows for the parameterization of geometry, such as PHIGS structures or Inventor Node Kits, we simply use functions that may be defined in the host language (in this case, C++):

```
Geometry&
block_with_ball(Transform& xform, Color& color)

    return (cube * scale(1,4,1) * color   // colored cube
        + sphere * xlt(0,2,0) * yellow)   // + yellow sphere
        * xform;   // all transformed by xform
```

We now have a standard C++ function that represents the desired parameterized geometry.

## 4.5  Expressiveness of the Interface

As a measure of expressiveness, it's useful to compare how one would achieve a comparable result through a number of different systems. Consider creating a geometry that consists of a cube with edges turned on and a blue sphere, all of which are designated as unpickable. In TBAG, this would be expressed quite naturally and succinctly as:

$$(cube * edges\_on + sphere * blue) * unpickable \qquad (12.1)$$

Note that in this expression, we specify what the geometry is, rather than specifying how to draw it.

In a traditional graphics system, like PHIGS, Hoops, or Doré, the Geometry in 12.1 would be expressed roughly as:

```
push pickability
set unpickable
push current edge flag
set edges on
execute cube
pop current edge flag
push current color
set color to blue
```

```
execute sphere
pop current color
pop pickability
```

Aside from being quite verbose, this latter expression forces the programmer to think in terms of a machine model of a graphics context and forces a description of how to draw the geometry.

The newer crop of object-oriented graphics systems, such as Inventor, GEO++, and GROOP, would express the Geometry more like:

```
c = new Cube;
c->set_edges_on(True);

s = new Sphere;
s->set_color(Blue);

g = new Group;
g->add(c);   // add the cube to the group
g->add(s);   // add the sphere to the group
g->set_pickable(False);   // make the entire group unpickable
```

While this is considerably more understandable than the PHIGS style, it is still quite verbose and less comprehensible when compared with TBAG's expression of the geometry. It also leaves less room for the implementation to transparently perform geometry optimizations.

Why is TBAG so much more succinct and expressive than other systems? One aspect of the answer lies in our use of the syntactic features available in C++ make expression of Geometry quite natural. But the more fundamental reason is that we don't have to worry about being able to edit geometry. All of the other cited systems have mechanisms that allow the editing of geometry, introducing considerable complexity into the entire interface.

## 5   Integration of the Geometry Layer into TBAG

The description of the geometry construction interface above focuses on creating static geometry values. A reader would be reasonably concerned about how this interface, with immutable values and no editing facilities, could be used to construct interactive, animated geometry. This section addresses that concern by describing the TBAG system itself. TBAG is a client of the Geometry-specific layer, and addresses issues that would be experienced by any system that built on top of the interface described above. TBAG provides mechanisms that let one express it time-varying (i.e., animated and/or interactive) geometry in ways virtually identical to expressing static geometry values. We provide a very brief description of the facilities available in TBAG for doing this. The reader is encouraged to consult [4] for more information.

TBAG is based on a very efficient local-propagation constraint solver, that, although it is by no means completely general, can solve an interesting and very useful subset of constraint problems. TBAG exposes the notion of a it constrainable, which is an entity that may be involved in a constraint relationship. Constrainables are parameterized according to the type of the value they hold, and this type parameterization is expressed with C++

templates. There is a primitive Real-valued constrainable called Time that represents absolute time in seconds, and it may be used in constructing other constrainables. Some examples:

```
// cone rotating about the Y axis by 1 radian per second
Constrainable<Geometry&> geo = cone * rot(y_axis, Time);

// Pulsating block with ball whose hue is determined by Time,
// and whose scale is determined by the absolute value
// of the sine of Time. This makes use of the function
// we defined in Section 4.4.
Constrainable<Geometry&> geo =
block_with_ball(uniform_scale(fabs(sin(Time))),
    hsv_color(Time, 1, 1))

// Constrainables may be parameterized as other types as well.
// Here, we construct a time-varying Point whose q and f
// are time-varying.
Constrainable<Point&> pt = spherical_point(Time, Time * 0.164, 1.0)
```

Note that many of the value construction functions that we saw in Section 3.3 are being used with constrainables as arguments. Even it block_with_ball, a function defined by an application programmer, is being used with constrainables. How does this work in a statically typed language like C++? TBAG provides a tool that processes header files and creates overloaded versions of the functions in the header files. These overloaded versions are chosen by the C++ compiler if constrainables are provided as arguments to them. This tool allows sets of functions that were written without TBAG in mind to be used from TBAG, with TBAG constrainables.

In addition to being able to be expressed in terms of Time, constrainables may be put into constraint relationships with other constrainables. The system maintains the constraint, even when the contents of one of the constrainables involved in the relationship changes. This is accomplished via the "assert" function. Some examples:

```
Constrainable<Transform&> xf1;
Constrainable<Transform&> xf2;

// Assert that the combination of xf1 and xf2 is the
// identity transform.
// This guarantees xf1 and xf2 to be inverses of each other.
assert(xf1 * xf2 == identity_trans);

// Create a geometry of two blocks_with_ball's, where one always
// has the inverse transform of the other.
Constrainable<Geometry&> geo = block_with_ball(xf1, red) +
                               block_with_ball(xf2, blue);

// Give xf1 an interesting trajectory. Because of its relationship
// to xf1, xf2 will automatically get the inverse trajectory,
// and thus both block_with_balls in geo will start moving.
```

```
assert(xf1 == rot(y_axis, Time) *
              uniform_scale(fabs(sin(Time)) *
              xlt(sin(Time), cos(Time * 3.0), sin(Time * -7.0))
```

Interaction is specified in much the same way as animation. The mouse, for instance, is abstracted as a time varying Point2D-valued constrainable. Asserting a constraint between the position of a geometry and the mouse constrainable causes the geometry to move when the mouse moves. Discrete events (for instance, a mouse button press) are dealt with by retracting some constraints and asserting others. For instance, when a mouse button is released, the constraint tying the geometry to the mouse can be retracted, and a constraint tying the geometry to its current position will be asserted.

These techniques for expressing relationships between different program entities, and the relationship between different entities and time, frees the programmer from having to concern himself with any notion of flow control. He does not need to write an animation loop, nor does he need to receive timer events or mouse motion events, he simply expresses relationships for the system to maintain.

Hopefully these examples make the point that the features available for constructing static geometry are available for creating interactive, animated geometry as well. Because of our approach, we do not need the editing facilities that most graphics systems provide (these are the same editing facilities that make the systems considerably more complex). For example, rather than replacing a transform within a hierarchical structure to affect animation, we simply express the animation up front, and the system conceptually creates an entire new geometry value at each frame. (It's important to realize that this construction of an entire new geometry value at each frame is purely conceptual. The actual implementation is smarter than that.)

## 6  Implementation of the Interface

We now turn our attention to how the interface described in the preceding sections is implemented. Remember that none of what we discuss here is visible to the application programmer. The primary implementation concept for the geometry layer of TBAG, from which most of the other implementation concepts flow, is that of rendering. When we speak of rendering, we mean in it in the broadest possible sense. Rendering refers to the processing of a geometry value in order to achieve some result. As mentioned earlier, we use rendering to draw geometry values into a frame buffer, perform ray intersection, extract bounding boxes, etc.

There is a single function, declared as

```
extern void render_geometry_in_context(Geometry& geo, Context& ctx);
```

that embodies all the rendering possibilities we are faced with. The specific action taken by render_geometry_in_context is dependent upon the specific types of geo and ctx.

To understand how this single function can be used to control all rendering possibilities, one must understand how Geometry and Context values are created and represented in the system, and how the multiple dispatching facility operates. The following sections discuss these issues, as well as the memory management techniques that we use to make our approach feasible, some non-obvious techniques that make good use of available computational power, and some geometry-specific optimizations we are able to perform because of the approach we take.

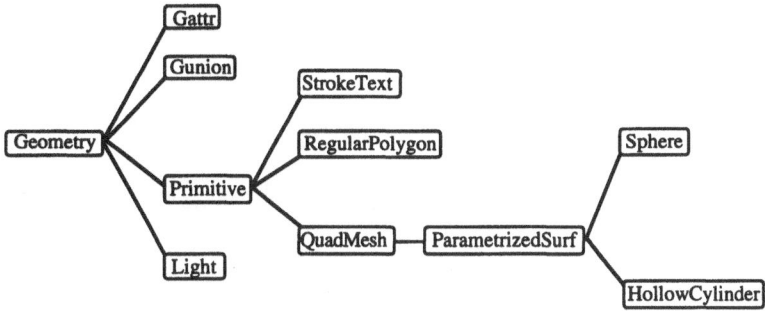

**Figure 1:** Partial class hierarchy for the `geometry` type

## 6.1 Representation of Geometry Values

Let's consider how geometry values are represented in the system. There is a class hierarchy extending from the Geometry abstract class that embodies all forms of geometry that may be created in the system. Here is a partial view of this hierarchy:

Remember, as discussed in Section 4.3, that this hierarchy is not visible to those programming in TBAG. It is visible solely to implementers and extenders.

As an example of how a Geometry value gets created, consider the combinational operator "+" (discussed in Section 3.4) applied to two Geometries to create a new Geometry. + is defined as:

```
Geometry&
operator+(Geometry& geo1, Geometry& geo2)
{
return *new Gunion(geo1, geo2);
}
```

and the Gunion subclass is defined as:

```
class Gunion : public Geometry {
  public:
    Gunion(Geometry& g1, Geometry& g2) : geo1(g1), geo2(g2)
DECLARE_TAG(Geometry);
Geometry& geo1;
Geometry& geo2;
};

DEFINE_TAG(Gunion, Geometry);
```

There are a few items to take note of here:

- Generally, construction and combination functions return references to new instances of Geometry subclasses.

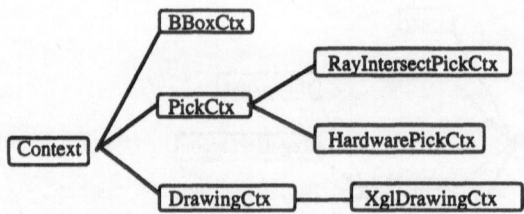

**Figure 2:** Partial class hierarchy for the `Context` type

- The `DECLARE_TAG(Geometry)` and `DEFINE_TAG(Gunion, Geometry)` declarations are used to provide run-time type information. The reason for this will be described further in Section 6.3.

- Note that there are no methods defined on our Gunion class. All interesting functionality will be provided via methods selected by multiple dispatching.

- The `Gattr` subclass shown in the figure is similar to the Gunion subclass, but represents attribution, and is constructed via the * operator on a Geometry and an Attributer.

## 6.2 Contexts and Their Representation

A "context" is a program entity that accumulates state during the processing (traversal) of a Geometry value. The system contains a number of different context types, each specialized for a different type of "rendering". Here is a partial class hierarchy:

A few notes:

- A BBoxCtx calculates the bounding box of the Geometry that's rendered into it.

- An XglDrawingCtx is a subclass of DrawingCtx, and uses SunSoft's XGL immediate mode 3D graphics library [13] to do the rendering into a frame buffer. Other subclasses may be added to use alternate 3D rendering engines.

- There are a couple of different approaches for picking. One uses the underlying hardware support (accessible through XGL), while the other does ray-intersection based picking. In our experience, ray intersection picking is both faster and is capable of providing more complete results, including surface intersection point and normal.

The representation of a Context includes member data reflecting the current state of the Geometry traversal. For instance, the BBoxCtx is expressed roughly as:

```
class BBoxCtx : public Context {
  public:
    DECLARE_TAG(Context);
    ...
    void swallow_bounding_box(BoundingBox& bbox);
    BoundingBox *current_bbox;
};

DEFINE_TAG(BBoxCtx, Context);
```

The `swallow_bounding_box()` method updates `current_bbox` to include the specified bounding box. When traversal of a Geometry is complete, `current_bbox` holds the Geometry's bounding box.

## 6.3 The Multiple Dispatching Facility

### Why we need multiple dispatching

The function `render_geometry_in_context` works by it multiply dispatching off of its two arguments, `geo` and it `ctx`. Multiple dispatching (sometimes referred to as *multiple polymorphism* or *multi-methods*) allows the code that actually gets selected to be executed (the "method") to be dependent upon the run-time types of two or more arguments of the "generic" function that was invoked. We borrow this terminology from CLOS, the CommonLisp Object System [8]. The "generic" function being discussed here is `render_geometry_in_context`.

C++ supports only single dispatching, meaning that, given a virtual function func, the expression

```
obj->func(arg)
```

selects the particular `func` method to be executed based solely upon the run-time type of `obj`. The run-time type of `arg` can play no part in determining which func gets selected. In TBAG, `render_geometry_in_context` must choose the particular method to execute by taking into account the runtime types of both `geo` and `ctx`.

Multiple dispatching is essential for TBAG to be able to be a truly extensible system. An extender of the system needs to be able to add both new Geometry subclasses and add new ways in which Geometry gets rendered (i.e., add new Context subclasses). If we only supported single dispatching, then we would either have to define our Geometry abstract class to have a member function per type of rendering we wanted to support:

```
class Geometry {
  public:
    virtual void render_to_xgl(XglDrawingCtx& ctx) = 0;
    virtual void render_for_bbox(BBoxCtx& ctx) = 0;
    ...
};
```

Or we would have to define our Context abstract class to have a member function per type of geometry subclass we wanted to support:

```
class Context {
  public:
    virtual void render_gunion(Gunion& geo) = 0;
    virtual void render_stroke_text(StrokeText& geo) = 0;
    ...
};
```

Both of these alternatives are completely unacceptable for a truly extensible system, since, in C++, it is impossible to add methods to an existing abstract class without altering header files and recompiling the entire system. So, we have created an efficient multiple dispatching facility that we use throughout the system.

Contrast this approach to extensibility with those offered by most other graphics systems. Most other systems only allow the introduction of new primitives and (occasionally) attributes via the subclassing of existing primitives and attribues. It is generally not possible for a system extender to add in a new type of operation.

We use multiple dispatching for more than just the `render_geometry_in_context` generic function. For example, `compose_transforms` takes two Transforms and composes them, returning a new Transform whose representation is dependent upon the argument's runtime types. For example, a rotation composed with a rotation yields another rotation, while a rotation composed with a scale returns a Transform represented by a 3x3 matrix. `compose_transforms` determines which method to invoke by multiply dispatching off of its two arguments.

Additionally, we use multiple dispatching to control the processing of attributes in contexts. For instance, the processing of a color may be ignored in a ray-intersection context, but must be honored in an XGL rendering context.

## Type tags

Since standard C++ doesn't currently expose any facility for portably retrieving run-time type information (RTTI), we need to provide our own facility for generating and accessing such information, in a portable fashion. The `DECLARE_TAG(AbstractClass)` and `DEFINE_TAG(Class, ParentClass)` macros used in conjunction with class definitions provide a per-class static "tag" that is unique across all tags declared to be part of `AbstractClass`. It also informs our run-time type facility that ParentClass is the most direct ancestor of the class in which the declaration is being made. In our implementation, the tag is simply a small integer. The static method `static_tag()` may be invoked on the class itself to retrieve the type tag of the class, while the method `tag()` may be used to retrieve the type tag of an object. Thus, to check if an object is of type `Gunion`, we could say:

```
Boolean is_gunion = (Gunion::static_tag() == obj->tag());
```

We need to supply `ParentClass` to the `DEFINE_TAG` macro in order for multiple dispatching to correctly reflect inheritance relationships amongst classes. As another example of the use of these macros, consider the declaration of the Sphere class, pictured in the class hierarchy in Figure 1.

```
class Sphere : public ParameterizedSurf {
public:
    ...
    DECLARE_TAG(Geometry, ParameterizedSurf);
};

DEFINE_TAG(Sphere, ParameterizedSurf);
```

Note that our inheritance specification currently supports only single inheritance. We have yet to find a requirement for multiple inheritance in our system, and multiple inheritance is a facility whose usefulness has been called into question many times in the past.

It's regrettable that we need to specify inheritance and declare tags at all, since this information is already known to the C++ compiler. However, as mentioned before, there is no portable way to access this information, thus we need to duplicate the information. Even more unfortunately, the proposed C++ extensions for run-time type information [12] do not provide all of the information that we need to support multiple dispatching (specifically, information about inheritance relationships is not accessible).

**Registering Methods**

In order for multiple dispatching to do the work we want it to do, we need to register methods to be executed with particular subclasses.

We do this via the REGISTER_DOUBLE_DISPATCH_METHOD macro. For instance, to register a method that extracts the bounding box out of a Sphere, we use:

```
REGISTER_DOUBLE_DISPATCH_METHOD(render_geometry_in_context,
    BboxCtx, Sphere, render_sphere_into_bbox_ctx);
```

A few comments:

- The first argument, render_geometry_in_context, is the generic function that this method is being registered for. It has been declared as a generic function elsewhere.

- Method registration occurs at system initialization time, prior to any generic functions being invoked.

- render_sphere_into_bbox_ctx is most appropriately thought of as a member function of both the BboxCtx class and the Sphere class, and should have the same access privileges that actual member functions of these classes have. However, since C++ does not recognize these methods as member functions, we need to define our classes such that instance data is declared public:, thus allowing these methods access to that data. This is why Gunion's geo1 and geo2 data members were declared public in Section 6.1.

The render_sphere_into_bbox_ctx function may be defined as:

```
static void
render_sphere_into_bbox_ctx(Sphere& geo, BboxCtx& ctx)
{
// sphere's are always unit dimensioned.
ctx.swallow_bounding_box(unit_bounding_box);
}
```

**The Method Table and Inheritance**

Conceptually, registering double dispatching methods on the generic function

`render_geometry_in_context()`

fills in a two-dimensional table of methods, with one axis representing the specific Geometry subtype and the other axis representing the specific Context subtype[5]. The method table may be sparsely populated, in that methods may not have been registered for every combination of argument types. It is the inheritance mechanism that determines which method to call if an empty table cell is reached by the dispatching facility. Consider the following simplified method table:

|   | A | B | C | D |
|---|---|---|---|---|
| X | 6 | 4 | 2 |   |
| Y | 5 | 3 | 1 |   |
| Z |   |   |   |   |

Here, with "$P \leftarrow Q$" meaning "P inherits from Q", we have
$$Z \leftarrow Y \leftarrow X$$
and
$$D \leftarrow C \leftarrow B \leftarrow A.$$
If we call a doubly dispatching function with arguments of type Y and of type C, conceptually the system will search for methods starting at #1 above, continuing in order to #6, stopping only when a method is found.

In practice, we use inheritance extensively. For instance, the method to render a Gunion object is the same regardless of the subclass of context used – simply render the geo1 component into the supplied context, then render the geo2 component into that context. Thus, we only define a Gunion rendering method on the abstract `Context` class, relying on inheritance to select this method for all other contexts.

As another example, consider the Sphere class. For rendering into an `XglDrawingCtx`, we inherit from the `ParameterizedSurf` class, which renders as a quadrilateral mesh. Since XGL doesn't support direct rendering of spheres, we can't do any better than rendering a Sphere as a parameterized surface. However, we do provide a method for rendering a Sphere into a `RayIntersect-PickingCtx`, since performing ray intersection against a sphere is much faster than performing it against a general parameterized surface.

Our extensibility goals set forth in the introduction are easily met by the approach we have chosen to take. Adding both new geometry subclasses and new contexts (embodying new styles of rendering) have been shown to be straightforward. The inheritance features described here also make it straightforward to re-use existing code.

**Implementing Inheritance Efficiently**

The previous discussion about the method table and the method selection process may lead the reader to believe that our implementation's computational complexity in method selection is $O(mn)$ with m being the number of arguments that we are dispatching off of (2, for double dispatching), and $n$ representing the average length of the inheritance chain

---

[5]In fact, our multiple dispatching facility is not restricted to just two dispatching arguments. A generic function that dispatched off of three arguments would conceptually have a 3D volume of methods.

that needs to be traversed for each argument until a registered method is found or until the root of the inheritance chain is hit.

In our implementation, this is not the case, and we achieve O($m$) performance, linear with the number of arguments being dispatched off of. We do this by eagerly filling in a sparse inheritance table during method selection. Specifically, if, prior to doing method selection, we have the following table:

|   | A | B | C | D |
|---|---|---|---|---|
| X | meth3 | meth5 |   |   |
| Y |   |   |   | meth9 |
| Z | meth7 |   |   |   |

where the filled in cells represent registered methods. Now, if we invoke a generic function with arguments of types C and Y, the inheritance semantics will cause method selection to search the table and come up with meth5. However, during this initial lookup, we fill in all the empty cells we encounter, and end up with this table:

|   | A | B | C | D |
|---|---|---|---|---|
| X | meth3 | meth5 | meth5 |   |
| Y |   | meth5 | meth5 | meth9 |
| Z | meth7 |   |   |   |

with the shaded cells being newly filled in with meth5. Now, subsequent calls with arguments of type C and Y (or C and X, or B and Y) will not require any table searching.

We are able to perform this optimization because of a rather benign restriction we place on the system: No methods may be registered with a generic function after that generic function has been invoked for the first time. If we didn't have this restriction, the eager filling in of the sparse table would have incorrect semantics in the event that a new method was registered later on. We have yet to encounter a situation where this restriction was troublesome.

As a measure of the computational efficiency of our approach, we examined the assembly code resulting from compiling our multiple dispatching facility. We found that, after the first invocation, a double dispatch requires just 53 SPARC instructions to find the appropriate method. If deemed necessary, this number can be halved by making changes that would result in a small decrease of flexibility.

### 6.4  Memory Management Techniques

As discussed in Section 5, one constructs an interactive animation in TBAG by using constrainables as arguments to functions. Consider displaying a cube that is being scaled by the absolute value of the sine of time and whose hue is varying with time:

```
cube * hsv_color(Time, 1, 1) * uniform_scale(fabs(sin(Time)))
```

If this is displayed starting at time t = 10.0, at a rate of 20 frames per second, the first five displayed frames would consist of the following geometries, respectively:

```
cube * hsv_color(10.00, 1, 1) * uniform_scale(fabs(sin(10.00)))
cube * hsv_color(10.05, 1, 1) * uniform_scale(fabs(sin(10.05)))
cube * hsv_color(10.10, 1, 1) * uniform_scale(fabs(sin(10.10)))
cube * hsv_color(10.15, 1, 1) * uniform_scale(fabs(sin(10.15)))
cube * hsv_color(10.20, 1, 1) * uniform_scale(fabs(sin(10.20)))
```

Given the earlier description of how geometry values are constructed, it should be clear that each of these expressions creates four new values – one Transform, one Color, and two Gattr Geometries (via the * operator). If values are allocated and constructed every frame, one would expect that an excessive amount of garbage will be created, and memory usage and allocation would become a major problem.

We avoid this potentially fatal problem by recognizing that, because of our functional, immutable approach, every value that is constructed during a frame is only needed for the duration of that frame. After the frame is displayed, the values are no longer needed. To exploit this fact, all TBAG objects derive from a base class that redefines the C++ new operator to, when appropriate, allocate from a "transient store". Thus, while in "transient mode", all TBAG objects are allocated sequentially from a small number of large chunks of memory. At the end of a frame, all of the created objects are collected simply by resetting a few pointers in the transient store. The next frame writes over the same chunks of memory.

## 6.5  Techniques for Computational Efficiency

A reader may understandably get the impression that evaluating the expression

$$cube * xlt(1,1,1) * rot(y\_axis, pi/3);$$ (12.2)

creates a Geometry value by translating each point in the vertex lists representing the cube by (1,1,1), then rotating each point around the Y-axis by $\pi/3$. Such an approach would be computationally prohibitive for non-trivial geometries, would not take advantage of the property that transforms compose with each other, and would not utilize any on-board graphics acceleration hardware that can deal with transforms directly.

Our system does not take this obvious approach. Rather, the expression in 12.2 above effectively evaluates into the binary tree shown in 3. When, for example, this representation is rendered into an XGL context, the translation and rotation transformations are composed and sent into the graphics hardware, making the best use of the available computational facilities. If this expression is part of a graphics animation, and the rotation amount is changing each frame, then a new binary tree will be built each frame. It turns out that, because of its simplicity, building such a tree is very inexpensive and, as explained earlier, all memory used in building it will be reclaimed the following frame.

## 6.6  Static Geometry Optimization

Consider rendering the expression cube * xlt(1,1,1) + cube * rot(y_axis, pi/4) to an XGL context. Such an operation involves setting the modeling transform to the translation, drawing a cube, setting the modeling transform to the rotation, and drawing another cube. This does not make particularly good use of the underlying graphics hardware, which is geared more for accepting large, batched geometric primitives. However, if

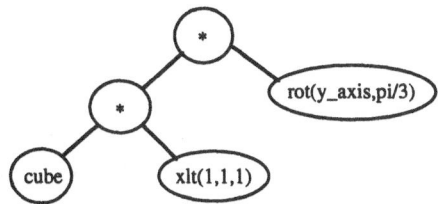

**Figure 3:** Representation of Expression 12.2

we explicitly ask for this geometry to be "optimized", it will be converted into a single "multi-simple polygon", a batched set of individual polygons. This is done by "pushing through" the transforms into the primitives themselves, and coalescing the resultant primitives into a single primitive. Not only does this make optimal use of the underlying graphics hardware, but it is also an optimization that a programmer would probably be unwilling to perform manually.

Note that this optimization is feasible only because we do not allow editing of a geometry value. If we did, then the original geometry would need to be retained, and any changes to it would somehow need to be forwarded to the optimized version.

In our current system, geometry optimization has to be invoked explicitly by the programmer, by applying the function optimize_geometry to a Geometry value. In the future, we intend to have this be implicit. Specifically, when a geometry becomes constant (e.g., a user was manipulating the geometry, but has since released it), the system will automatically invoke optimization. This is similar to the dynamic compilation that the Self system [2] performs after a function has been executed a suitable number of times, thus suggesting that the future usage pattern warrants accepting the cost of compiling that function, and will be a fairly straightforward addition to our system.

## 6.7 Implementation Statistics

The TBAG system is the result of approximately three calendar years and ten person-years of design and implementation. TBAG's geometry layer is a robust, mature, consistent, and full-featured system. It consists of 34 different Geometry subclasses, 12 Transform subclasses, 14 Context subclasses, over 100 Attributer subclasses, and over 15 other abstract data types. The geometry layer consists of about 20,000 lines of C++ code, all of which is consistent with the principles laid out in this paper. The system performs very well on both medium- and high-end graphics hardware – particularly on the SPARC-station 10ZX. Graphics performance is comparable to programs hand-coded in XGL. As an example, a comparison was done between rendering 500 spheres each tessellated into 50 quadrilaterals. On a SPARCstation 10ZX, the geometry specified in terms of TBAG operations rendered within 3% of the speed of the geometry specified more directly in terms of the underlying graphics library.

# 7  Additional Features

The geometry layer of the TBAG system has some additional interesting features that we have not seen in other systems. This section describes some of them.

## 7.1  Embedded Lights

Lights are first-class Geometry values in our system. Thus, they can be embedded directly
in geometry expressions and have attributes applied to them in the same way that any
other geometry can. In particular, they can be transformed along with the geometry. As
an example, consider the expression:

```
(cube + positional_light(yellow)) * xlt(1,1,1)
```

Here, positional_light(yellow) creates a positional light at the origin (all positional
lights are initially at the origin and may be transformed from there) that emits yellow
light. It is combined with a cube, and the entire compound geometry is translated to
$(1,1,1)$. Thus, we have a cube with a yellow light in the center of it, all at $(1,1,1)$.

Most other interactive 3D graphics systems either force lights to be specified in world
coordinates, thus they cannot be part of the model itself (PHIGS takes this approach),
or, as is the case with Inventor, lights only affect the objects that come after them in the
display hierarchy. This latter approach forces geometry description to be order-dependent
(thus eliminating opportunities for optimizations based on primitive re-ordering), and
hence non-declarative.

## 7.2  Embedded Shadow Planes

We also provide a "shadow plane" geometry that, like a light, may be trivially combined
with other geometries. A shadow plane should be thought of as an invisible plane initially
in the XY plane at $z = 0$. It may be transformed from that position into other positions.
For each light source in the scene, every other geometry casts a shadows onto each shadow
plane. On a SPARCstation 10ZX, this is all accomplished at interactive frame rates for
reasonably complex scenes.

## 7.3  Support for Interaction

TBAG supports the specification of geometry values that have their own behavior under
interaction. *Manipulators* are packaged up as Attributers, and may be used to attribute
geometry (just as colors and transforms attribute geometry) so that the geometry behaves
in a way dictated by the manipulator when it is interacted with. Most other systems de-
couple the behavior of an object under interaction from the specification of the appearance
of that object, making for less declarative applications. Inventor is a notable exception,
as it allows interaction nodes to be part of its graphs.

## 7.4  Integration of Sound

We have integrated audio support into our system in a manner entirely consistent with
our geometry system, and sound and geometry can easily be combined together to create
intriguing applications. For instance, the expression:

```
chirping_sound * frequency(1.2) * amplitude(0.8)
```

creates a Sound value representing a bird chirping (chirping_sound should be thought of
as a constant Sound, in the same manner that cube is a constant Geometry), attributed
with attributes stating that the sound should play back 20% faster than normal, and with
an amplitude of 80% of normal.

A Sound may be incorporated into a Geometry via the `sound_at_origin` construction function. `sound_at_origin` takes a Sound and returns a Geometry representing the specified sound at the 3D origin. This geometry can then be transformed to other places in the usual manner. The rendering of the resultant geometry takes into account the current "Listening Transform" (akin to the 3D graphics notion of viewing transform), and plays the sound in such a way that the listener experiences an approximation of the sound actually coming from the specified location.

We have used this facility to create an application that presents a 3D landscape of about 30 different sounds, each associated with a 3D icon. The user has the ability to navigate a pair of microphones through this landscape, hearing the sounds that are in the proximity of the microphones through stereo headphones.

2D imaging (and thus video, as time-varying 2D images), could integrate into our system in a similar fashion. This would allow arbitrary combinations of imaging and graphics media to be easily expressed. For example, texture mapping a wall in a 3D scene with an image produced from compositing a source image with the rendering of another 3D scene will be straightforward to express in our system. (Seeing that it can execute quickly on today's graphics and imaging hardware is another story!)

## 7.5  Network Distribution

TBAG provides a very simple way to create distributed, collaborative applications. Examples of such applications include:

- *Collaborative design:* three designers are all viewing the same geometry on workstations around the country. Modifications that any of the three make are witnessed by the other two, as they are happening.

- *Remote tutoring:* a professor is teaching a undergraduate physics course and presents an electronic illustration of spring forces in action. Students are watching this experiment live from their dorm rooms, their homes, or around the world may interact with the experiment on their computers, to get a better understanding of the physics of springs.

Not only are the distribution and collaboration aspects of these types of applications simple to construct in TBAG, but they also execute quite efficiently, using very little network bandwidth.

[4] discusses the implementation strategy for achieving this description of distribution and collaboration. However, to make it work, a requirement is placed on the Geometry-specific layer. Namely, all "values" described in Section 3 need to be able to "print" themselves into a machine-independent representation that can be interpreted on a remote machine. The interpretation of this machine-independent representation will create a new value whose behavior is indistinguishable from the old value.

The immutability of values makes providing the machine-independent printed representation somewhat easier. This is because the printed representation of a value is essentially an encoding of the expression that was evaluated to construct the value in the first place. If the values were mutable, then the expression that led to the value's creation would not necessarily reflect its current state.

## 8  Conclusion

In this paper, we've described the geometry layer of the TBAG system. We have presented a simple and general functional interface for programming 3D graphics that is fully accessible from C++. We've also described the design principles that underlie the interface, and discussed the advantages gained in succinctness and comprehensibility by presenting a functional interface to the programmer. In addition, we've shown how the interface is used from within the TBAG framework to create interactive, animated programs.

The presented interface poses some interesting challenges to the implementation. We have described our current implementation and explained how it supports the interface in both a time- and space-efficient manner, and how we provide general extensibility. In particular, a multiple dispatching facility that accounts for the inherent extensibility and much of the computational efficiency of our approach was explained in depth.

We have also discussed a number of interesting features of our system including embedded lights and shadow planes, support for interaction, integration with sound, and aspects of TBAG's transparent support for network distribution.

## Acknowledgements

Thanks go to Leon Shirman, Srikanth Subramaniam, Ajay Sreekanth, and Tom Meyer for their help developing, commenting on, and using the TBAG system. Doug Gehringer, Randy Pausch, Russell Pflughaupt, and Matthias Wloka commented on earlier drafts of this paper. We'd also like to thank Matt Pérez for his support of this project.

## References

[1] Kavi Arya. A Functional Approach to Animation. In *Computer Graphics Forum, 5(4)*, pages 297–311, December 1986.

[2] Craig Chambers, David Ungar, and Elgin Lee. An Efficient Implementation of Self, a Dynamically-Typed Object-Oriented Language Based on Prototypes. In *Lisp and Symbolic Computation 4*, pages 243–281, 1991.

[3] Roger B. Dannenberg, Christopher Lee Fraley, and Peter Velikonja. Fugue: A Functional Language for Sound Synthesis. In *IEEE Computer, July 1991*, 1991.

[4] Conal Elliott, Greg Schechter, Ricky Yeung, and Salim Abi-Ezzi. TBAG: A High Level Framework for Interactive, Animated 3D Graphics Applications. In *Computer Graphics (SIGGRAPH '94 Proceedings), volume 28(2)*, July 1994.

[5] A.J. Field and P.G. Harrison. *Functional Programming*. Addison Wesley, Reading, Mass., 1988.

[6] Rich Gossweiler, Shuichi Koga Chris Long, and Randy Pausch. Virtual Environment Research Platform. In *IEEE Symposium on Research Frontiers in Virtual Reality*, October 1993.

[7] International Standard ISO/IEC 9592. *Programmer's Hierarchical Interactive Graphics System (PHIGS)*, 1989.

[8] Sonya E. Keene. *Object-Oriented Programming in Common Lisp*. Addison Wesley, Reading, Mass., 1989.

[9] Larry Koved and Wayne L. Wooten. GROOP: An object-oriented toolkit for animated 3D graphics. In *OOPSLA 93 Proceedings*, October 1993.

[10] Kubota Pacific Computer, Inc. *Doré Programmer's Guide, Release 5.0*, 1991.

[11] Paul S. Strauss and Rikk Carey. An Object-Oriented 3D Graphics Toolkit. In *Computer Graphics (SIGGRAPH '92 Proceedings), volume 26(2)*, July 1992.

[12] Bjarne Stroustrup and Dmitry Lenkov. Run-Time Type Identification for C++ (Revised yet again). Technical report, ANSI document x3j16/92-0121, WG21/N0198, 1992.

[13] Sun Microsystems, Inc. *Solaris XGL 3.0 Reference Manual*, 1992.

[14] Mark A. Tarlton and P. Nong Tarlton. A framework for dynamic visual applications. In *1992 Symposium on Interactive 3D Graphics*, pages 161–164, 1992.

[15] Garry Wiegand and Bob Covey. HOOPS Reference Manual, Version 3.0. Technical report, Ithaca Software, 1991.

[16] Peter Wisskirchen. *Object-Oriented Graphics: From GKS and PHIGS to Object-Oriented Systems*. Springer-Verlag, Berlin, 1990.

# Authors' Addresses

Ekkehard Beier
TU Ilmenau
Dep. of Computer Graphics
Am Ehrenberg, PSF 327
D-98684 Ilmenau
GERMANY
ekki@prakinf.tu-ilmenau.de

Edwin Blake
Computer Science
University of Cape Town
Rondebosch 7700
Cape Town
SOUTH AFRICA
edwin@cs.uct.ac.za

Peter Bouwman
Hans de Bruin
FEW, Department of Computer Science
Erasmus University
P.O. Box 1738
NL-3000 Rotterdam
THE NETHERLANDS
{bouwman,debruin}@cs.few.eur.nl

Dennis Dingeldein
Computer Graphics Center (ZGDV)
Wilhelminenstr. 7
D-64283 Darmstadt
GERMANY
dingelde@igd.fhg.de

Parris K. Egbert
Travis L. Hilton
Computer Science Department
3328 TMCB
Brigham Young University
Provo, Utah 84602
USA
egbert@cs.byu.edu, hilto@cs.byu.edu

Dieter Fellner
Institut fuer Informatik III
Roemerstr. 164
D-53117 Bonn
GERMANY
dieter@cs.uni-bonn.de

Steve Freeman
Rank Xerox Research Centre
6, chemin de Maupertuis
38240 Meylan
FRANCE
Steve.Freeman@xerox.fr

Quinton Hoole
Computer Science
University of Cape Town
Rondebosch 7700
Cape Town
South Africa
quinton@cs.uct.ac.za

R.L. Grimsdale
VLSI & Computer Graphics Group
School of Engineering
University of Sussex
Brighton BN1 9QT
UK

Alwin Groene
Wilhelm-Schickard-Institut fuer Informatik
Universitaet Tuebingen
Graphisch-Interaktive Systeme
Auf der Morgenstelle 10/C9
D-72076 Tuebingen
GERMANY
alwin@gris.informatik.uni-tuebingen.de

Reinhard Klein
University of Tuebingen
WSI/GRIS
Auf der Morgenstelle 10
D-72076 Tuebingen
GERMANY

I.J. Palmer
Department of Computing
University of Bradford
Bradford BD7 1DP
UK
I.J.Palmer@comp.brad.ac.uk

Greg Schechter
Conal Elliot
Ricky Yeung
Microsoft Corporation
One Microsoft Way
Redmond, WA 98052-6399
USA
gregsc@microsoft.com

Philipp Slusallek
Andreas Kolb
Guenther Greiner
University of Erlangen
Graphische Datenverarbeitung
Am Weichselgarten 9
D-91058 Erlangen
GERMANY
slusallek@informatik.uni-erlangen.de

Remco Veltkamp
CWI, IS
Kruislaan 413
1098 SJ Amsterdam
THE NETHERLANDS
remco@cwi.nl

Peter Wisskirchen
GMD
Schloss Birlinghoven
D-53757 St. Augustin
GERMANY
wisskirchen@gmd.de

# Focus on Computer Graphics
(Formerly EurographicSeminars)

Advances in Computer Graphics Hardware III. Edited by A. A. M. Kuijk.
VIII, 214 pages, 88 figs., 1991

Advances in Object-Oriented Graphics I. Edited by E. H. Blake, P. Wisskirchen.
X, 218 pages, 74 figs., 1991

Advances in Computer Graphics Hardware IV. Edited by R. L. Grimsdale,
W. Straßer. VIII, 276 pages, 124 figs., 1991

Advances in Computer Graphics VI. Images: Synthesis, Analysis, and Interaction.
Edited by G. Garcia, I. Herman. IX, 449 pages, 186 figs., 1991

Intelligent CAD Systems III. Practical Experience and Evaluation. Edited by
P. J. W. ten Hagen, P. J. Veerkamp. X, 270 pages, 116 figs., 1991

Graphics and Communications. Edited by D. B. Arnold,
R. A. Day, D. A. Duce, C. Fuhrhop, J. R. Gallop, R. Maybury, D. C. Sutcliffe.
VIII, 274 pages, 84 figs., 1991

Photorealism in Computer Graphics. Edited by K. Bouatouch, C. Bouville.
XVI, 230 pages, 118 figs., 1992

Advances in Computer Graphics Hardware V. Rendering, Ray Tracing and
Visualization Systems. Edited by R. L. Grimsdale, A. Kaufman.
VIII, 174 pages, 97 figs., 1992

Multimedia. Systems, Interaction and Applications. Edited by L. Kjelldahl.
VIII, 355 pages, 129 figs., 1992. Out of print

Advances in Scientific Visualization. Edited by F. H. Post, A. J. S. Hin.
X, 212 pages, 141 figs., 47 in color, 1992

Computer Graphics and Mathematics. Edited by B. Falcidieno, I. Herman,
C. Pienovi. VII, 318 pages, 159 figs., 8 in color, 1992

Rendering, Visualization and Rasterization Hardware. Edited by A. Kaufman.
VIII, 196 pages, 100 figs., 1993

Visualization in Scientific Computing. Edited by M. Grave, Y. Le Lous,
W. T. Hewitt. XI, 218 pages, 120 figs., 1994

Photorealistic Rendering in Computer Graphics. Edited by P. Brunet,
F. W. Jansen. X, 286 pages, 175 figs., 1994

From Object Modelling to Advanced Visual Communication. Edited by
S. Coquillart, W. Straßer, P. Stucki. VII, 305 pages, 128 figs., 38 in color, 1994

Photorealistic Rendering Techniques. Edited by G. Sakas, P. Shirley, S. Müller.
X, 448 pages, 155 figs., 16 color plates, 1995

Interactive Systems: Design, Specification, and Verification.
Edited by F. Paternó. X, 447 pages, 176 figs., 1995

Object-oriented and Mixed Programming Paradigms. New Directions in Computer
Graphics. Edited by P. Wisskirchen.
X, 196 pages, 68 figs, 1996